Arab..

Learn the
Easy Way

A quick step-by-step approach

Arabic
Learn the Easy Way

A quick step-by-step approach

Amir Jamal

GOODWORD

First published 2014
© Goodword Books 2014

Goodword Books
1, Nizamuddin West Market, New Delhi-110 013
Tel. +9111-4182-7083, Mob. +91-8588822672
email: info@goodwordbooks.com
www.goodwordbooks.com

Goodword Books, Chennai
324, Triplicane High Road
Triplicane, Chennai-600005
Tel. +9144-4352-4599
Mob. +91-9790853944, 9600105558
email: chennaigoodword@gmail.com

Goodword Books, Hyderabad
2-48/182, Plot No. 182, Street No. 22
Telecom Nagar Colony, Gachi Bawli
Hyderabad-500032
Mob. 9448651644
email: hyd.goodword@gmail.com

Islamic Vision Ltd.
426-434 Coventry Road, Small Heath
Birmingham B10 0UG, U.K.
Tel. 121-773-0137
e-mail: info@ipci-iv.co.uk
www.islamicvision.co.uk

IB Publisher Inc.
81 Bloomingdale Rd, Hicksville
NY 11801, USA
Tel. 516-933-1000
Toll Free: 1-888-560-3222
email: info@ibpublisher.com
www.ibpublisher.com

Printed in India

Contents

ARABIC: LEARN THE EASY WAY

6

8 ARABIC: LEARN THE EASY WAY

Foreword

A good teacher in the making showed me his first draft of this book in hand and I felt so good to see my student graduating from a teacher to a writer, though at first I thought that this young man's attempt to simplify Arabic grammar for beginners and others must have been futile, and I was most unwilling to go through it and give my time to correcting it. However, as a teacher I could not refuse outright. When I began to read it, I found that the author had really done a good job. I read his first draft and made suggestions about removing some topics and adding some others more essential for beginners. He took my advice in good part and promptly carried out my suggestions. He has included 46 lessons in the first of the series he proposes to bring out on Arabic grammar. The beauty of these lessons lies in the fact that the author chose topics and constructed his lessons without borrowing texts from other books on classical literature, which authors normally do to spare themselves same effort. He knows and understands very well that through a borrowed text he cannot put across his point as simply and adequately as should be done at the beginner's level, where repetition and simplification are absolute necessities. His explaining a point through English is straight forward and his examples and texts are relevant to daily life.

Besides the lessons, he has also given an adequate number of exercises. I am sure Arabic students will find this book very useful.

S.A. Rahman

(Former Chairperson)

CAAS, SLL and CS

Jawaharlal Nehru University

Introduction

Arabic is spoken by more than two-hundred and eighty million people around the globe and it is the main language of most of the Middle East. Its global importance has redoubled in today's world because of the growing significance of Middle Eastern affairs in our daily lives. Most importantly, Arabic also plays a major role in the Islamic faith because the Holy Quran was revealed to the Prophet Muhammad (PBUH) in this very language. Apart from its religious aspect, currently this language has become helpful in dealing with the international market. Consequently, Arabic is opening up innumerable employment possibilities in many industries such as oil, travel, finance and translation, to name but a few.

Recently, we have seen that the number of Arabic students has been rising steadily, not only in the traditional Arabic Madrasas but also in schools, colleges and universities. With this ever increasing number of Arabic students, there is a need for simplified Arabic grammar books to guide and assist them in learning the language so that they may achieve their goals.

In India, Arabic learners may be divided into two categories. One, those studing in the Madrasas who study Arabic and Islamic sciences. Two, the students who study in schools, colleges and universities who aspire to securing jobs in the national or international markets.

While there is no dearth of suitable teaching material for the Madrasa students, we require material to teach non-Madrasa students which will be suitable for them and will cater to their needs.

With this in mind, many scholars and Arabic teachers have written books on Arabic grammar, using English as the medium. I believe a variety of such books does help in the process of learning and hence, I am adding one more to this list in as simple way as I think would be genuinley helpful to learners. I have included in this book all the essential grammar points that would give learners a good grip of the language.

This book is the first of my proposed two volumes in which I deal with topics which are absolutely essential for students of modern Arabic.

The lessons of the book comprise topics in Arabic with their equivalents in English. Each lesson consists of text, explanation, definitions and examples. I have also provided at the end of each lesson the glossary of the lesson and necessary exercises. The plurals of the nouns are given in brackets, while the verbs and their verbal nouns are separated by dashes (-). The feminine by convention (مُؤَّنَثٌ سَمَاعِيٌّ) is shown by f. or fem.

I hope that the users of this book will benefit in the way I have envisaged.

For any suggestions for further improvements or for any queries, I may be contacted at my email: amirjamalsheikh@gmail.com

In conclusion I would like to extend my heartfelt thanks to all those who have helped me to write this book. I am specially grateful to Prof. S. A. Rahman, former chairperson of the Centre of Arabic and African studies, Jawaharlal Nehru University, New Delhi, who is one of my many able teachers. He inspires me to work hard for my students at all times. It was very kind of him to have gone through the manuscript of this book and the suggestions he gave me about how to bring out this book in its present form proved very useful.

Finally, I express my gratitude to Allah the Almighty who has always blessed me with His mercy and given me the strength to work.

Amir Jamal

LESSON 1

Letters of the Alphabet حُرُوْفُ الْأَبْجَدِيَّةِ

❧❀❧

There are 28 letters in the Arabic alphabet:

أ	ب	ت	ث	ج	ح	خ
(ʾalif/ألف)	(bâ'/باء)	(tâ'/تاء)	(thâ'/ثاء)	(jîm/جيم)	(ḥâ'/حاء)	(khâ'/خاء)
د	ذ	ر	ز	س	ش	ص
(dâl/دال)	(dhâl/ذال)	(râ'/راء)	(zây/زاى)	(sîn/سين)	(shîn/شين)	(ṣâd/صاد)
ض	ط	ظ	ع	غ	ف	ق
(ḍâd/ضاد)	(ṭâ'/طاء)	(ẓâ'/ظاء)	('ayn/عين)	(ghayn/غين)	(fâ'/فاء)	(qâf/قاف)
ك	ل	م	ن	ه/ة	و	ي
(kâf/كاف)	(lâm/لام)	(mîm/ميم)	(nûn/نون)	hâ'/هاء	(wâw/واو)	(yâ'/ياء)

Note:

(i) For all practical purposes there are two more letters: ة
i . e. the round ta and ء i.e. hamza. Generally, they are considered to be another form of the normal stretched ta 'ت' and alif 'ا' respectively.

(ii) Arabic is written and read horizontally from right to left.

Exercise:

(i) Read the letters of the Arabic alphabet.

(ii) Learn the names of the letters of the Arabic alphabet and memorize them in the order in which they appear.

LESSON 2

Names, Sounds and Different Shapes
of the Letters
أَسْمَاءٌ وَأَصْوَاتٌ وَأَشْكَالٌ مُخْتَلِفَةٌ لِلْحُرُوفِ

+‹§§›+

In Arabic, most letters change their forms depending
on their placement in the word - whether initial or medial or
terminal, as shown hereunder:

Name	Independent	Initial	Medial	Terminal	Transliteration
'alif/الف	ا	-	-	ـا	a
bâ'/باء	ب	بـ	ـبـ	ـب	b
tâ'/تاء	ت	تـ	ـتـ	ـت	t
thâ'/ثاء	ث	ثـ	ـثـ	ـث	th
jîm/جيم	ج	جـ	ـجـ	ـج	j
hâ'/حاء	ح	حـ	ـحـ	ـح	ḥ
khâ'/خاء	خ	خـ	ـخـ	ـخ	kh
dâl/دال	د	-	-	ـد	d
dhâl/ذال	ذ	-	-	ـذ	dh
râ'/راء	ر	-	-	ـر	r
zây/زاى	ز	-	-	ـز	z
sîn/سين	س	سـ	ـسـ	ـس	s
shîn/شين	ش	شـ	ـشـ	ـش	sh
ṣâd/صاد	ص	صـ	ـصـ	ـص	ṣ

Name	Independent	Initial	Medial	Terminal	Transliteration
ḍâd/ضاد	ض	ضـ	ـضـ	ـض	ḍ
ṭâ'/طاء	ط	ط	ـطـ	ـط	ṭ
ẓâ'/ظاء	ظ	ظ	ـظـ	ـظ	ẓ
'ayn/عين	ع	عـ	ـعـ	ـع	'
ghayn/غين	غ	غـ	ـغـ	ـغ	gh
fâ'/فاء	ف	فـ	ـفـ	ـف	f
qâf/قاف	ق	قـ	ـقـ	ـق	q
kâf/كاف	ك	كـ	ـكـ	ـك	k
lâm/لام	ل	لـ	ـلـ	ـل	l
mîm/ميم	م	مـ	ـمـ	ـم	m
nûn/نون	ن	نـ	ـنـ	ـن	n
hâ'/هاء	ه	هـ	ـهـ	ـه	h
wâw/واو	و	–	–	ـو	w (u, aw, au)
yâ'/ياء	ي	يـ	ـيـ	ـي ي	y (i, ay, ai)
hamza/همزة	أ ا	أ	ـئـ	ء ؤ أ ئ	'

Exercise:

1. Read and write the letters.
2. Memorize the names, sounds and different forms of the letters.

LESSON 3

Vowels حَرَكَاتٌ

+✵✵✵+

In order to make syllables and to use them in speaking, we need vowels between the consonants. In Arabic, we have 6 vowels; 3 long vowels and 3 short vowels, while two diphthongs are also used. They are:

ــَ (a)	fatha/فتحة	makes a sound like u in cut	SHORT
ــِ (i)	kasra/كسرة	makes a sound like i in sit	
ــُ (u)	damma/ضمة	makes a sound like u in put	VOWELS
ا ــَ (a)		makes a sound like ar (a:) in arm	LONG
ي ــِ (i)	حُرُوفُ الْمَدِّ	makes a sound like ee in need	
و ــُ (u)		makes a sound like oo in noon	VOWELS
ــَ و	الصَّوْتُ	makes a sound like ow in how	DIPHTHONGS
ــَ ي	بِالْحَرَكَتَيْنِ	makes a sound like i in kite	

Note: The absence of a vowel is represented by a small circle which is placed above a letter, i.e. ــْ and is called sukûn (سُكُونٌ).

Exercise:
1. Learn the short vowels and the sounds they make.
2. Learn the long vowels and the sounds they make.
3. Learn the diphthongs and the sounds they make.

LESSON 4

How are the Short Vowels Placed?
كَيْفَ تُوضَعُ الْحَرَكَاتُ؟

✦✦✦

a <-> َ

أَ	بَ	تَ	ثَ	جَ	حَ	خَ
دَ	ذَ	رَ	زَ	سَ	شَ	صَ
ضَ	طَ	ظَ	عَ	غَ	فَ	قَ
كَ	لَ	مَ	نَ	هَ/ةَ	وَ	يَ

i <-> ِ

إِ	بِ	تِ	ثِ	جِ	حِ	خِ
دِ	ذِ	رِ	زِ	سِ	شِ	صِ
ضِ	طِ	ظِ	عِ	غِ	فِ	قِ
كِ	لِ	مِ	نِ	هِ/ةِ	وِ	يِ

u <-> ُ

أُ	بُ	تُ	ثُ	جُ	حُ	خُ
دُ	ذُ	رُ	زُ	سُ	شُ	صُ
ضُ	طُ	ظُ	عُ	غُ	فُ	قُ

يْ	وْ	هُـ/هْ	نْ	مْ	لْ	كْ

ـْ

خْ	حْ	جْ	ثْ	تْ	بْ	أْ
صْ	شْ	سْ	زْ	رْ	ذْ	دْ
قْ	فْ	غْ	عْ	ظْ	طْ	ضْ
يْ	وْ	هُـ/هْ	نْ	مْ	لْ	كْ

Note: Sukûn is always placed above a letter.

Exercise:

1. Read and write the letters with the vowel points carefully.
2. Memorize the vowel points and the sounds they produce.
3. Try to pronounce each combination of letters below:

أَ شَ رَ	نَ تَ جَ	وَ رِمَ	زَ هُ رَ	حَ سِ بَ	كَ تَ بَ
أَشَرَ	نَتَجَ	وَرِمَ	زَهُرَ	حَسِبَ	كَتَبَ
طَ هَ رَ	جَ رَحَ	خَ لَ قَ	صَ لِ عَ	ثَ قُ لَ	كَ رُمَ
طَهَرَ	جَرَحَ	خَلَقَ	صَلِعَ	ثَقُلَ	كَرُمَ
غَ لَ ظَ	ذَ رَفَ	قَ تَ لَ	يَ ضَ عُ	يَ جِ دُ	سَ مِ عَ
غَلَظَ	ذَرَفَ	قَتَلَ	يَضَعُ	يَجِدُ	سَمِعَ

4. Write two words each according to the instructions given below and pronounce them correctly.

(a) Consisting of two letters with ‗ above the first and ‗ on the second. (Example: هَلْ).

(b) Consisting of two letters, with ‗ below the first and ‗ on the second. (Example: مِنْ).

(c) Consisting of two letters, with ‗ above the first and ‗ on the second. (Example: قُلْ).

(d) Consisting of three letters, using any of the short vowels and ‗ above the second. (Example: جَمْعٌ).

(e) Consisting of four letters, using any of the short vowels and ‗ above the second letter. (Example: مَصْنَعٌ).

GLOSSARY	الْكَلِمَاتُ الْعَسِيرَةُ
to saw	أَشَرَ - يَأْشُرُ - أَشْرٌ
to be heavy	ثَقُلَ - يَثْقُلُ - ثِقَلٌ
to wound	جَرَحَ - يَجْرَحُ - جَرْحٌ
to regard, consider	حَسِبَ - يَحْسِبُ - حِسْبَانٌ
to create, make	خَلَقَ - يَخْلُقُ - خَلْقٌ
to shed (tears)	ذَرَفَ - يَذْرِفُ - ذَرْفٌ
to shine, give light	زَهَرَ - يَزْهَرُ - زُهُورٌ
to hear, listen	سَمِعَ - يَسْمَعُ - سَمْعٌ
to be bald	صَلِعَ - يَصْلَعُ - صَلَعٌ

to be or become thick	غَلُظَ - يَغْلُظُ - غِلَظٌ
to kill	قَتَلَ - يَقْتُلُ - قَتْلٌ
to be noble, be generous	كَرُمَ - يَكْرُمُ - كَرَامَةٌ
to result, bring forth	نَتَجَ - يَنْتِجُ - نِتَاجٌ
to find	وَجَدَ - يَجِدُ - وِجْدَانٌ
to swell	وَرِمَ - يَرِمُ - وَرَمٌ
to lay, put down, place	وَضَعَ - يَضَعُ - وَضْعٌ
to be pure	طَهُرَ - يَطْهُرُ - طُهْرٌ
to write	كَتَبَ - يَكْتُبُ - كِتَابَةٌ

LESSON 5

Places of Origination of the Arabic Letters
مَخَارِجُ الْحُرُوْفِ الْعَرَبِيَّةِ

+≶≷+

To know the place of origination of any Arabic letter, we place a sukûn (ـْ) on it preceded by Alif (أ) with a ـَ i.e. (أَ) and then pronounce it. For example, saying أَبْ will tell us the origination of بَاء and that it is a labial sound, i.e. it is produced with the lips. The place from where the letter is pronounced is called مَخْرَجٌ in Arabic.

NAME	LETTER	PLACE OF ORIGINATION
The Aerial Letters الْحُرُوْفُ الْهَوَائِيَّةُ	ا و ي	Originate from the emptiness of the mouth (when used as long vowels).
The Guttural Letters الْحُرُوْفُ الْحَلْقِيَّةُ	ء ه	Originate from the back of the throat (Larynx).
	ح ع	Originate from the centre of the throat.
	خ غ	Originate from the upper portion of the throat.
Vellar Letters الْحَرْفَانِ اللَّهَوِيَّانِ	ق ك	Originate when the back of the tongue rises and touches the soft palate.

Palatal Letters الْحُرُوْفُ الشَّجَرِيَّةُ	ج ش ي	Originate when the centre of the tongue touches the upper palate. Originates when the tongue curves up and the two sides go up and touch the top of the mouth.
The letter الْحَرْفُ ُض '	ض	Originates when the upturned side of the tongue touches the gum of the upper back teeth.
The Liquids الْحُرُوْفُ الذَّوْلَقِيَّةُ	ر ل ن	Originate when the tip of the tongue touches the upper hard palate.
The Dental Letters الْحُرُوْفُ النِّطْعِيَّةُ	ت د ط	Originate when the tip of the tongue touches the gums of the upper two teeth.
The Gingival Letters الْحُرُوْفُ اللِّثَوِيَّةُ	ث ذ ظ	Originate when the tip of the tongue touches the edge of the upper two teeth.
Tip of the Tongue الْحُرُوْفُ الأَسْلِيَّةُ	ز س ص	Originate when the tip of the tongue rises towards the upper palate, touching the gums behind the upper two front teeth.

| The Labial Letters الْحُرُوْفُ الشَّفَوِيَّةُ | ب م ف | Originate from the lips. Originates when the inner portion of the bottom lip meets the edge on the two upper front teeth. |
| | و | Originates by incomplete touching of the lips (lips must also be rounded)- |

Rule:

The place from which the sound of a letter originates is called مَخْرَجٌ.

Exercise:

1. Memorise the places of origination of letters.
2. Write ﹾ over all the letters and precede them with an alif with fatha (ﹷ) i.e. (أ) and pronounce them.

LESSON 6

Orthographic Signs عَلَامَاتٌ أُخْرَى لِلتَّهْجِيَةِ

+⟨⟩+

Apart from fatha, kasra and damma, there are some other signs which are used in Arabic to pronounce a word. They are:

(1) ــْ : Sukûn (سُكُوْنٌ)

Used to indicate the absence of a vowel, it is placed above the letter, e.g.,

هَلْ (interrogative particle to ask questions)

بَلْ (rather; even; but, however, yet)

أَمْ (or)

(2) ــّ : Shaddah (شَدَّةٌ) or Tashdîd (تَشْدِيْدٌ)

This is used to represent the doubling of a letter. If the same letter occurs twice in a word with the first one with a سُكُوْنٌ and the second with some حَرَكَةٌ, the letter is written only once and shaddah is written above it and read twice, e.g.,

مَ رْ رَ	==>	مَرَّ	(to pass, go)
فَ رْ رَ	==>	فَرَّ	(to flee)
جَ دْ دَ	==>	جَدَّ	(to make every effort)

Note: The letter which holds the shadda is called mushaddad (مُشَدَّدٌ).

(3) ـٰ : Madda (مَدَّةٌ)

It indicates to stretching the reciting sounds. It is used
when an alif occurs after hamza (ء). The hamza (ء) is not
written. Instead a maddah sign (ـٰ) is put on the alif
which serves the same purpose, e.g.

قُرْءَانٌ   ==>   قُرْآنٌ   (Quran)

مِءَاتٌ   ==>   مِآتٌ   (hundreds)

مَءَارِبُ   ==>   مَآرِبُ   (wishes)

(4) ٰ : Alif Maqsûra (أَلِفٌ مَقْصُوْرَةٌ)   or Short Alif

The sound of Alif Maqsûra (أَلِفٌ مَقْصُوْرَةٌ) is just like the
full alif. Sometimes, for some reason, the full alif is not
written. In that case a short alif is written above the
letter which gives the sound of alif, e.g.

سِوىٰ (except)   زَكوٰة   Zakât

عَلىٰ (on)   صَلوٰة   Salât

إلىٰ (to)

كِسْرىٰ (Khosrau designation of the Persian king in
general).

Note: Sometimes أَلِفٌ مَقْصُوْرَةٌ is represented by a فَتْحَةٌ on
the preceeding letter.

Exercise:

1. Learn the orthographic signs which are mentioned in this lesson.

2. Write five words each as directed:

    (a) with ˌ on any of the letters.

    (b) with ˝ on any of the letters.

    (c) with ¯ on any of the letters.

    (d) with ' on any of the letters.

إِسْتِخْدَامُ الْحَرَكَاتِ الطَّوِيْلَةِ Use of Long Vowels

A long vowel is formed when a short vowel's sound is stretched. Every short vowel produces a long vowel similar to its sound.

فَتْحَةٌ produces the sound of silent ا

خَا	حَا	جَا	ثَا	تَا	بَا	ءَا
صَا	شَا	سَا	زَا	رَا	ذَا	دَا
قَا	فَا	غَا	عَا	ظَا	طَا	ضَا
يَا	وَا	هَا	نَا	مَا	لَا	كَا

كَسْرَةٌ produces the sound of silent ي

خِي	حِي	جِي	ثِي	تِي	بِي	اِي
صِي	شِي	سِي	زِي	رِي	ذِي	دِي
قِي	فِي	غِي	عِي	ظِي	طِي	ضِي
يِي	وِي	هِي	نِي	مِي	لِي	كِي

ضَمَّةٌ produces the sound of silent و

خُو	حُو	جُو	ثُو	تُو	بُو	أُو
صُو	شُو	سُو	زُو	رُو	ذُو	دُو
قُو	فُو	غُو	عُو	ظُو	طُو	ضُو
يُو	وُو	هُو	نُو	مُو	لُو	كُو

Exercise:

1. Read and write all the Arabic letters with long vowels.

2. Read the following words.

مَالَ - قِيلَ - خِلَالَ - يَطُوْلُ - مُسَافِرُوْنَ

مُجَاهِدُوْنَ - تَعَالَ - طِوَالَ - بَاعَ - يُزِيْلُ

جَالَ - يُجْرَحُوْنَ - مُتَرْجِمُوْنَ - سَاكِنِيْنَ

مُوْقِنِيْنَ - تَقُوْلُوْنَ - طِيْلَةَ - مَائِلُوْنَ

GLOSSARY	الْكَلِمَاتُ الْعَسِيْرَةُ
to incline, lean	مَالَ - يَمِيْلُ - مَيْلٌ
to say, speak	قَالَ - يَقُوْلُ - قَوْلٌ
during	خِلَالَ
to be or become long or tall	طَالَ - يَطُوْلُ - طُوْلٌ
traveller, passenger	مُسَافِرٌ (مُسَافِرُوْنَ)
fighter	مُجَاهِدٌ (مُجَاهِدُوْنَ)
come (here)!	تَعَالَ
throughout	طِوَالَ
to sell	بَاعَ - يَبِيْعُ - بَيْعٌ
to cause to cease, remove	أَزَالَ - يُزِيْلُ - إِزَالَةٌ
to roam, wander about	جَالَ - يَجُوْلُ - جَوْلٌ

to wound	جَرَحَ - يَجْرَحُ - جَرْحٌ
translator	مُتَرْجِمٌ (مُتَرْجِمُوْنَ)
dweller, inhabitant	سَاكِنٌ (سَاكِنُوْنَ)
convinced, certain, sure	مُوْقِنٌ (مُوْقِنُوْنَ)
throughout	طِيْلَةَ
inclining	مَائِلٌ (مَائِلُوْنَ)

LESSON 8

Use of Diphthongs إِسْتِخْدَامُ الْفَتْحَةِ قَبْلَ وْ/ يْ

۞

ـَ وْ

خَوْ	حَوْ	جَوْ	ثَوْ	تَوْ	بَوْ	أَوْ
صَوْ	شَوْ	سَوْ	زَوْ	رَوْ	ذَوْ	دَوْ
قَوْ	فَوْ	غَوْ	عَوْ	ظَوْ	طَوْ	ضَوْ
يَوْ	وَوْ	هَوْ	نَوْ	مَوْ	لَوْ	كَوْ

ـَ يْ

خَيْ	حَيْ	جَيْ	ثَيْ	تَيْ	بَيْ	أَيْ
صَيْ	شَيْ	سَيْ	زَيْ	رَيْ	ذَيْ	دَيْ
قَيْ	فَيْ	غَيْ	عَيْ	ظَيْ	طَيْ	ضَيْ
يَيْ	وَيْ	هَيْ	نَيْ	مَيْ	لَيْ	كَيْ

Exercise:

1. Read and write letters with diphthongs.

2. Read the following words correctly.

رَأَيْنَا - جَرَوْنَ - حَكَيْتَ - كَسَوْتُمَا

يَبْقَوْنَ - مَشَيْتُمْ - قَلَيْتِ - سَقَيْتُ

رَمَيْتُنَّ - هَوَيْنَا - مَحَوْنَ - يَبْقَيْنَ

GLOSSARY	الْكَلِمَاتُ الْعَسِيْرَةُ
to see	رَأَى - يَرَى - رُؤْيَةٌ
to flow	جَرَى - يَجْرِي - جَرْيٌ
to tell	حَكَى - يَحْكِي - حِكَايَةٌ
to clothe	كَسَا - يَكْسُو - كَسْوٌ
to remain, stay	بَقِيَ - يَبْقَى - بَقَاءٌ
to walk	مَشَى - يَمْشِي - مَشْيٌ
to fry	قَلَى - يَقْلِي - قَلْيٌ
to irrigate	سَقَى - يَسْقِي - سَقْيٌ
to throw	رَمَى - يَرْمِي - رَمْيٌ
to fall	هَوَى - يَهْوِي - هُوِيٌّ
to love	هَوِيَ - يَهْوَى - هَوًى
to wipe off	مَحَا - يَمْحُو - مَحْوٌ
to remain, stay	بَقِيَ - يَبْقَى - بَقَاءٌ

LESSON 9

The Nunnation التَّنْوِيْنُ

In Arabic, in order to express indefiniteness of nouns and adjectives, the nunnation (التَّنْوِيْنُ) is used. The nunnation is denoted by writing the short vowel twice above or below the last letter of the word, as the case may be.

تَنْوِيْنُ الْفَتْحَةِ ـً produces a sound like 'un', as in <u>un</u>dated.

تَنْوِيْنُ الْكَسْرَةِ ـٍ produces a sound like 'in', as in <u>in</u>corporate.

تَنْوِيْنُ الضَّمَّةِ ـٌ produces a sound like 'un', as in S<u>unn</u>i.

Note:

1. The letter which holds التَّنْوِيْنُ is called مُنَوَّنٌ.

2. The vowel sign ـَ, when doubled is called فَتْحَتَانِ or تَنْوِيْنُ الْفَتْحَةِ.

3. The vowel sign ـِ, when doubled is called كَسْرَتَانِ or تَنْوِيْنُ الْكَسْرَةِ.

4. The vowel sign ـُ, when doubled is called ضَمَّتَانِ or تَنْوِيْنُ الضَّمَّةِ.

Exercise:

1. Learn the signs of nunnation and their names.

LESSON 10

How is the Nunnation Put?

كَيْفَ يُوْضَعُ التَّنْوِيْنُ؟

As we have read in the previous lesson, the nunnation is denoted by writing a short vowel sign twice above or below the last letter, but in the case of فَتْحَتَانِ, an extra alif (ا) is also added, except with 'ء' and 'ة' as shown in the table below.

فَتْحَتَانِ (ـً)

خَا	حَا	جَا	ثَا	تَا - ةً	بَا	ءً
صًا	شًا	سًا	زًا	رًا	ذَا	دَا
قًا	فًا	غًا	عًا	ظًا	طًا	ضًا
يًا	وًا	هًا	نًا	مًا	لاً	كًا

كَسْرَتَانِ (ـٍ)

خٍ	حٍ	جٍ	ثٍ	تٍ - ةٍ	بٍ	ءٍ
صٍ	شٍ	سٍ	زٍ	رٍ	ذٍ	دٍ

قٍ	فٍ	غٍ	عٍ	ظٍ	طٍ	ضٍ
يٍ	وٍ	هٍ	نٍ	مٍ	لٍ	كٍ

ضَمَّتَانِ (ــٌ)

خٌ	حٌ	جٌ	ثٌ	تٌ - ةٌ	بٌ	ءٌ
صٌ	شٌ	سٌ	زٌ	رٌ	ذٌ	دٌ
قٌ	فٌ	غٌ	عٌ	ظٌ	طٌ	ضٌ
ئٌ	وٌ	هٌ	نٌ	مٌ	لٌ	كٌ

Note:

1. If the word ends with التَّاءُ الْمَرْبُوطَةُ (ة), double vowels are placed below or above it as the case may be, e.g.

(bomb) قُنْبُلَةٍ - قُنْبُلَةً - قُنْبُلَةٌ

(date) تَمْرَةٍ - تَمْرَةً - تَمْرَةٌ

2. When an indefinite noun or adjective is preceded by أَلْ, it becomes definite and it carries a single vowel point, e.g.

الْوَرَقِ - وَرَقٍ   الْوَرَقَ - وَرَقًا   الْوَرَقُ - وَرَقٌ

Exercise:

1. Read the Arabic letters with the تَنْوِيْنٌ.

2. Read each of the combinations of letters given below:

جُرْحًا	وَقْتًا	شَوْكَةً	جِرَابًا	طَعَامًا
حَاكِمٍ	نَاعِمٍ	عُصْفُورٍ	أَرْضٍ	سَنَةٍ
غُرَابٌ	رَجُلٌ	مَلِكٌ	زَهْرَةٌ	جَرَسٌ

3. Write 5 words each as follows:

      (a) with فَتْحَتَانِ.

      (b) with كَسْرَتَانِ.

      (c) with ضَمَّتَانِ.

      (d) with 'أَلْ.

GLOSSARY	الْكَلِمَاتُ الْعَسِيرَةُ
food	طَعَامٌ (أَطْعِمَةٌ)
sack, bag, travelling bag	جِرَابٌ (أَجْرِبَةٌ، جُرُبٌ)
fork	شَوْكَةٌ (أَشْوَاكٌ)
time	وَقْتٌ (أَوْقَاتٌ)
wound	جُرْحٌ (جِرَاحٌ، جُرُوحٌ)
year	سَنَةٌ (سَنَوَاتٌ)
earth	أَرْضٌ (أَرَاضٍ) fem.
sparrow	عُصْفُورٌ (عَصَافِيرُ)
soft	نَاعِمٌ
ruler	حَاكِمٌ (حُكَّامٌ، حَاكِمُونَ)

bell	جَرَسٌ (أَجْرَاسٌ)
flower	زَهْرَةٌ (زُهُوْرٌ)
king	مَلِكٌ (مُلُوْكٌ)
man	رَجُلٌ (رِجَالٌ)
crow	غُرَابٌ (غِرْبَانٌ)

LESSON 11

The Sun Letters الْحُرُوْفُ الشَّمْسِيَّةُ

+≶≷+

The letters of the Arabic alphabet are divided into two groups of fourteen letters each. They are the Sun letters and the Moon letters. In this lesson we shall talk about the Sun letters. They are as follows:

س	ز	ر	ذ	د	ث	ت
ن	ل	ظ	ط	ض	ص	ش

When the definite article أَلْ is attached to an indefinite word, the last letter of the word accepts only single فَتْحَةٌ or ضَمَّةٌ or كَسْرَةٌ. The alif of ال is directly linked to the sun letter, which doubles the sound and ل, though written, remains silent.

شَجَرَةٌ (tree) ---> الشَّجَرَةُ (the tree)

However, if the definite article 'ال' is preceded by a word or preposition, alif is not pronounced, either e.g.

تَحْتَ الشَّجَرَةِ (under the tree)

Here are examples of all the Sun Letters:

DEFINITE ARTICLE PRECEDED BY LETTER/WORD	DEFINITE ARTICLE ATTACHED TO WORD	SUN LETTER
عَلَى التَّاجِ (on the crown)	التَّاجُ (crown)	ت

(in the snow) فِي الثَّلْجِ	(snow, ice) الثَّلْجُ	ث
(for the religion) لِلدِّيْنِ	(religion) الدِّيْنُ	د
(by the tail) بِالذَّيْلِ	(tail) الذَّيْلُ	ذ
(and the sand) وَالرَّمْلُ	(sand) الرَّمْلُ	ر
(in the oil) فِي الزَّيْتِ	(oil) الزَّيْتُ	ز
(in the dawn) فِي السَّحَرِ	(dawn) السَّحَرُ	س
(in the net) فِي الشَّبَكَةِ	(net) الشَّبَكَةُ	ش
(by hunting) بِالصَّيْدِ	(hunting) الصَّيْدُ	ص
(in the light) فِي الضَّوْءِ	(light) الضَّوْءُ	ض
(naturally) بِالطَّبْعِ	(nature) الطَّبْعُ	ط
(and the gazelle) وَالظَّبْيُ	(gazelle) الظَّبْيُ	ظ
(in the night) فِي اللَّيْلِ	(night) اللَّيْلُ	ل
(on the fire) عَلَى النَّارِ	(fire) النَّارُ	ن

Exercise:

1. Memorize the sun letters.

2. Read the following words.

الشَّامُ - الذُّبَابُ - فِي الدَّارِ - بِالثَّمَنِ - التِّيْنُ

(Syria)   (fly)   (in the house)   (with the money)   (fig)

إِلَى اللِّقَاءِ - فِي السَّابِقِ - مَعَ الزَّمِيْلِ - سِنُّ الرُّشْدِ

(goodbye)   (formerly)   (with the colleague)   (majority)

وَقْتُ الظُّهْرِ   -   تَحْتَ النَّظَرِ   -   شَرِكَةُ التَّأْمِيْنِ

(noon, midday)   (under consideration)   (insurance company)

الصَّحَابَةُ   -   فِى الطَّرِيْقِ

(the companions of the Prophet Muhammad)   (in the way)

3. Write five words each as directed:

   (a) Beginning with a sun letter without الـ.

   (b) Beginning with a sun letter with الـ.

   (c) Beginning with a sun letter attached with الـ and preceded by a particle.

LESSON 12

The Moon Letters الْحُرُوْفُ الْقَمَرِيَّةُ

+§§+

You have already learned that the letters of the Arabic alphabet are divided into two groups; the Sun letters and the Moon letters. We have discussed the Sun letters in the previous lesson. Now we come to the second group of 14 letters, i.e. the Moon letters. The Moon Letters are as follows:

أ	ب	ج	ح	خ	ع	غ
ف	ق	ك	م	هـ	و	ي

When the definite article أَلْ is attached to an indefinite word beginning with a moon letter, the ل of أَلْ is fully and clearly pronounced. In case it is preceded by a word, the last letter of this word is linked to ل of أَلْ, e.g.

بَابٌ (door) --> الْبَابُ (the door)

الْبَابُ + عَلَى <-- عَلَى الْبَابِ (on the door)

Here are examples of all the Moon Letters:

DEFINITE ARTICLE PRECEDED BY LETTER/WORD	DEFINITE ARTICLE ATTACHED TO WORD	MOON LETTER
بِالْأَمْرِ (by the order)	الْأَمْرُ (the order)	أ
فِي الْبَيْتِ (in the house)	الْبَيْتُ (the house)	ب

ج	الْجَمَلُ (the camel)	عَلَى الْجَمَلِ (on the camel)
ح	الْحَاكِمُ (the ruler)	أَمْرُ الْحَاكِمِ (order of the ruler)
خ	الْخِتَامُ (end)	فِي الْخِتَامِ (at the end)
ع	الْعَيْنُ (the spring)	فِي الْعَيْنِ (in the spring)
غ	الْغُرَابُ (the crow)	لِلْغُرَابِ (for the crow)
ف	الْفُنْدُقُ (the hotel)	فِي الْفُنْدُقِ (in the hotel)
ق	الْقَوْمُ (the people man)	لِلْقَوْمِ (for the people)
ك	الْكَرِيْمُ (noble)	اِبْنُ الْكَرِيْمِ (son of the noble man)
م	الْمَطَرُ (the rain)	فِي الْمَطَرِ (in the rain)
ه	الْهَاتِفُ (the telephone)	بِالْهَاتِفِ (by telephone)
و	الْوَطَنُ (the country)	حُبُّ الْوَطَنِ (patriotism)
ي	الْيَقِيْنُ (the certainty)	بِالْيَقِيْنِ (with certainty)

Exercise:

1. Memorize the moon letters.
2. Read the following words.

الْأَرْنَبُ - فِي الْبَحْرِ - الْخَيْلُ - عَلَى الْجِسْرِ

(on the bridge) (the horse) (in the sea) (the rabbit)

عِلْمُ الْحَيَاةِ - الْيُسْرىٰ - مِنَ الْغُرْفَةِ - الْقَاهِرَةُ

(Cairo) (from the room) (the left (hand)) (biology)

يَوْمُ الْفَصْلِ - الْمَطَرُ - خِيَانَةُ الْوَعْدِ

(breach of promise) (the rain) (the day of judgement)

عَمُوْدُ الْكَهْرَبَاءِ - حَدِيْثُ الْعَهْدِ - الْهَيْكَلُ

       (temple)   (recent)   (electric pole)

3. Write five words each as directed.

(a) Beginning with a moon letter without ال.

(b) Beginning with a moon letter with ال.

(c) Beginning with a moon letter with ال preceded by a word or a particle.

LESSON 13

The Complete Sentence اَلْجُمْلَةُ الْمُفِيدَةُ

+⟨⟩+

Examples:

The breeze is refreshing.	النَّسِيْمُ مُنْعِشٌ۔
Health is a boon.	الصِّحَّةُ نِعْمَةٌ۔
Hamid ate an apple.	أَكَلَ حَامِدٌ تُفَّاحَةً۔
The merchant sold the wool.	بَاعَ التَّاجِرُ الصُّوْفَ۔
The student went to school.	ذَهَبَ التِّلْمِيْذُ إِلَى الْمَدْرَسَةِ۔
The child slept in the cradle.	نَامَ الطِّفْلُ فِي الْمَهْدِ۔

Discussion:

If we look at the first sentence, we find that it is made up of two words. The first one is "النَّسِيْمُ", while the second one is "مُنْعِشٌ-" If we take the first word, i.e. "النَّسِيْمُ" alone, we get to know only its meaning i.e. the breeze. Similarly, if we take the second word, i.e. "مُنْعِشٌ", it would mean only refreshing. But if we put both these words together as we see in the above examples, and say "النَّسِيْمُ مُنْعِشٌ" we get the complete sense, i.e. the breeze is refreshing. Therefore, a group of words giving complete meaning is called the complete sentence, i.e. الْجُمْلَةُ الْمُفِيدَةُ.

Rule:

1. A group of words giving complete meaning is called a complete sentence (الْجُمْلَةُ الْمُفِيْدَةُ).

2. A complete sentence (الْجُمْلَةُ الْمُفِيْدَةُ) may consist of two words at the minimum.

Exercise:

1. Choose a suitable word(s) and complete the sentences.

حَارٌّ (hot)	ذَهَبَ إِلَى (went)	مَحْبُوْبٌ (loved)
تَخْبِزُ (bakes)	فِي (in)	يَسْقِي (irrigates)

١) التِّلْمِيْذُ ـــــــ الْمَدْرَسَة ـ   ٢) الْبِنْتُ ـــــــ الْخُبْز ـ

٣) الْبُسْتَانِيُّ ـــــــ الْحَدِيْقَة ـ   ٤) الرَّجُلُ الْأَمِيْنُ ـــــــ ـ

٥) الْجَوُّ ـــــــ ـ   ٦) الْمَالُ ـــــــ الْخِزَانَة ـ

2. Use the following words in your own sentences.

صِدْقٌ ـ نَجْمٌ ـ قِطَّةٌ ـ نَهْرٌ

3. Make sentences, consisting of only two words, with each of the following words.

قَهْوَةٌ ـ سَمَاءٌ ـ دَمٌ ـ أَمِيْرَةٌ

4. Make two sentences of each category as follows:

   a) Consisting of two words.

   b) Consisting of three words.

   c) Consisting of four words.

5. Translate the following into Arabic.

   a) The boy is short.

b) The blood is red.

c) Aisha is tall.

d) The cat ate the mouse.

e) The child tore the magazine.

f) The mother cooks in the kitchen.

g) The doctor goes to the hospital.

h) The house is new.

i) The monument is old.

j) The worker works in the factory.

6. Translate the following into English.

١ ـ الْحُجْرَةُ نَظِيْفَةٌ ـ

٢ ـ السَّيْفُ قَاطِعٌ ـ

٣ ـ الْحِصَانُ نَشِيْطٌ ـ

٤ ـ الْإِمْتِحَانُ قَرِيْبٌ ـ

٥ ـ ذَهَبَتِ الْبِنْتُ إِلَى الْجَامِعَةِ ـ

٦ ـ كَسَرَ الطِّفْلُ الزُّجَاجَةَ ـ

٧ ـ قَاتَلَ الْجُنْدِيُّ فِي الْحَرْبِ ـ

٨ ـ قَرَأَ التِّلْمِيْذُ الدَّرْسَ ـ

GLOSSARY	الْكَلِمَاتُ الْعَسِيْرَةُ
bread	خُبْزٌ (أَخْبَازٌ)
gardener	بُسْتَانِيٌّ
honest	أَمِيْنٌ (أُمَنَاءُ)

weather	جَوٌّ (أَجْوَاءٌ)
safe	خِزَانَةٌ (خَزَائِنُ)
truth	صِدْقٌ
star	نَجْمٌ (نُجُوْمٌ)
cat	قِطَّةٌ (قِطَطٌ)
river	نَهْرٌ (أَنْهَارٌ)
coffee	قَهْوَةٌ
sky	سَمَاءٌ
blood	دَمٌ (دِمَاءٌ)
princess	أَمِيْرَةٌ (أَمِيْرَاتٌ)
short	قَصِيْرٌ (قِصَارٌ)
red	أَحْمَرُ - حَمْرَاءُ f. (حُمْرٌ)
long	طَوِيْلٌ (طِوَالٌ)
to eat	أَكَلَ - يَأْكُلُ - أَكْلٌ
mouse	فَأْرٌ (فِيْرَانٌ)
child	طِفْلٌ (أَطْفَالٌ)
to tear	مَزَّقَ - يُمَزِّقُ - تَمْزِيْقٌ
magazine	مَجَلَّةٌ (مَجَلَّاتٌ)
mother	أُمٌّ (أُمَّهَاتٌ)
to cook	طَبَخَ - يَطْبُخُ - طَبْخٌ
kitchen	مَطْبَخٌ (مَطَابِخُ)

doctor	طَبِيبٌ (أَطِبَّاءُ)
to go	ذَهَبَ - يَذْهَبُ - ذَهَابٌ
hospital	مُسْتَشْفَى (مُسْتَشْفَيَاتٌ)
new	جَدِيدٌ (جُدُدٌ)
monument	عِمَارَةٌ (عِمَارَاتٌ)
old	قَدِيمٌ (قُدَمَاءُ)
worker	عَامِلٌ (عُمَّالٌ)
to work	عَمِلَ - يَعْمَلُ - عَمَلٌ
factory	مَصْنَعٌ (مَصَانِعُ)
room	حُجْرَةٌ (حُجُرَاتٌ)
clean	نَظِيْفٌ
sword	سَيْفٌ (سُيُوْفٌ)
cutting (sharp)	قَاطِعٌ
horse	حِصَانٌ (حُصْنٌ)
active	نَشِيْطٌ
to break	كَسَرَ - يَكْسِرُ - كَسْرٌ
glass bottle	زُجَاجَةٌ (زُجَاجَاتٌ)
to fight	قَاتَلَ - يُقَاتِلُ - مُقَاتَلَةٌ
soldier	جُنْدِيٌّ (جُنُوْدٌ)

LESSON 14

Parts of the Sentence أَجْزَاءُ الْجُمْلَةِ

+≽≼+

Examples:

Ashraf bought a camel.	اِشْتَرَى أَشْرَفُ جَمَلًا۔
Kashif is a hardworking boy.	كَاشِفٌ وَلَدٌ مُجْتَهِدٌ۔
The pigeon flies in the sky.	يَطِيْرُ الْحَمَامُ فِي السَّمَاءِ۔
The sparrow is a small bird.	الْعُصْفُوْرُ طَائِرٌ صَغِيْرٌ۔
Mumbai is a big city.	مُوْمْبَاى مَدِيْنَةٌ كَبِيْرَةٌ۔
The minister visited Cairo.	زَارَ الْوَزِيْرُ الْقَاهِرَةَ۔
The dog ate the bread.	أَكَلَ الْكَلْبُ الْخُبْزَ۔
The lion killed the cow.	اِفْتَرَسَ الْأَسَدُ الْبَقَرَةَ۔
The advocate read the will.	قَرَأَ الْمُحَامِي الْوَصِيَّةَ۔
Do you like poetry?	هَلْ تُحِبُّ الشِّعْرَ؟
The sun illuminates the earth.	تُنِيْرُ الشَّمْسُ الْأَرْضَ۔
The pen is on the desk.	الْقَلَمُ عَلَى الطَّاوِلَةِ۔

Discussion:

We read in the previous lesson that the sentence is a group of words placed in a certain order.

There are words which indicate people, like أَشْرَف, وَلَدٌ, كَاشِف and الْوَزِيْر and الْمُحَامِي or indicate birds and animals,

like الْحَمَامُ ,الْعُصْفُوْرُ ,الْكَلْبُ and الْأَسَدُ or indicate places, like
مُوْمْبَاى and الْقَاهِرَةُ, etc., or indicate things, like الْقَلَمُ and
الطَّاوِلَةُ or indicate any action, like الْقِرَاءَةُ ,الْكِتَابَةُ. All these
words give their meaning independently without the help of
any other word. Moreover, no tense is understood by them.
Therefore, we can say that the words which give their
meaning independently and indicate any person, animal,
place, thing or action, without showing any tense, are called
nouns (أَسْمَاءٌ).

Again, if we look at such words as اشْتَرَى ,يَطِيْرُ ,زَارَ,
أَكَلَ ,افْتَرَسَ ,قَرَأَ ,تُحِبُّ and تُنِيْرُ, we see that these words
indicate the occurence of an action at a particular time. For
example, the word 'اِشْتَرَى' indicates the occurrence of the
act of buying in the past. Whereas the word 'يَطِيْرُ' indicates
the act of flying in the present or future and so on. These
words are called verbs (أَفْعَالٌ).

There are words like فِي, and عَلَى which do not give
their full sense unless joined to a noun or a verb. They only
help in making sentences. These words are called particles
(حُرُوْفٌ).

Rule:

1. The word 'الْكَلِمَةُ' has three categories. They are as
   follows:
   a) Noun (إِسْمٌ)
   b) Verb (فِعْلٌ)

c) Particle (حَرْفٌ)

In Short:

a) A noun (إِسْمٌ) is a word which gives its meaning independently and indicates any person, animal, place, thing or action without showing any tense.

b) A verb (فِعْلٌ) is a word which indicates the occurrence or performance of an action at a particular time.

c) A particle (حَرْفٌ) is a word which does not give its meaning (sense) without the help of another word, e.g.

. فِي الْحُجْرَةِ , مِنَ الْبَيْتِ

Exercise:

1. Make two sentences each as follows:

a) Beginning with a noun (person).

b) Beginning with a noun (animal).

c) Beginning with a noun (thing).

d) Beginning with a verb.

e) Using a particle.

f) Consisting of only two nouns.

g) Consisting of a noun and a verb only.

h) Consisting of a noun, a verb and a particle.

2. Choose a suitable noun and fill in the blanks.

الدُّكَّان	الصَّحْرَاء	الْعُشْب	الْغُرْفَة	الأَرْض
(the shop)	(the desert)	(the grass)	(the room)	(the ground)

الْبَيْت	الْخَادِم	الطُّيُوْر	الصُّوَرَة	الْحِصَان
(the house)	(the servant)	(the birds)	(the picture)	(the horse)

١- الْمَاءُ نَادِرٌ فِي ــــــــــ -

٢- يَفْتَحُ التَّاجِرُ ــــــــــ -

٣- تَتَغَنَّى ــــــــــ -

٤- يَرْكَبُ الْجُنْدِىُّ ــــــــــ -

٥- يَخْدُمُ ــــــــــ الْمَالِكَ -

٦- تَكْنُسُ الْعَمَّةُ ــــــــــ -

٧- يَنْبُتُ ــــــــــ فِي الْمَيْدَانِ -

٨- يَحْرُثُ الْفَلَّاحُ ــــــــــ -

٩- هُوَ بَعِيْدٌ عَنْ ــــــــــ -

١٠- ــــــــــ مُعَلَّقَةٌ على الْحَائِطِ -

3. Choose a suitable verb and fill in the blanks.

يَشْرَبُ	يَقْتُلُ	جَرَّ	يَسُوْقُ	دَقَّ
(drinks)	(kills)	(pulled)	(drives)	(struck)
يَسْرِقُ	حَاصَرَ	يَخْبِزُ	يَدْعُوْ	غَطَّى
(steals)	(surrounded)	(bakes)	(calls)	(covered)

١- النَّمِرُ ــــــــــ الشَّاةَ -

٢- ــــــــــ الْجُنُوْدُ الْقَلْعَةَ -

٣- الْمَرِيْضُ ــــــــــ اللَّهَ -

٤- اللِّصُّ _____ الْمَالَ.

٥- الْخَبَّازُ _____ الْخُبْزَ.

٦- السَّائِقُ _____ السَّيَّارَةَ.

٧- الْفَرَّاشُ _____ الْجَرَسَ.

٨- _____ الْعَطْشَانُ الْمَاءَ.

٩- _____ السَّحَابُ السَّمَاءَ.

١٠- _____ الثَّوْرُ الْعَرَبَةَ.

4. Choose a suitable particle/preposition and fill in the blanks.

عَلَى	مِنْ	إِلَى	فِي	عَنْ
(on)	(from)	(to)	(in)	(about)

لِ		بِ	
(for)		(by, at, with, in)	

١- يَتَأَلَّمُ الطَّائِرُ _____ الْقَفَصِ.

٢- سَافَرَ نَبِيلٌ _____ الْمَدِينَةِ.

٣- بَحَثْتُ _____ النَّجَّارِ الْمَاهِرِ.

٤- أَرْسَلَ الْخَادِمُ الرِّسَالَةَ _____ الْمُدِيرِ.

٥- كَسَرْتُ اللَّوْزَةَ _____ الْحَجَرِ.

٦- جَرَيْنَا _____ بَيْتِهِ _____ بَيْتِنَا.

٧- يَمْكُثُ الْمُسَافِرُ _____ الْفُنْدُقِ.

٨- اِنْتَظَرَ الْمَرِيضُ _____ الطَّبِيبِ.

٩- سَافَرْتَ _____ الْبَاصِ.

١٠- يَقْبِضُ الْبُولِيسُ _____ الْقَاتِلِ.

5. Translate the following into Arabic.

   a) He broke the mirror.

   b) The boy stood on the dais.

   c) Birds chirped in the morning.

   d) The train is fast.

   e) The girl wrote a letter.

   f) Kolkata is a big city.

   g) The sun rises in the east.

   h) The tiger chased the lamb.

   i) The apple is red.

   j) The money is in the pocket.

6. Translate the following into English.

١ ـ إِسْتَرَاحَ الْمُسَافِرُ تَحْتَ الشَّجَرَةِ.

٢ ـ الشَّجَرَةُ مُثْمِرَةٌ.

٣ ـ الْهَوَاءُ صَافٍ.

٤ ـ تَفَتَّحَ زَهْرُ الْوَرْدِ.

٥ ـ إِشْتَرَى الْجَزَّارُ الْكَبْشَ.

٦ ـ أَدْلَى الْوَزِيرُ بِالْخِطَابِ.

٧ ـ الشَّايِ فِي الْفِنْجَانِ.

٨ ـ تُعْطِي الْجَامُوسَةُ اللَّبَنَ.

٩ ـ بَحَثَتِ الشُّرْطَةُ عَنِ السَّارِقِ.

١٠ ـ نَظَرَتِ الْأُمُّ إِلَى طِفْلِهَا.

GLOSSARY	الْكَلِمَاتُ الْعَسِيْرَةُ
mirror	مِرْآةٌ (مَرَايَا)
to break	كَسَرَ - يَكْسِرُ - كَسْرٌ
to stand	وَقَفَ - يَقِفُ - وُقُوفٌ
dais	مِنَصَّةٌ
to chirp, sing	تَغَنَّى - يَتَغَنَّى - تَغَنٍّ
lamb	حَمَلٌ (حُمْلَانٌ)
to chase	طَارَدَ - يُطَارِدُ - مُطَارَدَةٌ
tiger	نَمِرٌ (نُمُرٌ)
to take rest	اِسْتِرَاحَ - يَسْتَرِيْحُ - اِسْتِرَاحَةٌ
butcher	جَزَّارٌ (جَزَّارُوْنَ)
male sheep	كَبْشٌ
to deliver a speech	أَدْلَى بِخِطَابٍ
she buffalo	جَامُوْسَةٌ

LESSON 15

The Subject and the Predicate الْمُبْتَدَأُ وَالْخَبَرُ

◆❖◆

Examples:

The infant is sleeping.	الرَّضِيْعُ نَائِمٌ۔
The snow is falling.	الثَّلْجُ سَاقِطٌ۔
The house is near.	الْمَنْزِلُ قَرِيْبٌ۔
The garden is beautiful.	الْحَدِيْقَةُ جَمِيْلَةٌ۔
Allah is merciful.	اللهُ رَحِيْمٌ۔
The girl is hardworking.	الْبِنْتُ مُجْتَهِدَةٌ۔
The weight is heavy.	الْوَزْنُ ثَقِيْلٌ۔
The knowledge is beneficial.	الْعِلْمُ نَافِعٌ۔
The rate is high.	السِّعْرُ رَفِيْعٌ۔
Iraq is distant.	الْعِرَاقُ بَعِيْدٌ۔

Discussion:

Look at the examples above. They are all sentences made up of two parts. The first part in each sentence is a noun (therefore the sentence is a nominal sentence). The first part, about which something is said in the remaining part, is called the subjects (الْمُبْتَدَأُ)

The second part which gives us some information

and makes us understand the meaning of the sentence by providing the information about the subject (الْمُبْتَدَأُ) is called the predicates (الْخَبَرُ).

Rule:

1. The noun by which a nominal sentence begins is called the subject, i.e. 'الْمُبْتَدَأُ'.

2. The part of a nominal sentence which provides the information about the subject 'الْمُبْتَدَأُ' is called the predicate 'الْخَبَرُ'.

Exercise:

1. Pick out the subjects and the predicates from the following sentences:

٢- الْحَرُّ شَدِيدٌ۔	١- الْحُجْرَةُ نَظِيْفَةٌ۔
٤- الْعِنَبُ حَامِضٌ۔	٣- الدَّرْسُ سَهْلٌ۔
٦- الرِّوَايَةُ طَوِيْلَةٌ۔	٥- الْبِنْتُ جَمِيْلَةٌ۔
٨- الطَّرِيْقُ ضَيِّقٌ۔	٧- الْأَرْضُ وَاسِعَةٌ۔
١٠- النَّجَاحُ قَرِيْبٌ۔	٩- اللَّيْلُ مُقْمِرٌ۔

2. Translate the sentences given in exercise no.1 into English.

3. Give the predicate (الْخَبَرُ) to each of the following subjects (الْمُبْتَدَأُ).

١) الْكِذْبُ ٢) النَّعْلُ ٣) الْجَمَلُ

٤) الْعَصِيْرُ ٥) الطَّاوِلَةُ ٦) السَّيَّارَةُ

٧) الْبَيْتُ ٨) الْقَامُوْسُ ٩) الْوِسَادَةُ

4. Give the subject (الْمُبْتَدَأُ) to each of the following predicates (الْخَبَرُ).

١) مُثْمِرٌ ٢) فَسِيْحَةٌ ٣) مُنْعِشٌ

٤) قَاطِعٌ ٥) مُجْتَهِدٌ ٦) لَامِعَةٌ

٧) مَمْلُوْءَةٌ ٨) بَسِيْطٌ ٩) صَعْبٌ

5. Make three sentences each as directed.

a) consisting of subject and predicate.

b) with الْقِرْدُ (the monkey) as subject.

c) with السَّاعَةُ (the clock) as subject.

6. Translate the following into Arabic.

a) The bucket is small.

b) The earth is moving.

c) The notebook is new.

d) The clown is laughing.

e) The computer is fast.

f) The pilot is active.

g) The hair is black.

h) The bangle is beautiful.

i) The ocean is deep.

j) The song is sweet.

7. Translate the following into English.

١) الْبَيَانُ وَاضِحٌ۔

٢) زَيْدٌ كَرِيمٌ۔

٣) الثَّرِيُّ مَسْرُورٌ۔

٤) الْفَقِيرُ مِسْكِينٌ۔

٥) الْإِبْنُ مُطِيعٌ۔

٦) الْكُوَيْتُ دَوْلَةٌ عَرَبِيَّةٌ۔

٧) الْقَامُوسُ مُفِيدٌ۔

٨) الْمَوْتُ مَحْتُومٌ۔

٩) الْوَرَقُ خَفِيفٌ۔

١٠) الأَرْضُ مُسْتَدِيرَةٌ۔

GLOSSARY	الْكَلِمَاتُ الْعَسِيرَةُ
sour, acid	حَامِضٌ
shoe; horseshoe	نَعْلٌ (نِعَالٌ)
bucket	سَطْلٌ (سُطُولٌ)
clown	مُهَرِّجٌ
pilot	طَيَّارٌ (طَيَّارُونَ)
bracelet, armlet, bangle	سِوَارٌ (أَسْوِرَةٌ)
inevitable, destined	مَحْتُومٌ
round; circular	مُسْتَدِيرَةٌ

LESSON 16

The Nominal Sentence الْجُمْلَةُ الْإِسْمِيّةُ

+<><>+

Examples:

The room is closed.	الْحُجْرَةُ مُغْلَقَةٌ۔
The journey is tiring.	السَّفَرُ مُتْعِبٌ۔
The man is generous.	الرَّجُلُ سَخِيٌّ.
The mango is delicious.	الْأَنْبَجُ لَذِيذٌ۔
The mother is dear.	الْأُمُّ مَحْبُوْبَةٌ۔
The tree is fruitful.	الشَّجَرَةُ مُثْمِرَةٌ۔
The princess is a spinster.	الْأَمِيْرَةُ عَانِسٌ۔
The Negro is strong.	الزَّنْجِيُّ قَوِيٌّ۔

Discussion:

Look at the examples above. They all are sentences giving complete information to the reader. Further observation tells us that they are made up of two parts. The first one is a subject and the second one is a predicate. As each sentence begins with a noun, it is called a Nominal Sentence الْجُمْلَةُ الْإِسْمِيّةُ.

Rule:

1. The sentence that begins with a noun is called a
Nominal Sentence 'الْجُمْلَةُ الإِسْمِيَّةُ'.

2. The Nominal Sentence has two parts i.e. subject 'مُبْتَدَأٌ'
and predicate 'خَبَرٌ'.

Exercise:

1. Write a suitable predicate for each of the following
subjects.

٦ ـ الْخَنْجَرُ	١ ـ النَّارُ
٧ ـ الطَّالِبَةُ	٢ ـ الْبُلْبُلُ
٨ ـ الثَّلْجُ	٣ ـ السَّلَّةُ
٩ ـ الأُسْتَاذُ	٤ ـ الْفِيلُ
١٠ـ السُّلَحْفَاةُ	٥ ـ الْكَوْكَبُ

2. Write a suitable subject for each of the following
predicates.

٦ ـ وَسِخٌ	١ ـ سَرِيعٌ
٧ ـ حَسَنَةٌ	٢ ـ مُفِيدَةٌ
٨ ـ حُلْوٌ	٣ ـ رَفِيعٌ
٩ ـ كَبِيرٌ	٤ ـ بَطِيئٌ
١٠ ـ حَادَّةٌ	٥ ـ نَظِيفٌ

3. Make two nominal sentences each as directed:

a) with a noun (person) as subject.

b) with a noun (animal) as subject.

c) with a noun (plant) as subject.

4. Underline the words that are subjects in the following sentences.

٦ـ اللَّبُوءَةُ مُفْتَرِسَةٌ.   ١ـ الْقِطَارُ وَاقِفٌ.

٧ـ الْغَضَبُ شَدِيدٌ.   ٢ـ الثَّوْبُ قَصِيرٌ.

٨ـ الشَّمْسُ طَالِعَةٌ.   ٣ـ الْمُسَافِرُ جَوْعَانٌ.

٩ـ الْوَطَنُ بَعِيدٌ.   ٤ـ الْقِطَّةُ لَاعِبَةٌ.

١٠ـ الْبِئْرُ جَافَّةٌ.   ٥ـ النَّاجِحُ فَرِحٌ.

5. Underline the words that are predicates in the following sentences.

٦ـ الْمَاءُ جَارٍ.   ١ـ الْوَلَدُ شَابٌّ.

٧ـ الصَّدِيقُ مُخْلِصٌ.   ٢ـ السَّيَّارَةُ سَرِيعَةٌ.

٨ـ الْأُمُّ قَلِقَةٌ.   ٣ـ الْأَوْلَادُ نَائِمُوْنَ.

٩ـ الْبَحْرُ هَائِجٌ.   ٤ـ الْبَيْتُ وَاسِعٌ.

١٠ـ الْجَامِعَةُ مُغْلَقَةٌ.   ٥ـ الْفِنْجَانُ فَارِغٌ.

6. Translate the following into Arabic.

a) The crowd is big.

b) The rabbit is quick.

c) The night is dark.

d) The prince is cruel.

e) The governor is coming.

f) The apricot is bitter.

g) The news is old.

h) The shepherd is frightened.

i) The saleswoman is busy.

j) The volcano is active.

7. Translate the following into English.

١) الْمَطَرُ نَازِلٌ۔

٢) الْأَسْعَارُ مُرْتَفِعَةٌ۔

٣) الرِّيَاضَةُ مُفِيْدَةٌ۔

٤) الْفَوْزُ قَرِيْبٌ۔

٥) الْاِوَزُّ فِي الْبِرْكَةِ۔

٦) الْحَاسُوْبُ سَرِيْعٌ۔

٧) التَّعَاوُنُ وَاجِبٌ۔

٨) الْخَطِيْبُ عَلَى الْمِنْبَرِ۔

٩) السُّفُنُ سَائِرَةٌ فِي الْبِحَارِ۔

١٠) السَّاعَةُ مُعَلَّقَةٌ عَلَى الْحَائِطِ۔

GLOSSARY	الْكَلِمَاتُ الْعَسِيْرَةُ
lioness	لَبُؤَةٌ (لَبَآتٌ)
rabbit	fem. أَرْنَبٌ (أَرَانِبُ)
prince	أَمِيْرٌ (أُمَرَاءُ)
governor	مُحَافِظٌ (مُحَافِظُوْنَ)
apricot	مِشْمِش

volcano	بُرْكَانٌ (بَرَاكِيْنُ)
active	نَشِيْطٌ (نِشَاطٌ)
goose	إِوَزٌّ
cooperation	تَعَاوُنٌ

LESSON 17

The Verbal Sentence الْجُمْلَةُ الْفِعْلِيَّةُ

+❖+

Examples:

The wind blew.	هَبَّتِ الرِّيْحُ.
The teacher came.	حَضَرَ الْمُعَلِّمُ.
The hen lays eggs.	تَبِيْضُ الدَّجَاجَةُ.
The camel knelt down.	بَرَكَ الْجَمَلُ.
Wash your face.	اِغْسِلْ وَجْهَكَ.
Open the window.	اِفْتَحِ النَّافِذَةَ.
She wrote with the pencil.	كَتَبَتْ بِقَلَمِ الرَّصَاصِ.
I know his address.	أَعْرِفُ عُنْوَانَهُ.
The ducklings follow the mother.	تَتْبَعُ الْأَفْرَاخُ الْأُمَّ.
The writer edited the book.	حَرَّرَ الْكَاتِبُ الْكِتَابَ.

Discussion:

Look at the examples above. They are all sentences giving complete information to the reader. Further observation tells us that they all begin with a verb. Some sentences have a perfect verb, some have an imperfect verb while the remaining have an imperative verb. This type of sentence which begins with a verb is known as verbal sentence ٬ جُمْلَةٌ فِعْلِيَّةٌ.

Rule:

1. Every sentence which begins with a verb of any kind is known as verbal sentence اَلْجُمْلَةُ الْفِعْلِيَّةُ'.

Exercise:

1. Give a doer (subject) for each of the following verbs.

٦_ يَعْلُوْ		١_ اِسْتِرَاحَ
٧_ تَتَجَلَّى		٢_ تَفَتَّحَتْ
٨_ نَمَا		٣_ أَوْرَقَ
٩_ تَشْتَعِلُ		٤_ صَفَا
١٠_ يَبْكِي		٥_ تَيَسَّرَ

2. Write a suitable perfect verb for each of the following nouns.

٦_ الْأَمِيْرَةُ		١_ الْحِصَانُ
٧_ الْمُسَافِرُ		٢_ النُّوْرُ
٨_ الْقَمْحُ		٣_ الْبَلَدُ
٩_ النَّغْمَةُ		٤_ الْمُبَارَاةُ
١٠_ الْقَارِبُ		٥_ الثَّعْلَبُ

3. Write a suitable imperfect tense for each of the following nouns.

٦_ الْبَائِعُ		١_ الْغُرَابُ
٧_ النُّزْهَةُ		٢_ الْعِلْمُ
٨_ الْمَطْبَخُ		٣_ الْحَفْلَةُ
٩_ الشَّايِ		٤_ الشَّأْنُ
١٠_ الْعَدُوُّ		٥_ السُّوْقُ

4. Make two verbal sentences each as follows:

  a) Consisting of a perfect verb and a doer only.

  b) Consisting of an imperfect verb and a doer only.

  c) Consisting of a perfect verb, a doer and an object.

  d) Consisting of an imperfect verb, a doer and an object.

  e) Having الْمَحَطَّةُ (the station) as subject.

5. Translate the following into Arabic.

  a) The servant found the watch.

  b) She came late.

  c) Carelessness caused the accident.

  d) The judge gave a bad judgement.

  e) We got a good result.

  f) Close the shop early.

  g) The child folded the newspaper.

  h) My wife lost her necklace.

  i) The spy betrayed his country.

  j) The policeman lit a cigarette.

6. Translate the following into English.

١) رَأَيْتُ التِّمْسَاحَ فِي الْبِرْكَةِ۔

٢) وَضَعَ الدَّوَاةَ عَلَى الطَّاوِلَةِ۔

٣) تَبْكِي الْأَرْمَلَةُ۔

٤) تَعِبَ الْمُصَارِعُ۔

٥) تَدْفَعُ الْأُمُّ الْأُجْرَةَ.

٦) رَكِبَ الدَّرَّاجَةَ النَّارِيَّةَ.

٧) جِئْنَا مِنْ فِلَسْطِينَ.

٨) يُحَلِّقُ النَّسْرُ فِي السَّمَاءِ.

٩) أَكَلْتُمُ الْبَطَاطِسَ.

١٠) إِشْتَرَى الابْنُ اللُّعْبَةَ.

GLOSSARY	الْكَلِمَاتُ الْعَسِيْرَةُ
carelessness	إِهْمَالٌ
necklace	قِلَادَةٌ (قَلَائِدُ)
spy	جَاسُوسٌ (جَوَاسِيْسُ)
betray	خَانَ - يَخُوْنُ - خِيَانَةٌ
cigarette	سِيْجَارَةٌ (سَجَائِرُ)
crocodile	تِمْسَاحٌ (تَمَاسِيْحُ)
wrestler	مُصَارِعٌ (مُصَارِعُوْنَ)
Palestine	فِلَسْطِينُ
to hover	حَلَّقَ - يُحَلِّقُ - تَحْلِيْقٌ
potato	بَطَاطِسُ

LESSON 18

The Past Tense Verb (The Perfect Tense Verb)
الْفِعْلُ الْمَاضِي

Examples:

The boy laughed.	ضَحِكَ الْوَلَدُ۔
The crow flew.	طَارَ الْغُرَابُ۔
The child became happy.	فَرِحَ الطِّفْلُ۔
The train stopped.	وَقَفَ الْقِطَارُ۔
The rain fell.	نَزَلَ الْمَطَرُ۔
The goat sat down.	رَبَضَتِ الشَّاةُ۔
The grandmother slept.	نَامَتِ الْجَدَّةُ۔
The match started.	بَدَأَتِ الْمُبَارَاةُ۔
The girl feared.	خَافَتِ الْبِنْتُ۔
The wind blew.	هَبَّتِ الرِّيْحُ۔

Discussion:

Look at the examples above. You will find that the first word of each sentence is a verb, and it indicates the occurrence or performance of an action at a particular time. On further study, you will find that each of them indicates a time in the past.

Hence, the word 'ضَحِكَ' in the first sentence indicates the occurrence of the action of laughing in the past. Similarly, the word 'طَارَ' in the second sentence shows the act of flying in the past and so on.

Therefore, each of these words is called a past tense verb (فِعْلٌ مَاضٍ).

Rule:

The Past Tense Verb (الْفِعْلُ الْمَاضِي) indicates the occurrence or performance of an action in the past.

Exercise:

1. Choose a suitable past tense verb from the given verbs for the nouns given below:

اشْتَدَّ (to be severe)	حَضَرَ (to attend)	نَامَ (to sleep)	ضَاعَ (to get lost)	نَضِجَ (to ripen)
ضَلَّ (to lose one's way)	سَهُلَ (to be easy)	اخْضَرَّ (to be green)	تَعِبَ (to be tired)	كَمُلَ (to be full)

الثَّمَرُ - الْقَامُوسُ - الْمُسَافِرُ - الْحَرُّ

الدَّرْسُ - الْكَلْبُ - الْوَزِيرُ - الْقَمَرُ

الْمَلْعَبُ - الْمَلَّاحُ

2. Fill in the blanks using the past tense verbs given below:

أَكَلَ	اسْتَرَاحَ	أَخَذَ	رَجَعَ	رَوَتْ
(to eat)	(to take rest)	(to take)	(to return)	(to tell)
سَاقَ	جَاءَ	إِنْكَسَرَ	طَلَعَتْ	إِنْعَقَدَ
(to drive)	(to come)	(to break itself)	(to rise)	(to be held)

١- _____ فَصْلُ الصَّيْفِ۔   ٢- _____ الزُّجَاجُ۔

٣- _____ الْعَامِلُ۔   ٤- _____ الْإِجْتِمَاعُ فِي الصَّبَاحِ۔

٥- _____ الشَّمْسُ۔   ٦- الرَّاعِي _____ غَنَمَهُ۔

٧- الْجَائِعُ _____ تَمْرًا۔   ٨- الْجَدَّةُ _____ قِصَصًا۔

٩- الْمُسَافِرُ _____ إِلَى بَيْتِهِ۔   ١٠- الطِّفْلُ _____ لُعْبَةً۔

3. Make ten sentences with the past tense verbs.

4. Translate the following into Arabic.

a) The thief fled.

b) The winter season arrived.

c) The woman sat on the chair.

d) The child lost the key.

e) The star shone in the sky.

f) The gatekeeper opened the factory.

g) He cut the wire.

h) The boy read a story.

i) The gardener irrigated the garden.

j) The swimmer dived into the pool.

5. Translate the following into English.

١) زَحَفَتِ السُّلَحْفَاةُ۔

٢) ضَعُفَتِ الْجَدَّةُ۔

٣) جَرَى النَّهْرُ۔

٤) أَحْرَقَتِ النَّارُ الْبَيْتَ۔

٥) قَدِمَ الْوَفْدُ۔

٦) كَسَرَتِ الْبِنْتُ الْقَدَحَ۔

٧) جَلَبَ الْخَادِمُ الْمَاءَ۔

٨) حَفَرَتِ الْآلَةُ الْأَرْضَ۔

٩) أَخَذَ الْمَرِيْضُ الدَّوَاءَ۔

١٠) حَفَرَ الْعُمَّالُ الْأَرْضَ۔

GLOSSARY	الْكَلِمَاتُ الْعَسِيْرَةُ
fruit	ثَمَرٌ (ثِمَارٌ)
dictionary	قَامُوسٌ (قَوَامِيْسُ)
passenger	مُسَافِرٌ (مُسَافِرُوْنَ)
heat	حَرٌّ
sailor	مَلَّاحٌ
shepherd	رَاعٍ (رُعَاةٌ)
sheep	غَنَمٌ (أَغْنَامٌ)
hungry	جَائِعٌ (جَائِعُوْنَ)
thief	سَارِقٌ (سَارِقُوْنَ)

to flee	فَرَّ - يَفِرُّ - فِرَارٌ
to lose	فَقَدَ - يَفْقِدُ - فُقْدَانٌ
key	مِفْتَاحٌ (مَفَاتِيْحُ)
string, wire	سِلْكٌ (أَسْلَاكٌ)
to dive (into)	غَاصَ - يَغُوْصُ - غَوْصٌ
to creep, crawl	زَحَفَ - يَزْحَفُ - زَحْفٌ
delegation	وَفْدٌ (وُفُوْدٌ)
medicine	دَوَاءٌ (أَدْوِيَةٌ)
to dig	حَفَرَ - يَحْفِرُ - حَفْرٌ

LESSON 19

Conjugation of the Past Tense Verb
(The Perfect Tense Verb)
تَصْرِيفُ الْفِعْلِ الْمَاضِي

+3E+

(1)

MASCULINE	Singular (مُفْرَدٌ)	he (it) went	ذَهَبَ
THIRD PERSON	Dual (مُثَنَّى)	they (two) went	ذَهَبَا
الْمُذَكَّرُ الْغَائِبُ	Plural (جَمْعٌ)	they went	ذَهَبُوا

(2)

FEMININE	Singular (مُفْرَدٌ)	she (it) went	ذَهَبَتْ
THIRD PERSON	Dual (مُثَنَّى)	they (two) went	ذَهَبَتَا
الْمُؤَنَّثُ الْغَائِبُ	Plural (جَمْعٌ)	they went	ذَهَبْنَ

(3)

MASCULINE	Singular (مُفْرَدٌ)	you went	ذَهَبْتَ
SECOND PERSON	Dual (مُثَنَّى)	you (two) went	ذَهَبْتُمَا
الْمُذَكَّرُ الْمُخَاطَبُ	Plural (جَمْعٌ)	you went	ذَهَبْتُمْ

(4)

FEMININE	Singular (مُفْرَدٌ)	you went	ذَهَبْتِ
SECOND PERSON	Dual (مُثَنَّى)	you (two) went	ذَهَبْتُمَا
الْمُؤَنَّثُ الْمُخَاطَبُ	Plural (جَمْعٌ)	you went	ذَهَبْتُنَّ

(5)

MSCLN. and FEM.	Singular (مُفْرَدٌ)	I went	ذَهَبْتُ
FIRST PERSON	Dual (مُثَنَّى)	we (two) went	ذَهَبْنَا
الْمُذَكَّرُ الْمُتَكَلِّمُ وَالْمُؤَنَّثُ الْمُتَكَلِّمُ	Plural (جَمْعٌ)	we went	ذَهَبْنَا

Discussion:

Look at the conjugation above, you will find that the verbs of groups (1) and (3) are used for the masculine gender. Group (1) indicates the third person and group (3) indicates the second person. Further observation tells us that the first verb of each of these two groups is used for the singular, the second verb for the dual and the third for the plural.

Similarly, the verbs of the groups (2) and (4) are used for the feminine gender. Group (2) indicates the third person and Group (4) indicates the second person. The first verb of each of these two groups is used for the singular, second verb is for the dual and the third is for the plural.

Now, looking at group (5) which is the last one, we find that it is for both masculine and feminine genders and it indicates the first person. The first verb is used for the singular, the second is for the dual and the third is for the plural.

Rule:

1. The original verb ' ذَهَبَ ' i.e. third person masculine singular remains the same, while the other patterns of conjugation are made by suffixing some letters.

2. We suffix ' ا ' to the original past tense verb (third person masucline singular) to denote the third person masculine dual and ' وْا ' preceded by ضَمَّةٌ of the last letter to denote the third person masculine plural.

3. We suffix ' تْ ' to the original past tense verb to denote the third person feminine singular, ' تَا ' for the third person feminine dual and ' نَ ' adding سُكُوْنٌ to the last letter of the verb for the third person feminine plural.

4. We suffix ' تَ ' to the original past tense verb to denote the second person masculine singular, ' تُمَا ' for the second person masculine dual and 'تُمْ' for the second preson masuline plural.

5. We suffix ' تِ ' to the original past tense verb to denote the second person feminine singular, ' تُمَا ' for the second person feminine dual and 'تُنَّ' for the second person feminine plural.

6. We suffix ' تُ ' to the original past tense verb to denote the first person masculine and feminine singular both and 'نَا' for the first person both masculine and feminine dual and again 'نَا' for the first person both masculine and feminine plural.

Exercise:

1. Write the conjugation of the following verbs:

سَمِعَ - ضَرَبَ - فَتَحَ

حَسِبَ - كَرُمَ - نَصَرَ

2. Fill in the blanks with a suitable past tense verb from the verbs given below:

أَتَى	كَتَبْتِ	غَرَسَ	نَبُلْنَ	اِجْتَهَدَ
صَفَا	رَمَّ	ذَاعَ	حَسُنَ	ذَهَبْتُ

١- ــــــــــ النَّجَّارُ الْكُرْسِيَّ- ٢- ــــــــــ إِلَى اِنْجِلْتِرَا -

٣- صِيْتُهُ ــــــــــ - ٤- ــــــــــ الْجَوُّ -

٥- الْفَلَّاحُ ــــــــــ الْجَزَرَ - ٦- ــــــــــ خُلُقُهُ -

٧- ــــــــــ الضُّيُوْفُ- ٨- ــــــــــ الْعَامِلُ -

٩- الْأُمَّهَاتُ ــــــــــ - ١٠- أَنْتِ ــــــــــ الرِّسَالَةَ -

3. Write five sentences on "The Farmer" (الْفَلَّاحُ), each of which should have a past tense verb.

4. Write five sentences on "The Lady Teacher" (الْمُعَلِّمَةُ) each of which should have a past tense verb.

5. Write five sentences each of which should have a past tense verb, telling us about the things you did on the morning of Eid.

6. Translate the following into Arabic.

   a) The boy became tired.

   b) The robbers ran away.

c) The matter became easy.

d) The girl came to the river and filled the bucket.

e) The president flew to Germany.

f) He learnt the Quran by heart.

g) The lady bought the refrigerator.

h) The eye shed tears.

i) The water became warm.

j) The grandmother grabbed the stick.

7. Translate into Arabic.

I woke up early in the morning. I washed my hands and face. My mother also woke up. She prepared breakfast. My father took breakfast. I changed my clothes and went to school. My younger brother and sister also woke up, they cried. My mother gave them milk. My father left for the office. My mother stayed at home.

8. Translate the following into English.

١) جَلَسَتِ الضَّيْفَةُ عَلَى الأَرِيكَةِ۔

٢) زَارَ الطَّبِيبُ الْمَرِيضَ۔

٣) ذَهَبْتُ إِلَى الْمُكْتَبَةِ صَبَاحًا۔

٤) لَبِسَ سَاعِي الْبَرِيدِ الزِّيَّ الرَّسْمِيَّ۔

٥) بَاعَ الْبَقَّالُ الْحُبُوبَ۔

٦) سَقَطَتِ الْفَاكِهَةُ عَلَى الأَرْضِ۔

٧) الأَوْلَادُ لَعِبُوا كُرَةَ الْقَدَمِ۔

٨) شَخَّصَ الطَّبِيبُ الْمَرَضَ بِالْأَشِعَّةِ السِّينِيَّةِ۔

٩) كَسَرْتُمَا الدُّوْلَابَ۔

١٠) قَرَأْتِ الْمَجَلَّةَ۔

١١) الْقِطَارَانِ وَقَفَا عَلَى الْمَحَطَّةِ۔

١٢) شَرِبْتَ الْعَصِيْرَ۔

١٣) فَهِمْتُ الْقَضِيَّةَ۔

١٤) بَدَأْتُم الْمَشْرُوْعَ۔

١٥) فَتَحْنَا الْحُجْرَةَ۔

9. Translate into English.

نَجَحَ حَامِدٌ وَرَاشِدٌ فِي الْاِمْتِحَانِ - وَفَرِحَا - وَذَهَبَا إِلَى الْكُلِّيَّةِ وَقَابَلَا الْأُسْتَاذَ - أَثْنَى الْأُسْتَاذُ عَلَيْهِمَا - قَالَ : اِجْتَهَدْتُمَا فَنَجَحْتُمَا فِي الْاِمْتِحَانِ - مَنَحَتِ الْجَامِعَةُ لَهُمَا جَائِزَةً - عَلِمَ الْوَالِدُ وَالْوَالِدَةُ النَّبَأَ فَفَرِحَا - أَعَدَّتِ الْأُمُّ الطَّعَامَ اللَّذِيْذَ - أَكَلَتِ الْأُسْرَةُ الطَّعَامَ وَشَكَرُوا اللَّهَ - دَعَا حَامِدٌ رَاشِدًا إِلَى بَيْتِهِ - جَاءَ رَاشِدٌ وَلَقِيَ أَعْضَاءَ الْأُسْرَةِ - فَجَلَسَا فِي غُرْفَةِ الْاِسْتِقْبَالِ - جَاءَ الْخَادِمُ وَجَلَبَ الْمَاءَ- ثُمَّ أَتَى بِالشَّايِ وَالْكَعْكِ - فَأَكَلَا وَقَضَيَا وَقْتًا هَنِيئًا۔

GLOSSARY	الْكَلِمَاتُ الْعَسِيْرَةُ
carpenter	نَجَّارٌ (نَجَّارُوْنَ)
England	إِنْجِلْتَرَا
repute	صِيْتٌ
air; atmosphere	جَوٌّ (أَجْوَاءٌ)

to be, or become tired	تَعِبَ - يَتْعَبُ - تَعَبٌ
to be noble; be generous	كَرُمَ - يَكْرُمُ - كَرَمٌ
thief, robber	لِصٌّ (لُصُوْصٌ)
matter	أَمْرٌ (أُمُوْرٌ)
order	أَمْرٌ (أَوَامِرُ)
to beat, strike, hit	ضَرَبَ - يَضْرِبُ - ضَرْبٌ
to think, consider	حَسِبَ - يَحْسِبُ - حُسْبَانٌ
to fill	مَلَأَ - يَمْلَأُ - مَلْءٌ
to protect; learn by heart	حَفِظَ - يَحْفَظُ - حِفْظٌ
refrigerator	ثَلَّاجَةٌ (ثَلَّاجَاتٌ)
to shed (tears)	ذَرَفَ - يَذْرِفُ - ذَرْفٌ
to open; conquer	فَتَحَ - يَفْتَحُ - فَتْحٌ
to hear, listen	سَمِعَ - يَسْمَعُ - سَمْعٌ
to help	نَصَرَ - يَنْصُرُ - نَصْرٌ
to take, grab	أَخَذَ - يَأْخُذُ - أَخْذٌ
stick	fem. عَصًا (عِصِيٌّ)
to wash	غَسَلَ - يَغْسِلُ - غَسْلٌ
to change	بَدَّلَ - يُبَدِّلُ - تَبْدِيْلٌ
to cry	بَكَى - يَبْكِي - بُكَاءٌ
to stay	مَكَثَ - يَمْكُثُ - مُكُوْثٌ
sofa	أَرِيْكَةٌ (أَرَائِكُ)
uniform	زِيٌّ (أَزْيَاءٌ)

official	رَسْمِيٌّ
grains, cereals	حَبٌّ (حُبُوبٌ)
to diagnose a disease	شَخَّصَ - يُشَخِّصُ - تَشْخِيصٌ
x-ray	أَشِعَّةٌ سِيْنِيَّةٌ
cupboard	دُوْلَابٌ (دَوَالِيْبُ)
to come	قَدِمَ - يَقْدَمُ - قُدُوْمٌ
station	مَحَطَّةٌ (مَحَطَّاتٌ)
juice	عَصِيْرٌ
case, matter, affair	قَضِيَّةٌ (قَضَايَا)
project	مَشْرُوْعٌ (مَشَارِيعُ)
to meet	قَابَلَ - يُقَابِلُ - مُقَابَلَةٌ
to grant, give	مَنَحَ - يَمْنَحُ - مَنْحٌ
prize	جَائِزَةٌ (جَوَائِزُ)
members of the family	أَعْضَاءُ الْأُسْرَةِ
reception room, drawing room	غُرْفَةُ الْاِسْتِقْبَالِ
cake	كَعْكٌ
pleasant	هَنِيْئٌ

LESSON 20

The Present/Future Tense Verb
(The Imperfect Tense Verb)
الْفِعْلُ الْمُضَارِعُ

+᪥+

Examples:

The lazy person repents/will repent.	يَنْدَمُ الْكَسْلَانُ۔
The honest man speaks/will speak the truth.	يَصْدُقُ الْأَمِيْنُ۔
The snow falls/will fall.	يَسْقُطُ الثَّلْجُ۔
The judge passes the judgement/will pass the judgement.	يَحْكُمُ الْقَاضِي۔
The money is exhausted/will be exhausted.	يَنْفَدُ الْمَالُ۔
The lady teacher becomes angry/will become angry.	تَغْضَبُ الْمُعَلِّمَةُ۔
The tree becomes strong/will become strong.	تَمْتُنُ الشَّجَرَةُ۔
The maid serves/will serve.	تَخْدُمُ الْخَادِمَةُ۔
The sky is clear/will be clear.	تَصْفُوْ السَّمَاءُ۔
The flower blossoms/will blossom.	تَتَفَتَّحُ الزَّهْرَةُ۔
I learn the Quran by heart/will learn the Quran by heart.	أَحْفَظُ الْقُرْآنَ۔
I recite poetry/will recite poetry.	أَقُوْلُ الشِّعْرَ۔

| We respect the teacher/will respect the teacher. | نَحْتَرِمُ الأُسْتَاذَ۔ |
| We read the newspaper/will read the newspaper. | نَقْرَأُ الجَرِيْدَةَ۔ |

Discussion:

Look at the examples above. You will find that the first word of each sentence is a verb: it indicates the occurrence or performance of an action at a particular time. On further study, you will find that each of them indicates the present or future.

Hence, the word ' يَنْدَمُ ' in the first sentence indicates the performance of the action of repentance (نَدَامَةٌ) in the present or future time. Similarly, the word 'يَصْدُقُ' in the second sentence shows the performance of the action of speaking the truth (صِدْقٌ) in the present or future time, and so on.

Therefore, each of these words is called a present/future tense verb (فِعْلٌ مُضَارِعٌ).

The first letter of these verbs is either ي or ت or أ or ن, and all these four letter are called the letters of the present or future tense verb i.e. حُرُوْفُ الْمُضَارِع.

Rule:

1. The present or future tense verb (الْفِعْلُ الْمُضَارِعُ) is a verb

which   indicates the occurrence of the action in the present or future.

2. The present or future tense verbs should start with one of the letters of the present or future verb (حُرُوْفُ الْمُضَارِعِ) i.e. ن or أ or ت or ي.

Exercise:

1. Choose a suitable imperfect verb from the verbs in the table to make sentences with the nouns given below.

يَضْعُفُ	يَتَحَرَّكُ	يَفْسُدُ	يَرْتَفِعُ	يَفِرُّ
(to be weak)	(to move)	(to spoil)	(to rise)	(to flee)
يَجْرِي	يَقِفُ	يَبْكِي	يَنْزِلُ	يَسْقُطُ
(to run)	(to stop)	(to weep)	(to fall)	(to fall)

النَّخْلُ - الْبَاصُ - الْمَطَرُ - السِّعْرُ

اللَّبَنُ - الطِّفْلُ - السَّارِقُ - النَّهْرُ

الْجَدُّ - الْقِطَارُ

2. Fill in the blanks with a verb from the following table.

تَتَعَلَّمُ	تَغْسِلُ	يَعْمَلُ	يُدَرِّسُ	يَلْمَعُ
(to study)	(to wash)	(to work)	(to teach)	(to shine)
يَطِيْرُ	يَسْتَعِدُّ	يَقْرَأُ	يَشِبُّ	يَدْعُوْ
(to fly)	(to be ready)	(to read)	(to grow up)	(to call)

١ـ _____ الْغُلَامُ۔   ٢ـ _____ الْجَيْشُ لِلْحَرْبِ۔

٣ـ _____ الْقَارِئُ الْقُرْآنَ۔   ٤ـ _____ الْبَرْقُ۔

٥ـ _____ الصَّقْرُ فِي السَّمَاءِ۔   ٦ـ الْمُدَرِّسُ _____ الدَّرْسَ۔

٧ـ الْعَامِلُ _____ فِي الْمَصْنَعِ۔   ٨ـ _____ اللُّغَةَ الْعَرَبِيَّةَ۔

٩ـ الْمَلِكُ _____ الْوَزِيرَ۔   ١٠ـ الْغَسَّالَةُ _____ الْمَلَابِسَ۔

3. Make ten sentences beginning with imperfect tense verbs.

4. Translate the following into Arabic.

   a) The baby sleeps.

   b) The student will read a story.

   c) The clock strikes.

   d) The boy will kick the ball.

   e) Birds fly in the sky.

   f) The horse walks.

   g) The friends laugh.

   h) The sister will come back home.

   i) The leaves fall.

   j) The fire burns.

5. Translate the following into English.

١) تَرْبَحُ التِّجَارَةُ۔

٢) يَرِنُّ الْجَرَسُ۔

٣) يَنْمُو الْعُشْبُ۔

٤) يَصْرُخُ الْأَوْلَادُ۔

٥) تَظْهَرُ النَّتِيْجَةُ۔

٦) يَصْفِرُ الشُّرْطِيُّ الصَّفَّارَةَ۔

٧) نَذْهَبُ إِلَى حَدِيْقَةِ الْحَيَوَانَاتِ۔

٨) يَنْصَحُ الْأُسْتَاذُ الطَّالِبَ۔

٩) يَقْرِضُ الشَّاعِرُ الشِّعْرَ۔

١٠) تَعْجِنُ الْمَرْأَةُ الدَّقِيْقَ۔

GLOSSARY	الْكَلِمَاتُ الْعَسِيْرَةُ
date palm	نَخْلٌ، نَخِيْلٌ
thief	سَارِقٌ (سَرَقَةٌ)
rain	مَطَرٌ (أَمْطَارٌ)
grandfather	جَدٌّ (أَجْدَادٌ)
train	قِطَارٌ (قُطُرٌ)
boy	غُلَامٌ (غِلْمَانٌ)
army, troops	جَيْشٌ (جُيُوْشٌ)
lightning, flash of lightning	بَرْقٌ (بُرُوْقٌ)
falcon, hawk	صَقْرٌ (صُقُوْرٌ)
tower	بُرْجٌ (بُرُوْجٌ، أَبْرَاجٌ)
washing machine	غَسَّالَةٌ (غَسَّالَاتٌ)
he kicked the football	ضَرَبَ كُرَةَ الْقَدَمِ بِرِجْلِهِ
the clock struck four	دَقَّتِ السَّاعَةُ الرَّابِعَةَ
to benefit	رَبِحَ - يَرْبَحُ - رِبْحٌ
to grow	نَمَا - يَنْمُو - نُمُوٌّ

grass	عُشْبٌ (أَعْشَابٌ)
to whistle	صَفَرَ - يَصْفِرُ - صَفِيْرٌ
whistle	صَفَّارَةٌ (صَفَّارَاتٌ)
zoological garden	حَدِيْقَةُ الْحَيَوَانَاتِ
to compose poetry	قَرَضَ - يَقْرِضُ - قَرْضٌ
to knead (flour)	عَجَنَ - يَعْجِنُ - عَجْنٌ
flour	دَقِيْقٌ

LESSON 21

Conjugation of the Present/Future Tense Verb
(The Imperfect Tense Verb)
تَصْرِيْفُ الْفِعْلِ الْمُضَارِعِ

﴾۞﴿

(1)

MASCULINE	Singular (الْمُفْرَدُ)	he (it) goes/will go	يَذْهَبُ
THIRD PERSON	Dual (مُثَنًّى)	they (two) go/will go	يَذْهَبَانِ
الْمُذَكَّرُ الْغَائِبُ	Plural (جَمْعٌ)	they go/will go	يَذْهَبُوْنَ

(2)

FEMININE	Singular (مُفْرَدٌ)	she (it) goes/will go	تَذْهَبُ
THIRD PERSON	Dual (مُثَنًّى)	they (two) go/will go	تَذْهَبَانِ
الْمُؤَنَّثُ الْغَائِبُ	Plural (جَمْعٌ)	they go/will go	يَذْهَبْنَ

(3)

MASCULINE	Singular (مُفْرَدٌ)	you go/will go	تَذْهَبُ

SECOND PERSON	Dual (مُثَنًّى)	you (two) go/will go	تَذْهَبَانِ
الْمُذَكَّرُ الْمُخَاطَبُ	Plural (جَمْعٌ)	you go/will go	تَذْهَبُونَ

(4)

FEMININE	Singular (مُفْرَدٌ)	you go/will go	تَذْهَبِينَ
SECOND PERSON	Dual (مُثَنًّى)	you (two) go/will go	تَذْهَبَانِ
الْمُؤَنَّثُ الْمُخَاطَبُ	Plural (جَمْعٌ)	you go/will go	تَذْهَبْنَ

(5)

MASC. and FEM.	Singular (مُفْرَدٌ)	I go/will go	أَذْهَبُ
FIRST PERSON	Dual (مُثَنًّى)	we (two) go/will go	نَذْهَبُ
الْمُذَكَّرُ الْمُتَكَلِّمُ وَالْمُؤَنَّثُ الْمُتَكَلِّمُ	Plural (جَمْعٌ)	we go/will go	نَذْهَبُ

Discussion:

Look at the conjugation above. You will find that the verbs of groups (1) and (3) are used for the masculine. Group (1) indicates the third person and group (3) the second person. Further study tells us that the first verb of each of these two groups is used for singular, the second verb is for dual and the third is for plural.

Similarly, the verbs of groups (2) and (4) are used for the feminine. Group (2) indicates the third person and (4) group indicates the second. The first verb of each of these two groups is used for singular, the second verb is for dual and the third is for plural.

Now, looking at group (5), which is the last one, we find that it is for both masculine and feminine and it indicates the first person. The first verb is used for the singular, second is for the dual and the third is for the plural.

Rule:

1. We prefix ' يَ ' to the original past tense verb (which is considered to be the basic verb) to denote the third person masculine singular, prefix ' يَ ' and suffix 'انِ' to denote the third person masculine dual and prefix 'يَ' and suffix 'وْنَ' to denote the third person masculine plural.

2. We prefix ' تَ ' to the original past tense verb to denote the third person feminine singular, prefix ' تَ ' and suffix 'انِ' to denote the third person feminine dual and prefix ' يَ ' and suffix 'نَ' to denote the third person feminine plural.

3. We prefix ' تَ ' to the original past tense verb to denote the second person masculine singular, prefix 'تَ' and 'انِ'

to denote the second person masculine dual and prefix 'تَ' and suffix 'وْنَ' to denote the second person masuline plural.

4. We prefix ' تَ ' and suffix 'يْنَ' to the original past tense verb to denote the second person feminine singular, prefix 'تَ' and suffix 'انِ' to denote the second person feminine dual and prefix 'تَ' and suffix 'نَ' to denote the second person feminine plural.

5. We prefix ' أ ' to the original past tense verb to denote the first person masculine singular and feminine singular, prefix ' نَ ' to denote both the first person masculine dual and feminine dual and prefix 'نَ' again to denote both the first person masculine plural and feminine plural.

Exercise:

1. Write the conjugation of the following verbs.

يَسْمَعُ - يَضْرِبُ - يَذْهَبُ

يَحْسِبُ - يَكْرُمُ - يَنْصُرَ

2. Choose a suitable imperfect tense verb from the following table and fill in the blanks.

تُقْلِعُ	يَخِيْطُ	يَفْتَرِسُ	يَمْكُثُ	يَنْجَحُ
to take off	to stitch	to hunt	to stay	to succeed
يَقْدَمُ	يَعُوْدُ	يَأْمُرُ	يَكْثُرُ	يَنْدَمُ
to come	to return	to order	to be much	to repent

١- ـــــــــ الْعَمُّ فِي الْقَرْيَةِ۔   ٢- ـــــــــ الْعُشْبُ فِي الْغَابَةِ۔

٣- ـــــــــ الْوَفْدُ۔   ٤- ـــــــــ الطَّائِرَةُ۔

٥- ـــــــــ الْقَائِدُ الْجَيْشَ۔   ٦- الْمُسَافِرُ ـــــــــ فِي الْفُنْدُقِ۔

٧- ـــــــــ الْخَيَّاطُ الْقَمِيْصَ۔   ٨- ـــــــــ الْمُذْنِبُ ۔

٩- ـــــــــ النَّمِرُ الْغَزَالَ۔   ١٠- ـــــــــ الطَّالِبُ بِالْإِمْتِيَازِ۔

3. Write five sentences, everyone of which should contain an imperfect tense verb.

4. Translate the following into Arabic.

  a) The writer writes the book.

  b) The meeting will be held tomorrow.

  c) The girl collects the flowers.

  d) The driver drives the car.

  e) The snake creeps.

  f) The cashier receives the fees.

  g) The fence surrounds the building.

  h) The strong oppress the weak.

  i) The poet writes poetry.

  j) The star shines at night.

5. Translate into Arabic.

    The dove lives in a nest. It coos in the morning. It flies in the sky and brings food for the chicks. It catches insects and eats them. It makes the nest on trees, buildings and in bushes. It stays with its chicks in the night. It protects them from enemies. It covers them with its wings when it is cold. It fears snakes, eagles and cats. It sleeps early at night and wakes up early in the morning. It sings a sweet song.

6. Translate the following into English.

١) يَسْقِي الْبُسْتَانِيُّ الْحَدِيقَةَ۔

٢) يَطْرُقُ الْحَدَّادُ الْحَدِيدَ۔

٣) يَزُورُ الْفَنِّيُّ أَلْمَانِيَا۔

٤) يَنْقُدُ الْمُشْتَرِي الثَّمَنَ۔

٥) تَطْلُبُ الْجَدَّةُ الْمَاءَ۔

٦) يَمْرَضُ الْأَمِيرُ فِي اللَّيْلِ۔

٧) يَرُوقُ الْمَاءُ فِي النَّهْرِ۔

٨) تَسْرُعُ الطَّائِرَةُ۔

٩) يَنْدَمُ السَّارِقُ۔

١٠) تَخْجَلُ الْعَرُوسُ۔

١١) تَجْلِبِينَ الْقَهْوَةَ۔

١٢) تَشْرَعُ الْعَمَلَ۔

١٣) الْمُعَلِّمَتَانِ تُحَدِّثَانِ۔

١٤) أَمْشِي فِي مَمَرِّ الْمُشَاةِ۔

١٥) نَقْرَأُ الْقِصَّةَ۔

7. Translate into English.

خَالِدٌ تِلْمِيذٌ - إِنَّهُ يَسْتَيْقِظُ مُبَكِّرًا - وَيَذْهَبُ إِلَى الْمُدَرَسَةِ - وَيَدْرُسُ فِيهَا - هُوَ يَقْرَأُ الدَّرْسَ وَيَفْهَمُهُ - وَيَسْمَعُ كَلَامَ الْمُدَرِّسَ - وَيَكْتُبُ التَّمْرِينَاتِ - وَيَحْفَظُ الْقَوَاعِدَ - ثُمَّ يَلْعَبُ مَعَ الْأَصْدِقَاءِ - وَيَرْجِعُ إِلَى بَيْتِهِ - ثُمَّ يَتَنَاوَلُ الْغَدَاءَ وَيَنَامُ - يُسَاعِدُ وَالِدَيْهِ فِي عَمَلِهِمَا - وَيَجْلِبُ الْأَدَوَاتِ الْمَنْزِلِيَّةَ - تَفْرَحُ الْأُمُّ وَتُحِبُّهُ وَ تُلَاطِفُهُ - وَتُعْطِيهِ التَّمْرَ وَتُلْئِمُهُ - هِيَ تَجْعَلُ الْفَطِيرَ وَتُقَدِّمُ لَهُ - وَيَتَحَادَثُ الْوَلَدُ وَالْأُمُّ وَيَضْحَكَانِ - ثُمَّ يَجِيءُ الْأَبُ فَيَجْلِسُ - وَيَطْلُبُ الْمَاءَ - يَأْتِي خَالِدٌ

بِالْمَاءِ - فَيُقَدِّمُهُ لَهُ - وَيَشْرَبُ الْوَالِدُ الْمَاءَ وَيَفْرَحُ - ثُمَّ يَحِينُ وَقْتُ الْعَشَاءِ - فَيَأْكُلُ كُلُّهُمُ الْعَشَاءَ - وَيَشْكُرُونَ اللهَ وَيَنَامُونَ ـ

GLOSSARY	الْكَلِمَاتُ الْعَسِيرَةُ
paternal uncle	عَمٌّ (أَعْمَامٌ)
village	قَرْيَةٌ (قُرًى)
grass	عُشْبٌ (أَعْشَابٌ)
forest	غَابَةٌ (غَابَاتٌ)
delegation	وَفْدٌ (وُفُودٌ)
aeroplane	طَائِرَةٌ (طَائِرَاتٌ)
commander	قَائِدٌ (قُوَّادٌ)
army	جَيْشٌ (جُيُوشٌ)
hotel	فُنْدُقٌ (فَنَادِقُ)
tailor	خَيَّاطٌ (خَيَّاطُونَ)
sinner	مُذْنِبٌ (مُذْنِبُونَ)
gazelle	غَزَالٌ (غِزْلَانٌ)
with distinction	بِالِامْتِيَازِ
to gather, collect	جَمَعَ - يَجْمَعُ - جَمْعٌ
star	كَوْكَبٌ (كَوَاكِبُ)
cashier	صَرَّافٌ (صَرَّافُونَ)
to receive	اِسْتَلَمَ - يَسْتَلِمُ - اِسْتِلَامٌ
to surround, encompass	أَحَاطَ - يُحِيطُ - إِحَاطَةٌ بِ
wall, fence	سُورٌ (أَسْوَارٌ)
to oppress	ظَلَمَ - يَظْلِمُ - ظُلْمٌ

nest	عُشٌّ (أَعْشَاشٌ)
young bird, shoot	فَرْخٌ (أَفْرَاخٌ)
to catch, hunt	اِصْطَادَ - يَصْطَادَ - اِصْطِيَادٌ
dove	يَمَامَةٌ
enemy	عَدُوٌّ (أَعْدَاءُ)
viper, snake	أَفْعَى (أَفَاعٍ)
eagle	عُقَابٌ (عِقْبَانٌ)
irrigate	سَقَى - يَسْقِي - سَقْيٌ
to knock	طَرَقَ - يَطْرُقُ - طَرْقٌ
Germany	أَلْمَانِيَا
technician	فَنِّيٌّ (فَنِّيُّونَ)
ironsmith, blacksmith	حَدَّادٌ (حَدَّادُونَ)
to pay in cash	نَقَدَ - يَنْقُدُ - نَقْدٌ
to be clear, be pure	رَاقَ - يَرُوقُ - رَوْقٌ
to be ashamed	خَجِلَ - يَخْجَلُ - خَجَلٌ
bride	عَرُوسٌ (عَرَائِسُ)
footpath	مَمَرُّ الْمُشَاةِ
household things	الْأَدَوَاتُ الْمَنْزِلِيَّةُ
to kiss	لَثَمَ - يَلْثِمُ - لَثْمٌ
pastry	فَطِيرٌ
to offer, serve	قَدَّمَ - يُقَدِّمُ - تَقْدِيمٌ
to approach (time)	حَانَ - يَحِينُ - حَيْنٌ
dinner	عَشَاءٌ

LESSON 22

The Imperative Verb فِعْلُ الْأَمْرِ

+﴾﷽﴿+

Examples:

Write your lesson.	اُكْتُبْ دَرْسَكَ۔
Wash the utensil.	اِغْسِلِ الْإِنَاءَ۔
Give good news to your father.	بَشِّرِ وَالِدَكَ۔
Open the door.	اِفْتَحِ الْبَابَ۔
Entertain the guest.	أَكْرِمِ الضَّيْفَ۔
Attend the class.	أَحْضُرِ الْفَصْلَ۔
Wake up early.	اِسْتَيْقِظْ مُبَكِّرًا۔
Teach your daughter.	دَرِّسْ بِنْتَكَ۔
Sit on your seat.	اِجْلِسْ عَلَى مَقْعَدِكَ۔
Accept our gift.	تَقَبَّلْ تُحْفَتَنَا۔

Discussion:

Look at the examples above. You will find that the first word of each sentence is a verb: it indicates the occurrence or performance of an action. On further study, you will find that the speaker, i.e. the first person demands that the second person perform some action in the future. This type of verb, which is usually used for giving orders or making requests, is called the Imperative Verb (فِعْلُ الْأَمْرِ).

Hence, the verb 'اُكْتُبْ' in the first sentence has been used to express a command or give an order, i.e. second person (الْمُخَاطَبُ) has been asked to perform the action of writing (كِتَابَةٌ) in the future and is thus an imperative verb (فِعْلُ الْأَمْرِ).

Similarly, the verb 'اِغْسِلْ' in the second sentence where the second person (الْمُخَاطَبُ) has been asked to perform the action of washing is, therefore, also an imperative verb (فِعْلُ الْأَمْرِ), and so on.

Rule:

1. Imperative verb (فِعْلُ الْأَمْرِ) is a verb which is used for giving orders or making requests.

2. In case the last letter of the imperative is سُكُوْنٌ (ـْ) and we want to join it to some following word, the last letter of the imperative verb is given كَسْرَةٌ (ـِ) , e.g.

اِغْسِلِ الْإِنَاءَ <== اِغْسِلْ الْإِنَاءَ

Exercise:

1. Choose a suitable imperative verb and use it before the nouns given below.

اُكْتُبْ	كُلْ	اِسْمَعْ	اِقْرَأْ	قُلْ
write	eat	listen	read	say

شَغِّلْ	اِحْتَرِمْ	اِشْرَبْ	نَظِّفْ	اِفْتَحْ
start	respect	drink	clean	open

السَّيَّارَةَ - الْوَالِدَ - الرِّسَالَةَ - اللَّبَنَ

الرَّغِيْفَ - الشُّبَّاكَ - الْحُجْرَةَ - الصِّدْقَ

الْكِتَابَ - النَّصِيْحَةَ

2. Choose a suitable imperative verb from the verbs given below and fill in the blanks.

هَذِّبْ	اِفْتَحْ	اِشْرَبْ	اِجْعَلْ	أَكْمِلْ
educate	open	drink	make	finish
أَطْعِمْ	أَجِبْ	تَكَلَّمْ	اِرْكَبْ	اِسْتَعِدَّ
feed	answer	speak	ride on	prepare

١ـ _____ _____ ٢ـ بِاللُّغَةِ الْعَرَبِيَّةِ ـ _____ الْحُجْرَةَ.

٣ـ _____ أَبْنَاءَكَ. ٤ـ _____ لِلْاِمْتِحَانِ.

٥ـ _____ الْفَقِيْرَ. ٦ـ _____ وَاجِبَاتِكَ.

٧ـ _____ عَنِ الْأَسْئِلَةِ. ٨ـ _____ الشَّايَ.

٩ـ _____ الدَّوَاءَ. ١٠ـ _____ خَيْلَكَ.

3. Make ten sentences using an imperative verb in each sentence.

4. Translate the following into Arabic.

a) Serve your master.

b) Go and wash your face.

c) Take the pen and write the exercise.

d) Clean the table and arrange the books.

e) Visit the old monuments.

f) Wear new clothes.

g) Meet your relatives.

h) Read the newspaper.

i) Walk on the grass.

j) Drink milk.

5. Translate the following into English.

١) تَعَلَّمِ اللُّغَةَ الْعَرَبِيَّةَ۔

٢) تَجَهَّزْ لِلْحَفْلَةِ۔

٣) اِقْرَأِ الْقُرْآنَ۔

٤) اِدْفَعِ الثَّمَنَ۔

٥) أُنْظُرْ إِلَى السَّبُّورَةِ۔

٦) أُتْرُكِ اللَّعِبَ۔

٧) خُذِ الْكِتَابَ وَاقْرَإِ الدَّرْسَ۔

٨) أَلْقِ الْمَاءَ فِي الْكُوبِ۔

٩) تَرْجِمِ الْفِقْرَةَ إِلَى اللُّغَةِ الْعَرَبِيَّةِ۔

١٠) اِبْتَعِ الْقُمَاشَ۔

GLOSSARY	الْكَلِمَاتُ الْعَسِيرَةُ
flat loaf of bread; bun	رَغِيفٌ (أَرْغِفَةٌ)
truth; sincerity	صِدْقٌ
duty, obligation	وَاجِبٌ (وَاجِبَاتٌ)

to clean	نَظَّفَ - يُنَظِّفُ - تَنْظِيْفٌ
to arrange	رَتَّبَ - يُرَتِّبُ - تَرْتِيْبٌ
the old monuments	الْآثَارُ الْقَدِيْمَةُ
to wear	لَبِسَ - يَلْبَسُ - لُبْسٌ
to be ready, be prepared	تَجَهَّزَ - يَتَجَهَّزُ - تَجَهُّزٌ
event	حَفْلَةٌ (حَفْلَاتٌ)
to put, throw	أَلْقَى - يُلْقِي - إِلْقَاءٌ
to translate	تَرْجَمَ - يُتَرْجِمُ - تَرْجَمَةٌ
price, cost; value	ثَمَنٌ (أَثْمَانٌ)
paragraph, passage	فِقْرَةٌ (فِقْرَاتٌ)
to buy, purchase	إِبْتَاعَ - يَبْتَاعُ - اِبْتِيَاعٌ
fabric, cloth	قُمَاشٌ (أَقْمِشَةٌ)

LESSON 23

Conjugation of the Imperative Verb
تَصْرِيْفُ فِعْلِ الْأَمْرِ

+☙❀☙+

(1)

MASCULINE	Singular (الْمُفْرَدُ)	(You) Write	أُكْتُبْ
	Dual (الْمُثَنَّى)	(You) Write	أُكْتُبَا
الْمُذَكَّرُ	Plural (الْجَمْعُ)	(You) Write	أُكْتُبُوْا

(2)

FEMININE	Singular (الْمُفْرَدُ)	(You) Write	أُكْتُبِي
	Dual (الْمُثَنَّى)	(You) Write	أُكْتُبَا
الْمُؤَنَّثُ	Plural (الْجَمْعُ)	(You) Write	أُكْتُبْنَ

Discussion:

Look at the conjugation above. You will find that the verbs of group (1) are used for the masculine second person. The first verb of this group is used for the singular, the second verb is used for the dual and the third is used for the plural.

Similarly, the verbs of group (2) are used for the feminine second person. The first verb of this group is used for the singular, second verb is used for the dual and the third is used for the plural.

Rule:

1. The Imperative mood is formed from the second person of the imperfect verb.

2. To make the imperative moods, we drop 'letter of imperfect tense verb', then ضَمَّةٌ of the last letter is replaced by سُكُوْنٌ. If the first letter, after dropping the letter of imperfect verb, has سُكُوْنٌ, then an alif 'اِ' is prefixed to it. If the second original letter has ضَمَّةٌ on it, then ضَمَّةٌ is placed on this additional 'اِ'. If the second original letter has كَسْرَةٌ or فَتْحَةٌ, then كَسْرَةٌ is placed under this 'اِ'. Whenever this additional 'اِ' is preceded by any word whatsoever, this 'اِ' is dropped verbally, but not in writing. These rules apply to the simple triliteral verbs (فِعْلٌ ثُلَاثِيٌّ مُجَرَّدٌ). e.g.

أُكْتُبْ	<--	تَكْتُبُ
اِجْلِسْ	<--	تَجْلِسُ
اِذْهَبْ	<--	تَذْهَبُ

اِقْرَأِ الدَّرْسَ وَاكْتُبِ التَّمْرِيْنَاتِ ثُمَّ اذْهَبْ إِلَى الْبَيْتِ

3. The 'نْ' at the end of the masculine dual, masculine plural, feminine singular and feminine dual is dropped. In the case of masculine plural, an extra 'اِ' is written in place of 'نْ' but it is not pronounced. e.g.

أُكْتُبَا	<--	تَكْتُبَانِ
أُكْتُبُوا	<--	تَكْتُبُوْنَ
أُكْتُبِيْ	<--	تَكْتُبِيْنَ
أُكْتُبْنَ	<--	تَكْتُبْنَ

4. Where after dropping the letter of imperfect tense verb, the first of the remaining letters has a vowel sign, the alif 'ا' is not prefixed. Only the last letter is given سُكُوْنٌ (ْ), e.g.

صِلْ	<--	تَصِلُ
صِلَا	<--	تَصِلَانِ
صِلُوا	<--	تَصِلُوْنَ
صِلِي	<--	تَصِلِيْنَ
صِلَا	<--	تَصِلَانِ
صِلْنَ	<--	تَصِلْنَ

5. Imperatives of the verbs having hamza as their first letter, like أَخَذَ, أَكَلَ and أَمَرَ are made by dropping the 'letter of imperfect tense verb' and the original 'هَمْزَةٌ'. Other rules remain the same, e.g.

خُذْ	<--	تَأْخُذُ
خُذَا	<--	تَأْخُذَانِ
خُذُوا	<--	تَأْخُذُوْنَ
خُذِي	<--	تَأْخُذِيْنَ
خُذَا	<--	تَأْخُذَانِ
خُذْنَ	<--	تَأْخُذْنَ

6. But, if the imperative of the verb with أ as the first letter is preceded by وَ or فَ , its original هَمْزَةٌ is retained, e.g.

فَأْمُرْ	-	وَأْمُرْ
فَأْمُرَا	-	وَأْمُرَا
فَأْمُرُوا	-	وَأْمُرُوا
فَأْمُرِى	-	وَأْمُرِى
فَأْمُرَا	-	وَأْمُرَا
فَأْمُرْنَ	-	وَأْمُرْنَ

Exercise:

1. Make imperatives from the following verbs and write their conjugations.

يَسْمَعُ	-	يَضْرِبُ	-	يَفْتَحُ
يَحْسِبُ	-	يَجْلِسُ	-	يَنْصُرُ
يَقْرَأُ	-	يَسْأَلُ	-	يَأْكُلُ

2. Rewrite the following sentences after replacing the imperfect verbs by imperative verbs.

٢ـ تَرْحَمُوْنَ الْفُقَرَاءَ۔	١ـ تَخْدِمِيْنَ الْأُمَّ۔
٤ـ تَدْفَعْنَ أَجْرَ الْخَادِمِ۔	٣ـ تَذْخَرُوْنَ الْمَالَ۔
٦ـ تَشْكُرُ اللّٰهَ۔	٥ـ تَعْصِرَانِ الْعِنَبَ۔
٨ـ تَطْلُبِيْنَ الْعَمَلَ۔	٧ـ تَحْلِبُ الْبَقَرَةَ۔
١٠ـ تَكْفُلُ الْعَائِلَةَ۔	٩ـ تَبْدَآنِ الدَّرْسَ۔

3. Make six sentences with imperative verbs using all the six forms of the conjugation.

4. Give directions to your maidservant to make a cup of tea in five sentences.

5. Translate the following into Arabic.

a) Boys! Prepare for the examination.

b) Drive slowly.

c) Allow him to go.

d) Soldier! Fight the enemy.

e) Women! Search for good housemaids.

f) Butcher! Cut the meat.

g) Man! Ride the horse.

h) Suaad and Farha! Enter the house.

i) Maryam! Light the lamp.

j) O Allah! Accept our prayers.

6. Translate the following into English.

١) يَا أَيُّهَا الشُّرْطِيُّونَ! اِقْبِضُوا عَلَى اللِّصَّ۔

٢) اِلْحَقْ بِالْخِدْمَةِ۔

٣) يَا أَيُّهَا الْمَأْذُونُ الشَّرْعِيُّ! قُمْ بَعَقْدِ زَوَاجِ أَخِي۔

٤) يَا أَيُّهَا اللَّاعِبُونَ! اِشْرَبُوا الْمَاءَ۔

٥) يَا رَجُلُ! اِزْهَدْ فِي الدُّنْيَا۔

٦) يَا بِنْتَانِ! اِضْبِطَا أَوَاخِرَ الْكَلِمَاتِ ۔

٧) يَا صَدِيقُ! أُذْكُرِ اللَّهَ۔

٨) يَا صَائِمُونَ! اِفْرَحُوا ! سَيَكُونُ الْعِيْدُ غَدًا۔

٩) يَا اللَّهُ! أَجِرْنَا مِنَ النَّارِ۔

١٠) يَا سَيِّدَاتُ! عَلِّمْنَ بَنَاتِكُنَّ الْأَدَبَ۔

GLOSSARY	الْكَلِمَاتُ الْعَسِيرَةُ
to reach	وَصَلَ - يَصِلُ - وُصُوْلٌ
to put	وَضَعَ - يَضَعُ - وَضْعٌ
to find	وَجَدَ - يَجِدُ - وِجْدَانٌ
to take	أَخَذَ - يَأْخُذُ - أَخْذٌ
to eat	أَكَلَ - يَأْكُلُ - أَكْلٌ
to order, command	أَمَرَ - يَأْمُرُ - أَمْرٌ
to ask	سَأَلَ - يَسْأَلُ - سُؤَالٌ
to keep, preserve, save	ذَخَرَ - يَذْخَرُ - ذُخْرٌ
wage	أَجْرٌ (أُجُوْرٌ)
to pay, push	دَفَعَ - يَدْفَعُ - دَفْعٌ
to squeeze	عَصَرَ - يَعْصِرُ - عَصْرٌ
grapes	عِنَبٌ (أَعْنَابٌ)
to milk an animal	حَلَبَ - يَحْلِبُ - حَلْبٌ
family	عَائِلَةٌ (عَائِلَاتٌ)
to sponsor, support	كَفَلَ - يَكْفُلُ - كَفَالَةٌ
to drive (an automobile)	سَاقَ - يَسُوْقُ - سِيَاقَةٌ
slowly	بِبُطْئٍ
to allow	سَمَحَ - يَسْمَحُ - سَمَاحٌ (بِ ، لِ)
to search	بَحَثَ - يَبْحَثُ - بَحْثٌ (عن)
butcher	قَصَّابٌ (قَصَّابُوْنَ)
to girth	حَزَمَ - يَحْزِمُ - حَزْمٌ
to sieze	قَبَضَ - يَقْبِضُ - قَبْضٌ (على)

official authorized by the Qadi to perform civil marriages	الْمَاذُوْنُ الشَّرْعِيُّ
to vowelize	ضَبَطَ - يَضْبِطُ - ضَبْطٌ (الْكَلِمَةَ)
to renounce pleasure	زَهَدَ - يَزْهَدُ - زُهْدٌ
one who fasts	صَائِمٌ (صَائِمُوْنَ)
to teach	عَلَّمَ - يُعَلِّمُ - تَعْلِيْمٌ

LESSON 24

The Prohibitive Verb (The Negative Imperative)

فِعْلُ النَّهْيِ

◄۞►

Examples:

Do not play in the sun.	لَا تَلْعَبْ فِي ضَوْءِ الشَّمْسِ۔
Do not pluck the rose.	لَا تَقْطِفِ الْوَرْدَ۔
Do not go out while you are sick.	لَا تَخْرُجْ وَأَنْتَ مَرِيضٌ۔
Do not open the window.	لَا تَفْتَحْ الشُّبَّاكَ۔
Do not talk in the examination hall.	لَا تَتَكَلَّمْ فِي قَاعَةِ الْإِمْتِحَانِ۔
Do not eat hot food.	لَا تَأْكُلْ الطَّعَامَ الْحَارَّ۔
Do not beat your younger brother.	لَا تَضْرِبْ أَخَاكَ الصَّغِيْرَ۔
Do not abuse anyone.	لَا تَشْتِمْ أَحَداً۔
Do not sit before your father sits.	لَا تَجْلِسْ قَبْلَ أَنْ يَجْلِسَ أَبُوْكَ۔
Do not accompany evil-doers.	لَا تُرَافِقِ الْأَشْرَارَ۔

Discussion:

Look at the examples above. You will find that every sentence begins with 'لَا' followed by a verb in jussive mood (حَالَةُ الْجَزْمِ). On further study, you will find that the speaker, i.e. the first person addresses another person and orders him not to perform a certain action. This type of verb, which is usually used to prohibit, is called the prohibitive verb, or the negative imprative (فِعْلُ النَّهْي) and this 'لا' is called the prohibitive 'لا'.

Since, the verb 'تَلْعَبْ' along with prohibitive 'لا' in the first sentence is used to express a command of negation, i.e. the second person (اَلْمُخَاطَبُ) has been asked not to perform the action of playing (لُعْبٌ) in the present or future, it is a prohibitive verb or negative impratiove (فِعْلُ النَّهْي).

Similarly, the verb 'تَقْطِفْ' preceded by prohibitive 'لا' in the second sentence, which asks the second person (اَلْمُخَاطَبُ) not to perform the action of plucking (قَطْفٌ) in the present or future, is also a prohibitive verb or negative imperative (فِعْلُ النَّهْي). The same applies to the remaining sentences.

Rule:

1. The prohibitive verb or negative imperative (فِعْلُ النَّهْي), is a verb which is used for prohibiting or we can say that it is a verb by which another person is asked not to do something in the present or future.

2. The meaning of the prohibitive verb, or negative imprative is the opposite of that of the imperative verb.

While the imperative would mean "do", the prohibitive means "do not do". So we can say that the negative imperative is used to express prohibition.

3. The prohibitive verb is formed by using the prohibition particle (لَا), followed by an imperfect verb in the jussive mood (فِعْلٌ مُضَارِعٌ مَجْزُوْمٌ).

Exercise:

1. Write a suitable prohibitive verb before the nouns given below.

الْعَصِيْر - الْمَاء الْبَارِد - أَخَاكَ - الْكِتَاب

الْفَاكِهَة الْفَجَّة - الْحَيَوَان - الْبَاب - الزَّهْر

الْجِدَار - الثَّوْب الْمُمَزَّق

2. Fill in the blanks using a prohibitive verb.

٢- _____ السَّيَّارَة.		١- _____ وَلَدَكَ.	
٤- _____ السِّرّ.		٣- _____ بِالْبَاصِ.	
٦- _____ الْحَبْل.		٥- _____ الأُسْتَاذ.	
٨- _____ الْغَاوِيْن.		٧- _____ خِلَالَ الدَّرْسِ.	
١٠- _____ فِى أَدَاءِ وَاجِبِك.		٩- _____ الْجَار.	

3. Make five sentences beginning with a prohibitive verb.

4. Suppose you are a teacher, prohibit your students from doing five things in the examination hall.

5. Translate the following into Arabic.

a) Do not disobey your parents.

b) Do not look at others' mistakes.

c) Do not wear dirty clothes.

d) Do not shout in the class.

e) Do not go to playground.

f) Do not read this useless book.

g) Do not spit here.

h) Do not sell this bicycle.

i) Do not arrest this man, he is innocent.

j) Do not serve rice at this time.

6. Translate the following into English.

١) لَا تَدْرُسْ وَأَنْتَ تَعْبَانٌ۔

٢) لَا تَعْبُدُ غَيْرَ اللّٰهِ۔

٣) لَا تُرْسِلْ هٰذَا الطَّرْدَ۔

٤) لَا تَصْنَعْ الشَّايَ بِهٰذَا الْمَاءِ۔

٥) لَا تَرْفَعْ هٰذَا الصُّنْدُوْقَ الثَّقِيْلَ۔

٦) لَا تَدْخُلْ الْفَصْلَ! الْأُسْتَاذُ غَاضِبٌ عَلَيْكَ۔

٧) لَا تَسْمَعْ الْكَلَامَ الْفَارِغَ۔

٨) لَا تَكْسِرْ الْقَلَمَ۔

٩) لَا تَحْمِلْ هٰذِهِ الْحَقِيْبَةَ۔

١٠) لَا تَكْتُبْ عَلَى هٰذَا الْوَرَقِ۔

GLOSSARY	الْكَلِمَاتُ الْعَسِيْرَةُ
misguided	غَاوٍ (غَاوُوْنَ)
other	آخَرُ (آخَرُوْنَ)
useless	عَدِيْمُ الْفَائِدَةِ
to arrest	قَبَضَ - يَقْبِضُ - قَبْضٌ (عَلَى)
innocent	بَرِيْءٌ (أَبْرِيَاءُ)
to serve	قَدَّمَ - يُقَدِّمُ - تَقْدِيْمٌ
to worship	عَبَدَ - يَعْبُدُ - عِبَادَةٌ
useless talk	الْكَلَامُ الْفَارِغُ

LESSON 25

Conjugation of the Prohibitive Verb
تَصْرِيْفُ فِعْلِ النَّهْيِ

+◈◈◈+

MASCULINE	Singular (مُفْرَدٌ)	Do not write	لَا تَكْتُبْ
	Dual (مُثَنَّى)	Do not write	لَا تَكْتُبَا
الْمُذَكَّرُ	Plural (جَمْعٌ)	Do not write	لَا تَكْتُبُوْا

FEMININE	Singular (مُفْرَدٌ)	Do not write	لَا تَكْتُبِي
	Dual (مُثَنَّى)	Do not write	لَا تَكْتُبَا
الْمُؤَنَّثُ	Plural (جَمْعٌ)	Do not write	لَا تَكْتُبْنَ

Discussion:

Look at the conjugation above. You will find that the verbs of the first group are used for the masculine second person. The first verb of this group is used for the singular, the second is for the dual and the third is for the plural.

Similarly, the verbs of the second group are used for the feminine second person. The first verb of this group is used for the singular, the second is for the dual and the third is for the plural.

Rule:

1. The Prohibitive Verb is formed from second person of the imperfect verb.

2. To make the verb prohibitive, we prefix the 'لَا' of prohibition to the imperfect verb which changes the mood of the imperfect verb from indicative to jussive mood, e.g.

تَكْتُبُ   -->   لَا تَكْتُبْ

تَجْلِسُ   -->   لَا تَجْلِسْ

تَذْهَبُ   -->   لَا تَذْهَبْ

3. If there is 'نْ' at the end of the verb, this 'نْ' is dropped except the 'نْ' of the feminine plural. In the masculine plural, an extra 'ا' is written in place of 'نْ' but it is not pronounced, e.g.

تَكْتُبَانِ   -->   لَا تَكْتُبَا

تَكْتُبُوْنَ   -->   لَا تَكْتُبُوْا

تَكْتُبِيْنَ   -->   لَا تَكْتُبِي

تَكْتُبْنَ   -->   لَا تَكْتُبْنَ

4. If there is a weak letter 'حَرْفُ الْعِلَّةِ' (ا or و or ي) in the middle of the verb, it is removed in the masculine singular.

تَزُوْرُ --> لَا تَزُرْ

(لَا تَزُرْ - لَا تَزُوْرَا - لَا تَزُوْرُوْا - لَا تَزُوْرِي - لَا تَزُوْرَا - لَا تَزُرْنَ)

تَبِيْعُ --> لَا تَبِعْ

(لَا تَبِعْ - لَا تَبِيْعَا - لَا تَبِيْعُوْا - لَا تَبِيْعِي - لَا تَبِيْعَا - لَا تَبِعْنَ)

تَنَامُ --> لَا تَنَمْ

(لَا تَنَمْ - لَا تَنَامَا - لَا تَنَامُوْا - لَا تَنَامِي - لَا تَنَامَا - لَا تَنَمْنَ)

5. If there is a weak letter (حَرْفُ الْعِلَّةِ) (ا or و or ي) at the end
of the verb, it is removed in the masculine singular.

تَدْعُو   <--   لَا تَدْعُ

لَا تَدْعُ - لَا تَدْعُوَا - لَا تَدْعُو - لَا تَدْعِي - لَا تَدْعُوَا - لَا تَدْعُونَ

تَقْضِي   <--   لَا تَقْضِ

لَا تَقْضِ - لَا تَقْضِيَا - لَا تَقْضُوا - لَا تَقْضِي - لَا تَقْضِيَا - لَا تَقْضِينَ

تَرْضَى   <--   لَا تَرْضَ

لَا تَرْضَ - لَا تَرْضَيَا - لَا تَرْضَوا - لَا تَرْضَيْ - لَا تَرْضَيَا - لَا تَرْضَيْنَ

6. The geminated verb (الْفِعْلُ الْمُضَاعَفُ) is conjugated on the
   following pattern.

مَدَّ - يَمُدُّ (نَصَرَ - يَنْصُرُ)

لَا تَمُدَّ - لَا تَمُدَّا - لَا تَمُدُّوا - لَا تَمُدِّي - لَا تَمُدَّا - لَا تَمْدُدْنَ

لَا تَمْدُدْ - لَا تَمْدُدَا - لَا تَمْدُدُوا - لَا تَمْدُدِي - لَا تَمْدُدَا - لَا تَمْدُدْنَ

فَرَّ - يَفِرُّ (ضَرَبَ - يَضْرِبُ)

لَا تَفِرَّ - لَا تَفِرَّا - لَا تَفِرُّوا - لَا تَفِرِّي - لَا تَفِرَّا - لَا تَفْرِرْنَ

مَسَّ - يَمَسُّ (سَمِعَ - يَسْمَعُ)

لَا تَمَسَّ - لَا تَمَسَّا - لَا تَمَسُّوا - لَا تَمَسِّي - لَا تَمَسَّا - لَا تَمْسَسْنَ

Exercise:
1. Make prohibitive forms of the following verbs and write
   their conjugation.

تَتْرُكُ   -   تَجْلِسُ   -   تَذْكُرُ

تَفْتَحُ   -   تَلْبَسُ   -   تَأْمُرُ

تَرْجِعُ   -   تَرْكَبُ   -   تَشْرَبُ

2. Change the imperfect verbs into the prohibitive and vowelize them.

٢ـ تُبَدِّلُ غِطَاءَ الْوِسَادَةِ.   ١ـ تَخْدَعُ النَّاسَ.

٤ـ تَجْرَحُ يَدَكَ بِالسِّكِّينِ.   ٣ـ تَبْسُطَانِ السَّجَّادَةَ.

٦ـ تَحْضُرْنَ مُتَأَخِّرَاتٍ.   ٥ـ تَطْرُقَانِ الْبَابَ.

٨ـ تَغْضَبُ بِسُرْعَةٍ.   ٧ـ تَدْرُسِينَ فِي الضَّوْءِ الضَّئِيلِ.

١٠ـ تَفْشَلْنَ فِي الْإِمْتِحَانِ.   ٩ـ تَجْلِسُ فِي الشَّمْسِ.

3. Make six sentences beginning with a prohibitive verb, using all the six forms of the conjugation.

4. Suppose you are a teacher, forbid your students to do at least five things to make them good citizens.

5. Translate the following into Arabic.

  a) Do not cross the road before the light turns green.

  b) Do not accept bribes.

  c) Do not allow the children to play outside.

  d) Do not hide the secret from me.

  e) Do not cheat your brother.

  f) Do not fill this broken cup.

  g) Do not prevent me from giving in charity.

  h) Do not advise your elders.

  i) Do not move this heavy box alone.

  j) Do not sit on the road.

6. Translate the following into English.

١) لَا تَجْهَلُوا حُقُوقَ الْوَالِدَةِ.

٢) لَا تَكْنُسِي تِلْكَ الْحُجْرَةَ النَّظِيفَةَ.

٣) لَا تَغْسِلْنَ أَلْبِسَةً جَدِيدَةً.

٤) لَا تَرْكَبِ الْفِيلَ وَصَاحِبُهُ غَائِبٌ۔

٥) لَا تَقْلَقْ! سَيَتَغَيَّرُ الْوَقْتُ۔

٦) لَا تَسْمَحِ الأَوْلَادَ بِالْخُرُوجِ مِنَ الْفَصْلِ۔

٧) لَا تَهْرَعْ فِي الْأَكْلِ۔

٨) لَا تَفْرَحَا وَأَخُوكُمَا حَزِينٌ۔

٩) لَا تَعْبَثُوا بِالنَّارِ۔

١٠) لَا تَغْشِمِ الْمَسَاكِينَ۔

GLOSSARY	الْكَلِمَاتُ الْعَسِيرَةُ
to replace	بَدَّلَ - يُبَدِّلُ - تَبْدِيلٌ
cover	غِطَاءٌ (أَغْطِيَةٌ)
carpet	سَجَّادَةٌ (سَجَّادَاتٌ)
late	مُتَأَخِّرٌ (مُتَأَخِّرُونَ)
citizen	مُوَاطِنٌ (مُوَاطِنُونَ)
to cross	عَبَرَ - يَعْبُرُ - عُبُورٌ
bribe	رِشْوَةٌ
charity	صَدَقَةٌ (صَدَقَاتٌ)
to be upset	قَلِقَ - يَقْلَقُ - قَلَقٌ
to hurry	هَرَعَ - يَهْرَعُ - هَرَعٌ
to play (absent mindedly)	عَبِثَ - يَعْبَثُ - عَبَثٌ
to oppress	غَشَمَ - يَغْشِمُ - غَشْمٌ

LESSON 26

The Doer (The Subject) الْفَاعِلُ

❖

Examples:

The boy came.	جَاءَ الْوَلَدُ۔
The rose blossoms.	تَتَفَتَّحُ الْوَرْدَةُ۔
The water froze.	جَمَدَ الْمَاءُ۔
The fruit ripens.	تَنْضَجُ الْفَاكِهَةُ۔
The teacher became angry.	غَضِبَ الْأُسْتَاذُ۔
The peacock danced.	رَقَصَ الطَّاؤُوْسُ۔
The bag got torn.	تَمَزَّقَتِ الْحَقِيْبَةُ۔
The worker takes rest.	يَسْتَرِيْحُ الْعَامِلُ۔
The girl became happy.	فَرِحَتِ الْبِنْتُ۔

Discussion:

Look at the examples above. They are all sentences made up of a noun and a verb. In the first two sentences, we will find that the one who came is the boy 'الْوَلَدُ' and the thing which blossoms is the rose 'الْوَرْدَةُ'.

Hence, the boy is the one who performed the action of coming and the rose does the action of blossoming. Therefore, each of these two nouns is called the doer 'الْفَاعِلُ'

i.e. the subject of the verb. The doer, or the subject, takes
ضَمَّةٌ and it is said to be in the nominative case i.e. حَالَةُ
الرَّفْعِ. The same applies to the other sentences also.

Rule:

The doer الْفَاعِلُ is a noun اِسْمٌ in the nominative
case حَالَةُ الرَّفْعِ. The doer or the subject is the one
which/who performs the action of the verb.

Exercise:

1. Pick out the doer (الْفَاعِلُ) from the following sentences.

٢ـ يَتْعَبُ الْعَامِلُ.　　　　١ـ جَرَى النَّهْرُ.

٤ـ يَجُوعُ الْمُسَافِرُ.　　　　٣ـ لَعِبَ الْغُلَامُ.

٦ـ يَنْفَعُ الْعِلْمُ.　　　　٥ـ أَشْرَقَتِ الشَّمْسُ.

٨ـ تَحْدُثُ الْحَادِثَةُ.　　　　٧ـ أَتَى الطَّبِيبُ.

١٠ـ يَمْضِي الْوَقْتُ.　　　　٩ـ أَوْرَقَتِ الْأَشْجَارُ.

2. Give a doer (فَاعِلٌ) to each of the following verbs.

٣) اِحْمَرَّ　　٢) اِنْكَسَرَ　　١) رَبِحَ

٦) يَزْرَعُ　　٥) تَشْدُو　　٤) فَرِحَ

٩) يَنْهَضُ　　٨) عَدَا　　٧) خَافَ

3. Use the following nouns as doers in your sentences.

٣) الْمُوَظَّفُ　　٢) الْبُرْتُقَالُ　　١) السَّمَاءُ

٦) السَّاعَةُ　　٥) الْجَيْشُ　　٤) الذِّئْبُ

٩) السَّيْفُ　　٨) الْمُمَرِّضَةُ　　٧) الصَّدِيقُ

4. Make three sentences each as directed.

a) consisting of a perfect tense verb and a doer.

b) consisting of an imperfect verb and a doer.

c) having 'الشِّتَاءُ' as the doer.

d) having 'الْخَفِيْرُ' as doer.

5. Translate the following sentences into Arabic.

a) The examination commenced.

b) Aisha woke up.

c) The child sneezes.

d) The lawyer arrived.

e) The sky became dark.

f) The bottle broke.

g) The cat runs.

h) The pen fell down.

i) The hand swelled.

j) The ice melts.

6. Translate the following into English.

١) سَافَرَ عَزِيْزٌ۔

٢) يُصَمِّمُ الْمُهَنْدِسُوْنَ الْبِنَاءَ۔

٣) يَسْتَعِدُّ الطُّلَّابُ۔

٤) شَفَى اللهُ الْمُصَابَةَ۔

٥) يَظْهَرُ الصَّوْتُ۔

٦) تَصُوْمُ الْأُمَّهَاتُ۔

٧) تَأَلَّمَ الْمَرِيْضُ۔

٨) يَبْكِي الطِّفْلُ۔

٩) حَزِنَتِ الْفَقِيْرَةُ۔

١٠) تَبْتَسِمُ الْبِنْتُ۔

GLOSSARY	الْكَلِمَاتُ الْعَسِيْرَةُ
to be or become tired	تَعِبَ - يَتْعَبُ - تَعَبٌ
to be of use, be beneficial	نَفَعَ - يَنْفَعُ - نَفْعٌ
to rise	أَشْرَقَ - يُشْرِقُ - إِشْرَاقٌ
to happen, occur, take place	حَدَثَ - يَحْدُثُ - حُدُوْثٌ
to be leafy (tree)	أَوْرَقَ - يُوْرِقُ - إِيْرَاقٌ
to pass	مَضَى - يَمْضِي - مُضِيٌّ
to gain, profit	رَبِحَ - يَرْبَحُ - رِبْحٌ
to get broken	إِنْكَسَرَ - يَنْكَسِرُ - إِنْكِسَارٌ
to turn red	إِحْمَرَّ - يَحْمَرُّ - إِحْمِرَارٌ
to sow, plant, cultivate	زَرَعَ - يَزْرَعُ - زَرْعٌ
to run	عَدَا - يَعْدُوْ - عَدْوٌ
to rise	نَهَضَ - يَنْهَضُ - نُهُوْضٌ
orange	بُرْتُقَالٌ
jackal, wolf	ذِئْبٌ (ذِئَابٌ)
sword	سَيْفٌ (سُيُوْفٌ)

nurse (female)	مُمَرِّضَةٌ (مُمَرِّضَاتٌ)
winter	شِتَاءٌ
watchman, guard	خَفِيرٌ (خُفَرَاءُ)
to sneeze	عَطَسَ - يَعْطِسُ - عَطْسٌ
to commence	بَدَأَ - يَبْدَأُ - بَدْءٌ
to become black	اِسْوَدَّ - يَسْوَدُّ - اِسْوِدَادٌ
bottle	زُجَاجَةٌ (زُجَاجَاتٌ)
hand	fem. يَدٌ (أَيْدٍ، أَيَادٍ)
to melt	ذَابَ - يَذُوبُ - ذَوْبٌ ، ذَوَبَانٌ
snow, ice	ثَلْجٌ (ثُلُوجٌ)
to travel	سَافَرَ - يُسَافِرُ - مُسَافَرَةٌ
to design	صَمَّمَ - يُصَمِّمُ - تَصْمِيْمٌ
engineer	مُهَنْدِسٌ (مُهَنْدِسُوْنَ)
building	بِنَاءٌ (أَبْنِيَةٌ)
to cure	شَفَى - يَشْفِي - شِفَاءٌ
injured, sick	مُصَابٌ (مُصَابُوْنَ)

LESSON 27

The Object الْمَفْعُوْلُ بِهِ

✦✦✦

Examples:

The monkey ate the banana.	أَكَلَ الْقِرْدُ الْمَوْزَ۔
The girl obeyed the teacher.	أَطَاعَتِ الْبِنْتُ الْأُسْتَاذَ۔
The diligent person gets the prize.	يَنَالُ الْمُجْتَهِدُ الْجَائِزَةَ۔
The maid cleaned the room.	نَظَّفَتِ الْخَادِمَةُ الْحُجْرَةَ۔
The thief hides the money.	يَخْبَأُ اللِّصُّ الْمَالَ۔
The cat felt the cold.	أَحَسَّ الْقِطُّ الْبَرْدَ۔
The king rode on the horse.	رَكِبَ الْمَلِكُ الْحِصَانَ۔
The beggar woman stretches out her hand.	تَمُدُّ الْفَقِيْرَةُ يَدَهَا۔
The committee held the meeting.	عَقَدَتِ اللَّجْنَةُ الْإِجْتِمَاعَ۔
The porter lifted the suitcase.	رَفَعَ الْعَتَّالُ الشَّنْطَةَ۔

Discussion:

Look at the examples above. They are all sentences made up of a verb and two nouns. The first one is the noun which you have known earlier i.e. the subject 'الْفَاعِلُ' because the action is performed by him/it. In the first sentence the second noun is الْمَوْزَ and the action has been performed on it.

Hence, the action of eating is performed by the monkey 'الْقِرْدُ' and the effect is on the banana 'الْمَوْزَ'. Similarly, in the second sentence, where the action of obedience is performed by the girl 'الْبِنْتُ' the effect is on the teacher 'الْأُسْتَاذَ'.

Both monkey 'الْقِرْدُ' and girl 'الْبِنْتُ' are doers 'فَاعِلٌ', and the banana 'الْمَوْزَ' and teacher 'الْأُسْتَاذَ' are the nouns on which the action has been performed. Each one of these latter two words is classified as an object 'مَفْعُوْلٌ بِهِ'. And the same applies to other remaining examples.

It is to be noted that the object in Arabic is considered to be in the accusative case (حَالَةُ النَّصْبِ) and it is generally denoted by فَتْحَةٌ (ــَ) which is shown in the examples.

Rule:

The object, i.e. 'الْمَفْعُوْلُ بِهِ' is a noun which receives the action of the subject and is considered to be in the accusative case, i.e. 'حَالَةُ النَّصْبِ'.

Exercise:

1. Pick out the objects (الْمَفْعُولُ بِهِ) from the following sentences.

١- أَكَلَ الْحِصَانُ الشَّعِيرَ۔   ٢- دَفَعَ الرَّجُلُ الأُجْرَةَ۔

٣- وَزَنَ الْبَقَّالُ الأُرُزَّ۔   ٤- يَحْرُثُ الْفَلَّاحُ الأَرْضَ۔

٥- اِسْتَقْبَلَتِ الأُسْرَةُ الضَّيْفَ۔   ٦- يَبِيعُ الْفَاكِهَانِيُّ التُّفَّاحَ۔

٧- يُصَلِّحُ الإِسْكَافِيُّ الأَحْذِيَةَ۔   ٨- تَجْلِبُ الْجَارِيَةُ الْمَاءَ۔

٩- وَاجَهَ الْمُسَافِرُ الْمُشْكِلَةَ۔   ١٠- طَبَخَتِ الأُمُّ الطَّعَامَ۔

2. Translate the sentences given in exercise no.1 into English.

3. Use the following nouns as objects in your sentences.

٣) الْجَائِزَةُ   ٢) الْحُجْرَةُ   ١) الشَّاةُ

٦) الثَّعْلَبُ   ٥) اللَّبَنُ   ٤) السِّعْرُ

٩) الرِّوَايَةُ   ٨) السَّفِينَةُ   ٧) الصُّنْدُوقُ

4. Fill in the blanks with suitable objects.

٢) بَاعَ الْخُضَرِيُّ _____ -   ١) رَأَى الصَّائِمُ _____ -

٤) سَاقَ السَّائِقُ _____ -   ٣) رَكِبَ الْجُنْدِيُّ _____ -

٦) تُنْشِدُ الْبَنَاتُ _____ -   ٥) أَكَلَ الْمَرِيضُ _____ -

٨) أَخَذَ الْوَلَدُ _____ -   ٧) يَخِيطُ الْخَيَّاطُ _____ -

١٠) يَصِيدُ الصَّيَّادُ _____ -   ٩) أَوْضَحَ الْوَزِيرُ _____ -

5. Make three sentences each as directed.

    a) Consisting of a noun (person) as an object.

    b) Consisting of a noun (animal) as an object.

c) Consisting of a noun (plant) as an object.

d) Using 'اَلْجَرِيْدَةُ' (the newspaper) as an object.

e) Using 'اَلْأَنْبَجُ' (the mango) as an object.

6. Translate the following into Arabic.

a) The player kicked the ball.

b) The boy climbed up the tree.

c) The receptionist received the call.

d) The man drove the car.

e) The cow eats grass.

f) The servant opened the door.

g) The director listened to the issue.

h) The rickshaw puller pulled his rickshaw.

i) The girl ate ice-cream.

j) The severe cold killed the man.

7. Translate the following into English.

١) أَعْطَى الرَّجُلُ رُوْبِيَّةً لِلْفَقِيْرِ۔

٢) قَطَعَ الْجُرَذُ الْحَبْلَ۔

٣) قَبَّلْتُ جَدَّتِي عَلَى جَبِيْنِهَا۔

٤) غَادَرَ اللُّبْنَانِيُّ الْبِلَادَ۔

٥) رَأَتِ الْبِنْتُ الْفَرَاشَةَ۔

٦) تَجْمَعُ الْفَلَّاحَاتُ الْفَوَاكِهَ۔

٧) حَلَلْنَا حُجْرَةً۔

٨) قَضَيْتُ سَاعَةً فِي الْقَاعَةِ۔

٩) رَسَمَ الرَّسَّامُ الرَّسْمَ۔

١٠) أَدْخَلَ الرَّجُلُ الْإِبْنَ فِي الْمَدْرَسَةِ۔

GLOSSARY	الْكَلِمَاتُ الْعَسِيْرَةُ
rent; price	أُجْرَةٌ
fruit seller	فَاكِهَانِي
cobbler	إِسْكَافِيٌّ (أَسَاكِفَةٌ)
to face	وَاجَهَ - يُوَاجِهُ - مُوَاجَهَةٌ
box	صُنْدُوقٌ (صَنَادِيقُ)
ship	سَفِيْنَةٌ (سُفُنٌ)
novel	رِوَايَةٌ (رِوَايَاتٌ)
to kick	ضَرَبَ بِالْقَدَمِ
to rise, climb	صَعِدَ - يَصْعَدُ - صُعُوْدٌ
receptionist (lady)	مُوَظَّفَةُ الْإِسْتِقْبَالِ
telephonic call	مُكَالَمَةٌ (مُكَالَمَاتٌ)
director	مُدِيْرٌ (مُدَرَاءُ)
to refuse, disapprove	أَنْكَرَ - يُنْكِرُ - إِنْكَارٌ
to pull	جَرَّ - يَجُرُّ - جَرٌّ
rickshaw puller	سَائِقُ الْعَرَبَةِ الْهَوَائِيَّةِ
large rat	جُرَذٌ (جِرْذَانٌ)
to leave	غَادَرَ - يُغَادِرُ - مُغَادَرَةٌ
icecream	ايْسْكِرِيْمُ
severe	شَدِيْدٌ

Lebanese	لُبْنَانِيٌّ
butterfly	فَرَاشَةٌ (فَرَاشَاتٌ)
hall	قَاعَةٌ (قَاعَاتٌ)
artist	رَسَّامٌ (رَسَّامُوْنَ)
painting, sketch	رَسْمٌ (رُسُومٌ، رُسُوْمَاتٌ)

LESSON 28

Comparison between the Doer (Subject) and the Object

الْمُوَازَنَةُ بَيْنَ الْفَاعِلِ وَالْمَفْعُوْلِ بِهِ

+≷≷+

Examples:

The king rode on the elephant.	رَكِبَ الْمَلِكُ الْفِيْلَ۔
The lady smells the flower.	تَشُمُّ السَّيِّدَةُ الزَّهْرَةَ۔
The boy wrote the letter.	كَتَبَ الْوَلَدُ الرِّسَالَةَ۔
The maid ironed the shirt.	كَوَتِ الْخَادِمَةُ الْقَمِيْصَ۔
The butcher slaughtered the goat.	ذَبَحَ الْجَزَّارُ الشَّاةَ۔
The driver drives the car.	يَقُوْدُ السَّائِقُ السَّيَّارَةَ۔

Results:

After studying the above examples we come to some conclusions, which are as follows:

1. Every doer (subject) and every object is a noun.
2. The doer (subject) is that which performs the action of a verb.
3. The object is that on which some action is performed or which receives the action of a verb.
4. The doer (subject) is always in the nominative case (حَالَةُ الرَّفْعِ) and thus it carries ةٌ ضَمَّةً (ـُ) on its last letter.

5. The object is always considered to be in the accusative case (حَالَةُ النَّصْبِ) and thus it has فَتْحَةٌ (ـَ) on its last letter.

Exercise:

1. Pick the subjects and the objects from the following sentences and use them in your own sentences.

١ ـ كَتَمَ الصَّدِيْقُ السِّرَّ ـ   ٢ ـ تَبِعَتِ الْبِنْتُ الْمُعَلِّمَةَ ـ

٣ ـ يَمْنَحُ الْأُسْتَاذُ الْإِذْنَ ـ   ٤ ـ أَطْلَقَ الْبُوْلِيْسُ الرَّصَاصَ ـ

٥ ـ هَدَى الْمُرْشِدُ الْقَافِلَةَ ـ   ٦ ـ غَسَلَتِ الْأُخْتُ الْأَوَانِيَ ـ

٧ ـ خَنَقَ الْقَاتِلُ التَّاجِرَ ـ   ٨ ـ يَذْبَحُ الْجَزَّارُ الْكَبْشَ ـ

٩ ـ إِخْتَارَ الْحِزْبُ الزَّعِيْمَ ـ   ١٠ ـ تَقُصُّ الْجَدَّةُ قِصَّةً ـ

2. Translate the sentences given in exercise no.1 into English.

3. Use the following verbs in your own sentences providing them with a subject and an object.

قَرَضَ - جَرَّ - أَلَفَ - سَمِعَ - ذَرَفَ
يَبِيْعُ - يُتْعِبُ - يُنِيْرُ - يَمْلَأُ - يَخْلِطُ

4. Translate the following into Arabic.

Jijo is a washerman. He is very useful to society. He serves all the people. He washes their clothes. He gives good service. His life is very hard. He goes from door to door every week. He collects dirty clothes. He ties them into a bundle. He brings them home. He marks the clothes with a particular mark on every cloth. He then boils the cotton

clothes. He uses washing soda and soap. He also washes the
silken and woollen clothes. He uses special soap for them.
The next day he carries the wet clothes to the washing ghat.
There, he dries the clothes. He returns the clothes in one week.

5. Translate the following into English.

زُرْتُ صَدِيْقِي يَوْمَ الْأَحَدِ۔ فَرِحَ صَدِيْقِي بِزِيَارَتِي۔ فَقَامَ بِتَكْرِيْمِي۔
وَبَعْدَ أَنْ تَنَاوَلْنَا الْمَأْكُوْلَاتِ وَالْمَشْرُوْبَاتِ، أَرَدْنَا الذَّهَابَ إِلَى سَاحِلِ
الْبَحْرِ۔ صَحِبَنَا صَدِيْقٌ آخَرُ۔ فَذَهَبْنَا هُنَاكَ مَعًا۔ رَأَيْنَا هُنَاكَ رِجَالًا
وَنِسَاءً وَأَطْفَالًا فِي عَدَدٍ كَبِيْرٍ۔ كَانَ يَسْبَحُ بَعْضُهُمْ فِي الْبَحْرِ
وَالْأَطْفَالُ يَلْعَبُوْنَ فِي الْمَاءِ۔ وَقَابَلْنَا هُنَاكَ صَيَّادَ السَّمَكِ الَّذِي أَلْقَى
الشَّبَكَةَ فِي الْبَحْرِ۔ وَاصْطَادَ السَّمَكَ مِنَ الْبَحْرِ۔ ثُمَّ فَتَحْنَا الْحَقِيْبَةَ
وَأَخْرَجْنَا الطَّعَامَ، فَأَكَلْنَا الطَّعَامَ۔ وَفِي الْمَسَاءِ رَجَعْنَا إِلَى بَيْتِنَا
فَرِحِيْنَ وَتَعْبَانِيْنَ أَيْضًا۔

GLOSSARY	الْكَلِمَاتُ الْعَسِيْرَةُ
washerman	غَسَّالٌ (غَسَّالُوْنَ)
society	مُجْتَمَعٌ (مُجْتَمَعَاتٌ)
bundle	حُزْمَةٌ (حُزَمٌ)
mark	عَلَامَةٌ (عَلَامَاتٌ)
particular, special	خَاصٌّ
to boil	غَلَى - يَغْلِي - غَلْيٌ
cotton	قُطْنِيٌّ

silken	حَرِيْرِيٌّ
woollen	صُوْفِيٌّ
washing soda	صُوْدَا الْغَسِيْلِ
soap	صَابُونٌ (صَابُوْنَاتٌ)
wet	مُبَلَّلٌ
ghat (place for bathing and washing clothes in India)	الْغَاطُ
honouring, tribute	كَرَّمَ - يُكَرِّمُ - تَكْرِيْمٌ
to carry out	قَامَ - يَقُوْمُ - قِيَامٌ (بِ)
seashore	سَاحِلُ الْبَحْرِ
fisherman	صَيَّادُ السَّمَكِ
net	شَبَكَةٌ (شَبَكَاتٌ)
tired	تَعْبَانٌ (تَعْبَانُوْنَ)

LESSON 29

Subjunctive Mood of the Imperfect Tense Verb

نَصْبُ الْفِعْلِ الْمُضَارِعِ

Examples:

(that) أَنْ

I like to listen to poetry.	أُحِبُّ أَنْ أَسْمَعَ الشِّعْرَ-
He can break the box.	يَسْتَطِيْعُ أَنْ يَكْسِرَ الصُّنْدُوْقَ-
You intended to visit Kuwait.	أَرَدْتَ أَنْ تَزُوْرَ الْكُوَيْتَ-
(never) لَنْ	
Time will never return.	لَنْ يَرْجِعَ الْوَقْتُ-
The studious will never fail.	لَنْ يَفْشَلَ الْمُجْتَهِدُ-
The neglectful will never succeed.	لَنْ يَنْجَحَ الْمُهْمِلُ-
(so that) كَيْ	
He went to library so that he might study.	ذَهَبَ إِلَى الْمَكْتَبَةِ كَيْ يَتَعَلَّمَ-
She lay down so that she might take rest.	اِضْطَجَعَتْ كَيْ تَسْتَرِيْحَ-
I came so that I might congratulate you.	حَضَرْتُ كَيْ أُهَنِّئَكَ-

----

إِذَنْ (then)

I have been working hard for two months. Then you will succeed.	لَا أَزَالُ أَجْتَهِدُ مُنْذُ شَهْرَيْنِ - إِذَنْ تَفُوزَ۔
I will visit the Taj Mahal. Then I will accompany you.	سَأَزُورُ التَّاج مَحَل - إِذَنْ أُصَاحِبَكَ۔
The sky has become cloudy. Then it will rain.	غَامَتِ السَّمَاءُ - إِذَنْ سَيَنْزِلَ الْمَطَرُ۔

حَتَّى (till, until)

I read the lesson till I understand.	أَقْرَأُ الدَّرْسَ حَتَّى أَفْهَمَ۔
I eat till I am satiated.	آكُلُ حَتَّى أَشْبَعَ۔
Stir the spoon in the cup till the sugar is mixed.	حَرِّكِ الْمِلْعَقَةَ فِي الْفِنْجَانِ حَتَّى يَذُوبَ السُّكَّرُ۔

لِ (for)

I came out to buy fish.	خَرَجْتُ لِأَشْتَرِيَ السَّمَكَ۔
The girl worked hard to succeed in the examination.	اِجْتَهَدَتِ الْبِنْتُ لِتَفُوزَ فِي الْإِمْتِحَانِ۔
He opened the book to read a story.	فَتَحَ الْكِتَابَ لِيَقْرَأَ قِصَّةً۔

Discussion:

Look at the examples above. You will find that the imperfect verb is preceded by one of these particles; أَنْ, لَنْ, حَتَّى إِذَنْ, كَيْ and لِ, and that the imperfect verb has taken a فَتْحَةٌ (ـَ).

Hence, we say that these particles change the mood of the imperfect verb from the indicative to the subjunctive. In other words, these particles give فَتْحَةٌ (ـَ) to the imperfect verb and the verb is considered to be in the subjunctive mood i.e. حَالَةُ النَّصْبِ.

Rule:

1. The mood of the imperfect verb is changed from indicative to subjunctive when it is preceded by any of these particles i.e. أَنْ, لَنْ, كَيْ, إِذَنْ, حَتَّى and لِ.

2. When the vowel of the last letter of the imperfect verb is فَتْحَةٌ (ـَ), it is considered to be in the subjunctive mood, i.e. حَالَةُ النَّصْبِ.

Exercise:

1. Complete the following sentences with a suitable imperfect verb and put vowel point on its last letter.

١ـ أُحِبُّ أَنْ _____ ـ   ٢ـ أَرَدْتُ أَنْ _____ ـ

٣ـ الْمَيِّتُ لَنْ _____ ـ   ٤ـ لَنْ _____ الْفَقِيرُ ـ

٥ـ اِتَّجَرْتُ كَيْ _____ ـ   ٦ـ مَشَيْتُ كَيْ _____ ـ

٧ـ وَقَعَتِ النَّارُ إذَنْ _____   ٨ـ شَاهَدْتُ الْهِلَالَ إذَنْ _____ ـ

٩ـ يَتَدَرَّبُ حَتَّى _____ ـ   ١٠ـ اِنْتَظَرْنَا لَهُ حَتَّى _____ ـ

١١ـ أَخْرَجْتُ الْمِحْفَظَةَ لِ_____ الثَّمَنَ ـ

١٢ـ حَضَرْتُ الزَّوَاجَ لِ_____ الزَّوْجَيْنِ ـ

2. Fill in the blanks with a suitable particle and put a vowel
sign on the last letter of the imperfect verb.

١ـ الْبَخِيلُ _____ يُنْفِق ـ

٢ـ أَعْدَدْتُ الزَّادَ _____ أُسَافِر ـ

٣ـ يَجِبُ عَلَى الْوَلَدِ _____ يَحْتَرِم أَبَاهُ ـ

٤ـ سَأُقَابِلُ الْعَلَّامَةَ _____ أَسْتَفِيد مِنْهُ ـ

٥ـ لَاعَبْتُ مَعَهُ _____ يَفْرَح ـ

٦ـ اِلْتَحَقَ بِالْجَيْشِ _____ يَخْدُم الْوَطَنَ ـ

٧ـ جِئْتُ _____ أَزُور وَالِدَكَ ـ

٨ـ نُرِيدُ _____ نَرْتَحِل صَبَاحًا ـ

٩ـ تَغِيبُ عَنِ الدَّرْسِ _____ تَفْشَل ـ

١٠ـ قَرُبْتُ مِنَ النُّورِ _____ أَقْرَأ ـ

3. Write a complementary sentence for each of the following
sentences having an imperfect verb preceded by 'إذَنْ'.

١ـ سَأَبْنِي بَيْتًا ـ

٢ـ سَأُعْطِي الْفُقَرَاءَ ـ

٣ـ يُدَخِّنُ كَثِيرًا.

٤ـ لَعِبَ الأَوْلَادُ الْكِرِنْكِيْت طُوْلَ النَّهَارِ.

٥ـ نُسَافِرُ إِلَى مِصْرَ.

٦ـ غَادَرَ أَخُوْهُ.

٧ـ كَسَرَ الطِّفْلُ الزُّجَاجَ.

٨ـ قَتَلَ اللِّصُّ الْجَارَ.

٩ـ خَدَعَنِي ذَلِكَ التَّاجِرُ.

١٠ـ ظَلَّ الْمَطَرُ غَزِيرًا.

4. Make three sentences each as follows:

a) consisting of imperfect verb preceded by أَنْ.

b) consisting of imperfect verb preceded by لَنْ.

c) consisting of imperfect verb preceded by كَيْ.

d) consisting of imperfect verb preceded by إِذَنْ.

e) consisting of imperfect verb preceded by حَتَّى.

f) consisting of imperfect verb preceded by لِ .

5. Translate the following into Arabic.

a) He will never return.

b) I drank milk to make my body strong.

c) The cold is so severe here that water freezes.

d) I can lift this box.

e) The teacher explained so that the pupil might understand.

f) I have acquired a bachelor's degree. Then you will get the job.

7. Translate the following into English.

١) لَا تَشْرَبِ الشَّايَ حَتَّى يَبْرُدَ ـ

٢) اِبْتَعْتُ الْكِتَابَ لِأَقْرَأَهُ ـ

٣) خَافَ أَنْ يَفُوْتَهُ الْقِطَارُ ـ

٤) أُرِيدُ أَنْ أَلْعَبَ كُرَةَ الْقَدَمِ إِذَنْ نَلْعَبَ مَعَكَ ـ

٥) الْحَاسِدُ لَنْ يَنَالَ الْمَجْدَ ـ

٦) دَخَلْتُ مَكَّةَ الْمُكَرَّمَةَ كَيْ أَحُجَّ ـ

GLOSSARY	الْكَلِمَاتُ الْعَسِيرَةُ
to be trained	تَدَرَّبَ - يَتَدَرَّبُ - تَدَرُّبٌ
to trade, do business	اِتَّجَرَ - يَتَّجِرُ - اِتِّجَارٌ
to show mercy	رَأَفَ - يَرْأَفُ - رَأْفَةٌ (بِ)
drought	قَحْطٌ

LESSON 30

Jussive Mood of the Imperfect Tense Verb
جَزْمُ الْفِعْلِ الْمُضَارِعِ

+§§+

Examples:

Lam to show Negation in the Past
(did not, was not, had not) لَمْ

The boy did not take food.	لَمْ يَتَنَاوَلْ الْوَلَدُ الطَّعَامَ۔
I did not tell a lie.	لَمْ أَكْذِبْ۔
The glass did not break.	لَمْ يَنْكَسِرْ الزُّجَاجُ۔

Lamma to show Negation in the Past
(not yet) لَمَّا

The flower has not yet blossomed.	لَمَّا تَتَفَتَّحْ الزَّهْرَةُ۔
The sun has not yet risen.	لَمَّا تُشْرِقْ الشَّمْسُ۔
The matter is not yet completed.	لَمَّا يَكْتَمِلْ الْأَمْرُ۔

Lam to indicate a Command
(let) لِ

Let him do what he wants.	لِيَفْعَلْ مَا يَشَاءُ۔
Let them spend in the way of Allah.	لِيُنْفِقُوا فِي سَبِيلِ اللهِ۔

| Let the illiterate girl work hard. | لِتَجْتَهِدْ الْبِنْتُ الْجَاهِلَةُ۔ |

La to show Negation
(Do not) لَا

Do not beat the animals.	لا تَضْرِبْ الْحَيَوَانَ۔
Do not be slow in the work.	لا تَمَهَّلْ فِي الْعَمَلِ۔
Do not waste time.	لا تُضَيِّعْ الْوَقْتَ۔

The Particle of Condition
(if) إِنْ

If you drink cold water, you will fall sick.	إِنْ تَشْرَبْ الْمَاءَ الْبَارِدَ، تَمْرَضْ۔
If the teacher sits, I will sit.	إِنْ يَجْلِسْ الْأُسْتَاذُ، أَجْلِسْ۔
If you are lazy in your work, you will repent.	إِنْ تَكْسَلْ فِي العَمَلِ، تَنْدَمْ۔

Discussion:

Look at the examples above and in the previous pages. You will find that the imperfect verb is preceded by one of these particles; لَمْ, لَمَّا, لَامُ الْأَمْرِ, لَاءُ النَّهْي and إِنْ and that the imperfect verb has taken سُكُوْنٌ (ـْ).

Hence, we say that these particles change the mood of the imperfect verb from the indicative to the jussive mood. In other words, these particles place the verb after them in apocapate form (حَالَةُ الْجَزْمِ), i.e. they silence the last letter of the verb.

Note: The last letter of the imperfect verb, when it takes سُكُوْن (ـْ) if joined to the following word is given كَسْرَةٌ (ـِ), e.g. لَا تَقْرُبْ ==> لَا تَقْرُبِ الْحَيَوَانَ

Rule:

1. The mood of the imperfect verb is changed from indicative to jussive when it is preceded by any of these particles i.e. إِنْ and لَاءُ النَّهْي, لَامُ الْأَمْرِ, لَمَّا, لَمْ.

2. The last letter of the imperfect tense takes سُكُوْنٌ (ـْ) when it is preceded by any of these partilces لَمْ, لَمَّا, لَامُ الْأَمْرِ, لَاءُ النَّهْي and إِنْ and the verb is considered to be in the jussive mood (حَالَةُ الْجَزْمِ).

3. 'لَمْ' is a particle which is used to make the past tense negative.

4. 'لَمَّا' is a particle which gives the meaning of 'not yet'.

5. 'لَامُ الْأَمْرِ' is an indirect type of imperative which is used to exhort someone to do something. This may be used with all fourteen forms of the indicative imperfect verb.

6. As you have studied in the previous lesson, 'لَاءُ النَّهْي' is a particle which is used to prevent the performance of the action of the verb or it is used for negative orders or requests.

7. The particle إِنْ needs two imperfect verbs, the first verb is a condition for the occurrence of the second verb. The first verb is known as the verb of condition or protasis (فِعْلُ الشَّرْطِ) and the second verb is known to be the conclusion of a conditional sentence or apodosis i.e. (جَوَابُ الشَّرْطِ).

Exercise:

1. Introduce 'لَمْ' to the imperfect verb and mark سُكُونٌ (ـْ) on the last letter of the verb.

٢ـ النَّجَّارُ يَصْنَعُ الْكُرْسِيَّ.   ١ـ يُسَافِرُ الْأَبُ إِلَى لُبْنَانَ.

٤ـ الْقَافِلَةُ تُوَاصِلُ السَّيْرَ.   ٣ـ يَمْلِكُ الثَّرِيُّ قَصْرًا.

٦ـ يَرْكَبُ الرَّجُلُ الحِمَارَ.   ٥ـ تَكْتُمُ الْبِنْتُ السِّرَّ.

٨ـ تَتَمَتَّعُ الْفَتَاةُ بِالْجَوِّ الرَّائِقِ.   ٧ـ الْوَلَدُ يَتَسَلَّقُ الْأَشْجَارَ.

١٠ـ يَسْتَأْجِرُ الْمُسَافِرُ الْبَيْتَ.   ٩ـ يَلْبَسُ الْعَسْكَرِيُّ الزِّيَّ.

2. Introduce 'لَّمَا' to the imperfect verb and mark سُكُونٌ (ـْ) on the last letter.

٢ـ يَنْقَطِعُ الْمَطَرُ.   ١ـ يَحْضُرُ الْمُعَلِّمُ.

٤ـ تَهْبِطُ الطَّائِرَةُ.   ٣ـ يَتَحَرَّكُ الْقِطَارُ.

٦ـ يَتَّفِقُ الْوَزِيرُ.   ٥ـ يَتَّخِذُ الْمَجْلِسُ الْقَرَارَ.

٨ـ يُعْدِمُ الْجَلَّادُ الْمُجْرِمَ.   ٧ـ يَأْمُرُ الْأَمِيرُ.

١٠ـ تَبْدَأُ الْمُبَارَاةُ.   ٩ـ يَنْعَقِدُ الْإِجْتِمَاعُ.

3. Choose the appropriate imperfect verb, precede it by لَامُ الْأَمْرِ and fill in the blanks.

يَرْحَمُ - يُكْرِمُ - يَحْتَرِمُ - يَكْتُبُ - يَسْتَيْقِظُ

يُسْرِعُ - يُطْعِمُ - يُهَذِّبُ - يَرْجِعُ - يَدْفَعُ

١- _____ الضَّيْفَ۔

٢- _____ مُبَكِّرًا۔

٣- _____ الْجَائِعَ۔

٤- _____ بِخَطٍّ حَسَنٍ۔

٥- _____ عَلَى الْبُؤَسَاءِ۔

٦- _____ الزَّوْجَةُ الزَّوْجَ۔

٧- _____ الْغَائِبُ إِلَى أَهْلِهِ۔

٨- _____ الثَّمَنَ۔

٩- _____ أَوْلَادَهُ۔

١٠- _____ فِي أَدَاءِ الْفَرِيضَةِ۔

4. Fill in the blanks with appropriate imperfect verbs to give a negative order with لَاءُ النَّهْيِ.

تُرَافِقُ - تُكْثِرُ - تَحْتَقِرُ - تَرْتَكِبُ - تُقْلِقُ

تَسْمَعُ - تَجْلِسُ - تُقَلِّلُ - تُعَذِّبُ - تُضَيِّعُ

١- _____ فِي الصَّدَقَةِ۔

٢- _____ الْجَرِيمَةَ۔

٣- _____ الْفَقِيرَ۔

٤- _____ الْأَشْرَارَ۔

٥- _____ فِي مَجْرَى الْهَوَاءِ۔

٦- _____ فِي الْأَكْلِ۔

٧- _____ الْجِيرَانَ۔

٨- _____ الْوَقْتَ۔

٩- _____ الْكَلَامَ الْفَارِغَ۔

١٠- _____ الْحَيَوَانَ۔

5. Fill in the blanks with appropriate imperfect verbs given below to make conditional sentences.

تُسَافِرُ - يَبْتَعِدُ - تَمْرَضُ - تَعْمَلُ - تَلْعَبُ

تَقْرُبُ - يَغْضَبُ - تَحْتَرِمُ - يَحْسُنُ - تَجْتَهِدُ

١- إِنْ _____ مِنَ النَّارِ ، تُحْرِقْكَ۔

٢- إِنْ _____ ، تَنْجَحْ۔

٣- إِنْ _____ كِبَارَكَ، يَحْتَرِمْكَ صِغَارُكَ۔

٤- إِنْ تُجْهِدْ نَفْسَكَ، _____ ۔

٥- إِنْ _____ ، أُسَافِرْ مَعَكَ۔

٦- إِنْ _____ الْخَيْرَ، يَنْفَعْكَ فِي الْآخِرَةِ.

٧- إِنْ تَتَمَرَّنْ عَلَى الْكِتَابَةِ، _____ خَطُّكَ.

٨- إِنْ _____ بِالثَّعْلَبِ، هَجَمَ عَلَيْكَ.

٩- إِنْ تُوْلِمْ أَبَوَيْكَ، _____ عَلَيْكَ اللَّهُ.

١٠- إِنْ تَتَكَبَّرْ، _____ عَنْكَ النَّاسُ.

6. Make three sentences each as directed below.

a) consisting of imperfect verbs preceded by لَمْ.

b) consisting of imperfect verbs preceded by لَّا.

c) consisting of imperfect verbs preceded by لِ (لَامُ الْأَمْرِ).

d) consisting of imperfect verbs preceded by لَاءُ النَّهِي.

e) consisting of imperfect verbs preceded by إِنْ.

5. Translate the following into Arabic.

a) Do not eat fast.

b) He did not throw the ball.

c) The plane has not yet arrived.

d) He should pay his bills.

e) If you arrive on time, you will get a ticket.

f) Do not switch on the fan.

g) The gardener should water the plants.

h) The water has not yet frozen.

i) If you write neatly, you will get good marks.

j) The barber did not cut my hair.

7. Translate the following into English.

١) لَمْ تَثِبِ الضَّبُعُ.

٢) لا تَنَمْ وَقْتَ الْعَصْرِ.

٣) إِنْ يَنْزِلِ الْمَطَرُ، تَبْتَلِلْ.

٤) لَمَّا تُنَظِّفْ زَيْنَبُ الْكُوخَ۔

٥) لِيُشْرِفِ النَّاظِرُ عَلَى شُؤُونِ الْمَدْرَسَةِ۔

٦) لا تَحْزَنْ وَلا تَقْلَقْ۔

٧) لِيَقُلِ الْمَظْلُومُ حَالَهُ۔

٨) لَمَّا أُقَابِلِ السَّفِيرَ۔

٩) إِنْ تَسْمَعْ نَصِيحَتِي، تَنْتَفِعْ بِهَا۔

١٠) لَمْ تَنَلِ السَّيِّدَةُ الْوَظِيفَةَ۔

GLOSSARY	الْكَلِمَاتُ الْعَسِيرَةُ
to execute (s.o)	أَعْدَمَ - يُعْدِمُ - إِعْدَامٌ
fox	ثَعْلَبٌ (ثَعَالِبُ)
to attack	هَجَمَ - يَهْجُمُ - هُجُومٌ
bill	فَاتُورَةٌ (فَاتُورَاتٌ)
ticket	تَذْكِرَةٌ (تَذَاكِرُ)
to switch on	شَغَّلَ - يُشَغِّلُ - تَشْغِيلٌ
marks	عَلَامَةٌ (عَلَامَاتٌ)
barber	حَلَّاقٌ (حَلَّاقُونَ)
hyena	ضَبُعٌ (ضِبَاعٌ) fem.
to become wet	إِبْتَلَّ - يَبْتَلُّ - إِبْتِلَالٌ
hut	كُوخٌ (أَكْوَاخٌ)
the principal of the school	نَاظِرُ الْمَدْرَسَةِ

LESSON 31

Indicative Mood of the Imperfect Tense Verb
رَفْعُ الْفِعْلِ الْمُضَارِعِ

❖

Examples:

The heat becomes severe.	يَشْتَدُّ الْحَرُّ۔
The nightingale sings.	يُغَرِّدُ الْبُلْبُلُ۔
The rate becomes high.	يَرْتَفِعُ السِّعْرُ۔
The tree becomes leafy.	تُورِقُ الشَّجَرَةُ۔
The drunkard becomes intoxicated.	يَنْشَى السِّكِّيْرُ۔
The journalist travels.	يُسَافِرُ الصَّحَافِيُّ۔

Discussion:

Look at the examples above. Each one of them begins with an imperfect verb (فِعْلُ الْمُضَارِعُ) with the last letter of each verb having ضَمَّةٌ (ـُ). This is the simple indicative imperfect verb.

When an imperfect verb is not preceded by any particle which causes فَتْحَةٌ (ـَ) or سُكُوْنٌ (ـْ), it keeps its original ضَمَّةٌ and it is considered to be in the indicative mood.

Rule:

1. The imperfect verb takes ضَمَّةٌ (ـُ), if it is not preceded by any particle that causes فَتْحَةٌ (ـَ) or سُكُوْنٌ (ـْ) to the last letter.

2. The imperfect verb which takes ضَمَّةٌ (ـُ) is considered to be in the indicative mood.

Exercise:

1. Fill in the blanks with a suitable imperfect verb.

١- _____ الْجَائِعُ الطَّعَامَ.	٢- _____ الْبَرْدُ فِي الشِّتَاءِ.
٣- _____ الْأَشْجَارُ فِي الْغَابَةِ.	٤- _____ السَّمَكُ فِي الْبَحْرِ.
٥- _____ الْخَيَّاطُ الْمَلَابِسَ.	٦- _____ الْأُمُّ الصَّبِيَّ.
٧- _____ الْقَاضِي بَيْنَ النَّاسِ.	٨- _____ الْكَسْلَانُ الْعَمَلَ.
٩- _____ الْفَرَجُ بَعْدَ الضِّيْقِ.	١٠- _____ الْحَدَّادُ الْحَدِيْدَ.

2. Make three sentences each as directed below.
   a) with an indicative imperfect verb.
   b) with an indicative imperfect verb in the middle.

3. Write five sentences on the topic of 'الشُّرْطِيُّ', each having an indicative imperfect verb.

4. Write five sentences on the topic of 'النَّجَّارُ', each having an indicative imperfect verb.

5. Translate the following into Arabic.
   a) He listens to music.
   b) The secretary will send an e-mail.
   c) She always forgets her purse.

d) I play tennis.

e) The party will start in the evening.

f) The train leaves every morning.

g) The diplomat waits for the meeting.

h) He enjoys the opera.

i) The course will start in July.

j) Cats like milk.

6. Translate the following into English.

١) تُحَاوِلُ العَنْزَةُ الإِفْلَاتَ مِنَ الأَسَدِ۔

٢) يَقُوْمُ الْوَلَدُ بِالْعَمَلِ الرَّتِيْبِ۔

٣) يَبْحَثُ الِابْنُ الأُكْبَرُ عَنِ الْعَمَلِ۔

٤) تَمْلِكُ الأَمِيْرَةُ ثَرْوَةً كَبِيْرَةً۔

٥) سَنَعْقِدُ حَفْلَةً يَوْمَ الْجُمْعَةِ۔

٦) تُقَاسِي المَرِيْضَةُ أَلَمًا شَدِيْدًا۔

٧) يَلْهَثُ الْعَامِلُ مِنَ التَّعَبِ۔

٨) أَعْرِفُ تَقَالِيْدَ هٰذِهِ الْبِلَادِ۔

٩) يُلَقِّنُ الأَبُ ابْنَهُ مَبَادِئَ الْفَضِيْلَةِ۔

١٠) تَضَعُ الْفَلَّاحَةُ الرَّضِيْعَ عَلَى الظَّهْرِ۔

GLOSSARY	الْكَلِمَاتُ الْعَسِيْرَةُ
poverty, difficulty	ضِيْقٌ
relief	فَرَجٌ
music	مُوْسِيْقَى
e-mail	الْبَرِيْدُ الإِلَكْتِرَوْنِي

to forget	نَسِىَ - يَنْسَى - نِسْيَانٌ
to leave	غَادَرَ - يُغَادِرُ - مُغَادَرَةٌ
diplomat	دِبْلُوْمَاسِي
to enjoy	تَمَتَّعَ - يَتَمَتَّعُ - تَمَتُّعٌ (بِ)
opera	أُوْبِيْرَا
class	حَلَقَةٌ دِرَاسِيَّةٌ
escape	إِفْلَاتٌ
routine work	الْعَمَلُ الرَّتِيْبُ
to suffer, bear	قَاسَى - يُقَاسِي - مُقَاسَاةٌ
to be out of breath, pant	لَهَثَ - يَلْهَثُ - لَهْثٌ
tradition	تَقْلِيْدٌ (تَقَالِيْدُ)
to teach, instruct	لَقَّنَ - يُلَقِّنُ - تَلْقِيْنٌ
principle	مَبْدَأٌ (مَبَادِئُ)
virtue; merit	فَضِيْلَةٌ (فَضَائِلُ)

LESSON 32

Kana and its Sisters كَانَ وَ أَخَوَاتُهَا

❖

Examples:

كَانَ (was)

السَّارِقُ سَجِيْنٌ۔	كَانَ السَّارِقُ سَجِيْنًا۔
The thief is a prisoner.	The thief was a prisoner
الْقَمِيْصُ جَدِيْدٌ۔	كَانَ الْقَمِيْصُ جَدِيْدًا۔
The shirt is new.	The shirt was new.

صَارَ (to become)

الْقَمَرُ مُكْتَمِلٌ۔	صَارَ الْقَمَرُ مُكْتَمِلًا۔
The moon is full.	The moon became full.
الْمُوَاظِبُ نَاجِحٌ۔	صَارَ الْمُوَاظِبُ نَاجِحًا۔
The diligent person is successful.	The diligent person became successful.

لَيْسَ (not)

الفِنَاءُ وَاسِعٌ۔	لَيْسَ الفِنَاءُ وَاسِعًا۔
The courtyard is spacious.	The courtyard is not spacious.
الْكَلَامُ فَصِيْحٌ۔	لَيْسَ الْكَلَامُ فَصِيْحًا۔
The speech is intelligible.	The speech is not intelligible.

أَصْبَحَ (to become [in the morning])

الْمَطَرُ غَزِيْرٌ۔	أَصْبَحَ الْمَطَرُ غَزِيْرًا۔
The rain is copious.	The rain became copious.

الْعَامِلُ نَشِيطٌ۔	أَصْبَحَ الْعَامِلُ نَشِيطًا۔
The worker is active.	The worker became active.

(to become [in the evening]) أَمْسَى

الْفَاشِلُ حَزِينٌ۔	أَمْسَى الْفَاشِلُ حَزِينًا۔
The unsuccessful person is sad.	The unsuccessful person became sad.
الْبَرْدُ شَدِيدٌ۔	أَمْسَى الْبَرْدُ شَدِيدًا۔
The cold is severe.	The cold became severe.

(to become [in the forenoon]) أَضْحَى

النُّورُ سَاطِعٌ۔	أَضْحَى النُّورُ سَاطِعًا۔
The light is bright.	The light became bright.
الصَّانِعُ مَشْغُولٌ۔	أَضْحَى الصَّانِعُ مَشْغُولًا۔
The craftsman is busy.	The craftsman became busy.

(to become, continue to do s.th.) ظَلَّ

الْقِطَارُ مُتَحَرِّكٌ۔	ظَلَّ الْقِطَارُ مُتَحَرِّكًا۔
The train is moving.	The train kept moving.
النَّهْرُ فَاضٍ۔	ظَلَّ النَّهْرُ فَائِضًا۔
The river is flowing.	The river kept flowing.

(to spend the night) بَاتَ

الْخَفِيرُ مُتَنَبِّهٌ۔	بَاتَ الْخَفِيرُ مُتَنَبِّهًا۔
The watchman is awake.	The watchman spent the night awake.
الْمَرِيضُ مُضْطَرِبٌ۔	بَاتَ الْمَرِيضُ مُضْطَرِبًا۔
The patient is disturbed.	The patient spent the night disturbed.

Discussion:

Look at the examples above. You will find that the sentences of the section on left side are made up of the subject and predicate in the nominative case and the sentences of the section on right side begin with one of these verbs, i.e. ظَلَّ, أَضْحَى, أَمْسَى, أَصْبَحَ, لَيْسَ, صَارَ, كَانَ and بَاتَ and each one has two nouns; one has ضَمَّةٌ (ـُ) and the other has تَنْوِيْنُ الْفَتْحِ (ـً). Here, the question arises as to what has brought about this change? Indeed, the verbs which have been introduced into the sentence has caused this change. These verbs give ضَمَّةٌ (ـُ) to the first noun (which it already has) and فَتْحَةٌ (ـَ) or تَنْوِيْنُ الْفَتْحِ (ـً) to the other. The first noun remains in the nominative case and is called the noun (اِسْمٌ) of the verb which precedes while the other is in the accusative case and is called the predicate (خَبَرٌ) of the verb.

These verbs have their imperfect tenses and imperatives like any other verb, except لَيْسَ, which has neither imperfect tense nor the imperative.

Rule:

1. When كَانَ is introduced to the subject and predicate, it causes تَنْوِيْنُ الضَّمِّ (ـُ)or ضَمَّةٌ (ـُ) to the subject (which it already has) and تَنْوِيْنُ الْفَتْحِ (ـً) or فَتْحَةٌ (ـَ) to the

predicate. The subject is known as its noun (إِسْمُ كَانَ)
while the predicate is known as its predicate (خَبَرُ كَانَ) .

2. When كَانَ is introduced to the nominal sentence, the
case of the subject remains nominative while the case of
the predicate changes to the accusative case.

3. The verbs ظَلَّ, أَضْحَى, أَمْسَى, أَصْبَحَ, لَيْسَ, صَارَ and بَاتَ are
called sisters of كَانَ .

4. Each of these verbs has its imperfect tense and
imperative, except the verb لَيْسَ which has neither
imperfect form nor the imperative.

Exercise:

1. Use كَانَ with each of the following sentences and put a
vowel sign on the last letter of each word controlled by it.

١ـ السَّاعَةُ مَكْسُورَةٌ۔   ٢ـ الضَّيْفُ مُقْبِلٌ۔

٣ـ الْقَاعَةُ خَالِيَةٌ۔   ٤ـ الرِّدَاءُ مَمْدُودٌ۔

٥ـ الصَّخْرُ كَبِيرٌ۔   ٦ـ الضِّرْغَامُ مُفْتَرِسٌ۔

٧ـ الْقِطَّةُ لَاعِبَةٌ۔   ٨ـ الْفَاكِهَةُ طَازِجَةٌ۔

٩ـ الْحِلْيَةُ ثَمِينَةٌ۔   ١٠ـ الْبُسْتَانِيُّ مَشْغُولٌ۔

2. Use صَارَ before each of the following sentences and put a
vowel sign on the last letter of each word controlled by it.

١ـ الْجَوُّ مُعْتَدِلٌ۔   ٢ـ الْوَجْهُ جَمِيلٌ۔

٣ـ الشَّجَرَاتُ مُزْهِرَةٌ۔   ٤ـ الرَّجُلُ ثَرِيٌّ۔

٥ـ الْجَوَازُ مُجَدَّدٌ۔   ٦ـ الْوَلَدُ شَابٌّ۔

٧ـ الثَّوْبُ قَصِيرٌ۔   ٨ـ الْعَمُّ عَجُوزٌ۔

٩- التَّاجِرُ أَمِينٌ.   ١٠- الْخُطْبَةُ طَوِيلَةٌ.

3. Use لَيْسَ before each of the following sentences and put a vowel sign on the last letter of each word.

٢- الْعَصِيرُ حُلْوٌ.   ١- الشُّبَّاكُ مَفْتُوحٌ.

٤- الْمِذْيَاعُ جَدِيدٌ.   ٣- الْقَرْيَةُ قَرِيبَةٌ.

٦- الرِّسَالَةُ مُرْسَلَةٌ.   ٥- الْمُسْتَضِيفُ غَائِبٌ.

٨- الْخَالَةُ سَمِينَةٌ.   ٧- الْجِسْمُ قَوِيٌّ.

١٠- الْوَرَقُ خَفِيفٌ.   ٩- الْقَلَمُ ثَمِينٌ.

4. Use أَصْبَحَ before each of the following sentences and put a vowel sign on the last letter of each word controlled by it.

٢- الصَّوْتُ ضَعِيفٌ.   ١- الْقَلْبُ رَقِيقٌ.

٤- الثَّمَنُ رَخِيصٌ.   ٣- الشَّمْسُ طَالِعَةٌ.

٦- الدَّوَاةُ فَارِغَةٌ.   ٥- الْأَثَاثُ قَدِيمٌ.

٨- الْحَدِيثُ طَوِيلٌ.   ٧- النَّبَأُ مُنْتَشِرٌ.

١٠- الْبَحْرُ هَائِجٌ.   ٩- الْجَرِيدَةَ صَادِرَةٌ.

5. Fill in the blanks with a suitable word and put a vowel sign on its last letter.

٢- صَارَ الْفَطُورُ _____ -   ١- كَانَ السَّيِّدُ _____ -

٤- أَصْبَحَ السِّكِّينُ _____ -   ٣- لَيْسَ الْعَبْدُ _____ -

٦- بَاتَ الْمُتْعَبُ _____ -   ٥- ظَلَّ الْعَامِلُ _____ -

٨- أَضْحَى الثَّوْرُ _____ -   ٧- أَمْسَى الْحَزِينُ _____ -

6. Fill in the blanks with a suitable word and put a vowel sign on its last letter.

٢- صَارَ _____ عَمِيقًا.   ١- كَانَ _____ ثَقِيلًا.

٤- أَصْبَحَ _____ عَالِمًا.   ٣- لَيْسَ _____ أَمِينًا.

٥- يَظَلَّ ـــــــ مُنَوَّرًا۔   ٦- يَبِيْتُ ـــــــ مُتَأَلِّمًا۔

٧- يُمْسِي ـــــــ سُوْءًا۔   ٨- يُضْحِي ـــــــ مُبَارَكًا۔

7. Make two sentences each as directed below.

    a) with كَانَ, its noun, and its predicate.

    b) with صَارَ, its noun, and its predicate.

    c) with أَصْبَحَ, its noun, and its predicate.

    d) with بَاتَ, its noun, and its predicate.

    e) with لَيْسَ, its noun, and its predicate.

    f) with أَمْسَى, its noun, and its predicate.

    g) with ظَلَّ, its noun, and its predicate.

    h) with أَضْحَى, its noun, and its predicate.

8. Make two sentences each as follows.

    a) with يَكُوْنُ, its noun, and its predicate.

    b) with يَصِيْرُ, its noun, and its predicate.

    c) with يُصْبِحُ, its noun, and its predicate.

    d) with يَبِيْتُ, its noun, and its predicate.

    e) with يُمْسِي, its noun, and its predicate.

    f) with يَظَلُّ, its noun, and its predicate.

    g) with يُضْحِي, its noun, and its predicate.

9. Make two sentences each as per the instructions below.

    a) with كَانَ and having الْمُعَلِّمُ as its noun.

    b) with صَارَ and having اللِّبَاسُ as its noun.

    c) with لَيْسَ and having الْجَارُ as its noun.

    d) with بَاتَ and having الْمَرِيْضُ as its noun.

    e) with أَمْسَى and having الْحُجْرَةُ as its noun.

    f) with أَصْبَحَ and having الْعَامِلُ as its noun.

g) with ظَلَّ and having الْمَطَرُ as its noun.

h) with أَضْحَى and having الشَّجَرُ as its noun.

10. Translate the following into Arabic.

    a) Asad was tense before the examination.

    b) He became famous in this new city.

    c) My old school became a museum.

    d) He is not poor.

    e) The owl spent the night searching for food.

    f) My uncle became a priest.

    g) He later became very religious.

    h) I became acquainted with the new computer.

    i) I remained busy with the work the whole night.

    j) The library is not closed.

7. Translate the following into English.

١) كَانَ فَرِيقُنَا فَائِزًا۔

٢) أَمْسَى الْبَيْتُ مُظْلِمًا۔

٣) كَانَ الْفَصْلُ مُنْتَبِهًا وَهَادِئًا۔

٤) ظَلَّ الْقِطَارُ مُتَحَرِّكًا۔

٥) أَضْحَتِ الْآلَةُ صَدِئَةً۔

٦) يَصِيرُ الْجَوُّ بَارِدًا فِي اللَّيْلِ۔

٧) بَاتَتِ الْمُمَرِّضَةُ مُشْرِفَةً عَلَى الْمَرِيضِ۔

٨) لَيْسَتِ السِّبَاحَةُ عَمَلًا صَعْبًا ۔

٩) يَكُونُ السُّلُوكُ مُرْضِيًا ۔

١٠) تَظَلُّ الْأَوْرَاقُ سَاقِطَةً مِنَ الشَّجَرَةِ ۔

GLOSSARY	الكَلِمَاتُ العَسِيْرَةُ
cloak	رِدَاءٌ
ornament	جِلْيَةٌ (حِلًى)
blooming	مُزْهِرٌ
passport	جَوَازٌ (جَوَازَاتٌ)
renewed	مُجَدَّدٌ
radio set	مِذْيَاعٌ (مَذَايِيْعُ)
host	مُسْتَضِيْفٌ
dispatched	مُرْسَلٌ
light, thin	خَفِيْفٌ (خِفَافٌ)
fine, delicate	رَقِيْقٌ (رِقَاقٌ)
breakfast	فَطُوْرٌ
museum	مَتْحَفٌ (مَتَاحِفُ)
priest	كَاهِنٌ (كُهَّانٌ)
acquainted with	مُطَّلِعٌ (عَلَى)
rusty	صَدِئٌ
satisfactory, pleasing	مُرْضٍ

LESSON 33

Inna and its Sisters إِنَّ وَ أَخَوَاتُهَا

Examples:

(indeed, truly) إِنَّ

السَّرِيْرُ نَاعِمٌ۔	إِنَّ السَّرِيْرَ نَاعِمٌ۔
The bed is soft.	Indeed, the bed is soft.
النَّظَافَةُ ضَرُوْرِيَّةٌ۔	إِنَّ النَّظَافَةَ ضَرُوْرِيَّةٌ۔
Cleanliness is necessary.	Indeed, cleanliness is necessary.
(that) أَنَّ	
الْبَنْكُ مَفْتُوْحٌ۔	(سَمِعْتُ) أَنَّ الْبَنْكَ مَفْتُوْحٌ۔
The bank is open.	I heard that the bank is open.
الْوَزِيْرُ حَاضِرٌ۔	(أَخْبَرَ) أَنَّ الْوَزِيْرَ حَاضِرٌ۔
The minister is present.	He said that the minister is present.
(as if) كَأَنَّ	
الْهِرُّ أَسَدٌّ۔	كَأَنَّ الْهِرَّ أَسَدٌّ۔
The cat is lion.	As if the cat is lion.

كَأَنَّ الْأُسْتَاذَ وَالِدٌ۔	الْأُسْتَاذُ وَالِدٌ۔
As if the teacher is father.	The teacher is father.

لٰكِنَّ أَوْ وَلٰكِنَّ (but)	
(الْكِذْبُ مَكْرُوْهٌ) وَلٰكِنَّ الصِّدْقَ مَحْبُوْبٌ۔	الْكِذْبُ مَكْرُوْهٌ وَالصِّدْقُ مَحْبُوْبٌ۔
The lie is hated but the truth is lovable.	The lie is hated and the truth is lovable.
(الْكَلَامُ طَوِيْلٌ) وَلٰكِنَّ الْوَقْتَ قَلِيْلٌ۔	الْكَلَامُ طَوِيْلٌ وَالْوَقْتُ قَلِيْلٌ۔
The conversation is lengthy but the time is less.	The conversation is lengthy and the time is less.

لِأَنَّ (because)	
لَا أَخْرُجُ مِنَ الْبَيْتِ لِأَنَّ السَّمَاءَ مُمْطِرٌ۔	السَّمَاءُ مُمْطِرٌ۔
I do not go out of the house because it is raining.	It is raining.
لَا أَقْرَأُ لِأَنَّ الضَّوْءَ ضَئِيْلٌ۔	الضَّوْءُ ضَئِيْلٌ۔
I do not read because the light is dim.	The light is dim.

لَيْتَ (would that, I wish)	
لَيْتَ الْوَلَدَ مُؤَدَّبٌ۔ I wish (would) that the boy was disciplined.	الْوَلَدُ مُؤَدَّبٌ۔ The boy is disciplined.
لَيْتَ الْفَرَجَ قَرِيْبٌ۔	الْفَرَجُ قَرِيْبٌ۔
I wish the comfort was near.	The comfort is near.

لَعَلَّ (perhaps, may be)	
ـاَلْحَارِسُ غَائِبٌ۔ The watchman is absent.	لَعَلَّ الْحَارِسَ غَائِبٌ۔ Perhaps the watchman is absent.
الزُّجَاجُ مَكْسُوْرٌ۔ The glass is broken.	لَعَلَّ الزُّجَاجَ مَكْسُوْرٌ۔ Perhaps the glass is broken.

Discussion:

Look at the examples above. You will find that the sentences of the section on left side are made up of a subject and a predicate which are in the nominative case and the sentences of the section on the right side begin with one of these particles i.e. إِنَّ, أَنَّ, كَأَنَّ, لَكِنَّ, لِأَنَّ, لَيْتَ and لَعَلَّ and each sentence has two nouns; one has فَتْحَةٌ (ـَ) or تَنْوِيْنُ الْفَتْحِ (ـً) above it and the other has تَنْوِيْنٌ (ـٌ) above it. This has been caused by the particles which are introduced in the beginning of the subject and predicate. These particles cause ضَمَّةٌ (ـُ) to the first noun and فَتْحَةٌ (ـَ) or تَنْوِيْنُ الْفَتْحِ (ـً) to the second. So the first noun is considered to be in the accusative case and is called the noun (إِسْمٌ) of the particle which precedes it while the second part is said to be in the nominative case and is called the predicate (خَبَرٌ) of the particle.

Rule:

1. When any of إِنَّ, أَنَّ, كَأَنَّ, لَكِنَّ, لِأَنَّ, لَيْتَ and لَعَلَّ is introduced to the nominal sentence i.e. subject and predicate, they change the case of the subject from nominative into the accusative (i.e. ﹷ or ﹻ) and the predicate remains in the nominative case (i.e. ﹹ or ﹷ).

2. The particles إِنَّ, أَنَّ, كَأَنَّ, لَكِنَّ, لِأَنَّ, لَيْتَ and لَعَلَّ are also known as الْحُرُوفُ الْمُشَبَّهَةُ بِالْفِعْلِ.

3. The subject of the sentence is known as the noun of this particle (اِسْمُ الْحَرْفِ الْمُشَبَّهِ بِالْفِعْلِ) while the predicate is known as its predicate (خَبَرُ الْحَرْفِ الْمُشَبَّهِ بِالْفِعْلِ).

Exercise:

1. Use إِنَّ with the following sentences and put a vowel sign on the last letter of each word.

٢ـ الْاِسْمُ مَجْهُوْلٌ۔	١ـ الصَّبِيَّةُ لَاعِبَةٌ۔
٤ـ الطَّيْرُ مُتَغَرِّدٌ۔	٣ـ الْمَيْدَانُ وَاسِعٌ۔
٦ـ الْحَيَاةُ صَعْبَةٌ۔	٥ـ السَّفَرُ مُتْعِبٌ۔
٨ـ الْمَنْظَرُ جَمِيْلٌ۔	٧ـ الْاِبْنُ مُطِيْعٌ۔
١٠ـ الْكَلِمَةُ غَرِيْبَةٌ۔	٩ـ الضَّبَابُ مُتَكَاثِفٌ۔

2. Fill in the blanks with أَنَّ or لَكِنَّ or لِأَنَّ and put a vowel sign on the last letter of each noun.

١ـ وَجَدْتُ _____ الولد ذكيّ۔

٢ـ جَاءَ الضيوف _____ المستضيف غائب۔

٣ـ تَأَخَّرْتُ _____ القطار متأخر ـ

٤ـ الأُخْتُ مؤدبة _____ الأَخ فظّ ـ

٥ـ أخبر _____ الطير مطلق ـ

٦ـ لم أشرب الشاي _____ الشاي بارد ـ

٧ـ هل علمت _____ الامتحان قريب ـ

٨ـ أوضح _____ الأمر ليس كذلك ـ

٩ـ ضرب الأب الولد _____ الولد شرير ـ

١٠ـ ظنّ _____ الهدف سهل ـ

3. Use لَيْتَ with the following sentences and put a vowel sign on the last letter of each noun.

٢ـ الْمَنْزِلُ قَرِيبٌ ـ   ١ـ السُّؤَالُ سَهْلٌ ـ

٤ـ الطَّبَّاخُ نَظِيفٌ ـ   ٣ـ الْبِنْتُ مُهَذَّبَةٌ ـ

٦ـ اللِّبَاسُ جَاهِزٌ ـ   ٥ـ الطَّعَامُ لَذِيْذٌ ـ

٨ـ الْبَيْتُ كَبِيرٌ ـ   ٧ـ الْكِتَابُ مَوْجُودٌ ـ

١٠ـ الطَّرِيْقُ مَعْرُوفٌ ـ   ٩ـ الْفَرِيْقُ نَاجِحٌ ـ

4. Use لَعَلَّ with the following sentences and put a vowel sign on the last letter of each noun.

٢ـ الْمَلِكَة مُسَافِرَة ـ   ١ـ الدَّنَانِيْر مُنْتَثِرَة ـ

٤ـ النِّدَاء مَسْمُوْع ـ   ٣ـ الْجِبَال عَالِيَة ـ

٦ـ الطِّفْل خَائِف ـ   ٥ـ الأَمِيْر جَبَان ـ

٨ـ التَّاج ذَهَبِي ـ   ٧ـ الْقِصَّة مُمْتِعَة ـ

١٠ـ الْبَحْر هَائِج ـ   ٩ـ اللَّوْن مُتَغَيِّر ـ

5. Complete the following sentences with a suitable predicate and put a vowel sign on its last letter.

١ـ إِنَّ الْقَصْرَ ــــــــــ ـ   ٢ـ الْعَسَلُ حُلْوٌ وَلٰكِنَّ اللَّيْمُونَ ــــــ ـ

٣ـ لَعَلَّ السَّفِيرَ ــــــــــ ـ   ٤ـ كَأَنَّ الْبِنْتَ ــــــــ ـ

٥ـ لَيْتَ الْمُعَلِّمَ ــــــــــ   ٦ـ إِنَّ السَّرَابَ ــــــــ ـ

٧ـ حَامِدٌ صَغِيرٌ وَلٰكِنَّ رَاشِدًا ــــــ ـ   ٨ـ رَأَى أَنَّ الدَّهْرَ ــــــــ ـ

٩ـ كَأَنَّ الْكِتَابَ ــــــــ ـ   ١٠ـ لَيْتَ الثُّرْهَةَ ــــــــ ـ

١١ـ شَهِدَ أَنَّ اللِّصَّ ــــــــ ـ   ١٢ـ لَعَلَّ الْجَوْرَبَ ــــــــ ـ

6. Fill in the blanks with suitable nouns and put a vowel sign
   on the last letter of each of them.

١ـ إِنَّ ــــــــ شَدِيدٌ ـ   ٢ـ يَسُرُّنِي أَنَّ ــــــــ قَادِمَة ـ

٣ـ كَأَنَّ ــــــــ إِنْسَان ـ   ٤ـ لِأَنَّ ــــــــ قَوِيّ ـ

٥ـ الْأَرْنَبُ صَغِيرَةٌ وَلٰكِنَّ ــــــــ ضَخْم ـ

٦ـ عَرَفَ أَنَّ ــــــــ غَرِيب ـ   ٧ـ لَعَلَّ ــــــــ مَكْشُوف ـ

٨ـ إِنَّ الْخَبَرَ ــــــــ ـ   ٩ـ لَيْتَ الزَّهْرَة ــــــــ ـ

١٠ـ الْبَيْتُ ــــــــ وَلٰكِنَّ ــــــــ مُغْلَقَة ـ

١١ـ لِأَنَّ الْبِئْرُ ــــــــ ـ   ١٢ـ كَأَنَّ ــــــــ قَمَر ـ

7. Make two sentences each as directed.

    a) with إِنَّ .

    b) with أَنَّ .

    c) with كَأَنَّ .

    d) with وَلٰكِنَّ .

    e) with لِأَنَّ .

    f) with لَيْتَ .

    g) with لَعَلَّ .

8. Make six sentences on 'الْمُكْتَبَةُ' consisting of all the particles (إِنَّ وَأَخْوَاتُهَا).

9. Translate the following into Arabic.

    a) Indeed our generation is new.

    b) As if she was a nightingale.

    c) I came early but did not find a place.

    d) Perhaps Khalid won the prize.

    e) I wish my parents were here.

    f) I trust you because you are a good man.

    g) He explained that the company needed an accountant.

10. Translate the following into English.

١) لَيْتَ الصَّبْرَ سَهْلٌ۔

٢) حَاوَلْتُ أَنْ أُسَلِّيَهُ وَلَكِنَّ بُكَاءَهُ لَمْ يَتَوَقَّفْ۔

٣) مَا تَكَلَّمْتُ مَعَهُ لِأَنَّ خُلُقَهُ سَيِّئٌ۔

٤) لَمْ يَرْأَفْ بِالْمِسْكِينِ كَأَنَّ قَلْبَهُ حَجَرٌ۔

٥) يَبْدُو أَنَّ النَّائِبَ لَا يَعْلَمُ الْأَمْرَ۔

٦) لَعَلَّ الشَّاعِرَ يُشِيرُ إِلَى جَمَالِ الْحَدِيقَةِ۔

٧) إِنَّ الْمَقَالَةَ لِلشَّعْبِ۔

GLOSSARY	الْكَلِمَاتُ الْعَسِيْرَةُ
unknown; anonymous	مَجْهُولٌ
fog	ضَبَابٌ
rude	فَظٌّ (أَفْظَاظٌ)
to explain	أَوْضَحَ - يُوْضِحُ - إِيْضَاحٌ
coward	جَبَانٌ (جُبَنَاءُ)
mirage	سَرَابٌ
stocking; sock	جَوْرَبٌ (جَوَارِبُ)
generation	جِيْلٌ (أَجْيَالٌ)
nightingale	هَزَارُ (هَزَارَاتٌ)
nightingale	عَنْدَلِيْبٌ (عَنَادِلُ)
accountant	مُحَاسِبٌ (مُحَاسِبُوْنَ)

LESSON 34

Prepositions حُرُوْفُ الْجَرِّ

◄◄◊►►

Examples:

(1) from - مِنْ

The passenger came out of the station.	خَرَجَ الْمُسَافِرُ مِنَ الْمَحَطَّةِ۔
The thief flees the jail.	يَفِرُّ اللِّصُّ مِنَ السِّجْنِ۔

(2) to - إِلَى

The officer goes to the office.	يَذْهَبُ الْمُوَظَّفُ إِلَى الْمَكْتَبِ۔
The soldier returned home.	رَجَعَ الْجُنْدِيُّ إِلَى الْبَيْتِ۔

(3) from - عَنْ

The gazelle hid from the hunter.	اِخْتَفَى الْغَزَالُ عَنِ الصَّيَّادِ۔
The teacher asked about the absent student	سَأَلَ الْمُعَلِّمُ عَنِ التِّلْمِيْذِ الْغَائِبِ۔
The pious man abstains from sins.	يَكُفُّ الْعَفِيْفُ عَنِ الذُّنُوبِ۔

(4) on - عَلَى

The butterfly sits on the flower.	تَقَعُ الْفَرَاشَةُ عَلَى الزَّهْرَةِ۔
I put the book on the table.	وَضَعْتُ الْكِتَابَ عَلَى الطَّاوِلَةِ۔

(5) at, in - فِي	
The stars twinkle in the sky.	تَتَلَأْلَأُ النُّجُومُ فِي السَّمَاءِ۔
I walk in the garden.	أَتَنَزَّهُ فِي الْحَدِيْقَةِ۔

(6) by, at, with, in - بِ	
She cut the meat with a knife.	قَطَعَتِ اللَّحْمَ بِالسِّكِّيْنِ۔
He stayed in the city.	مَكَثَ بِالْمَدِيْنَةِ۔

(7) for - لِ	
The punishment is for the sinner.	الْعِقَابُ لِلْمُذْنِبِ۔
The respect is for the teacher.	الْإِحْتِرَامُ لِلْأُسْتَاذِ۔

Discussion:

Look at the examples above. You will find that the
sentences in the section on the right side end with a noun.
Each noun is preceded by a particle. In group (1) of the
examples, the last word is preceded by 'مِنْ', in group (2), it is
preceded by 'إِلَى'. Similarly, in group (3), it is preceded by
'عَنْ', in group (4), it is preceded by 'عَلَى', in group (5) it is
preceded by 'فِيْ', in group (6), it is preceded by 'بِ' and in
group (7), it is preceded by 'لِ'.

Moreover, the last letter of the nouns preceded by
any of these particles, has kasra (ِ) which is the sign of its
being in the genitive case. Hence, we can say that the nouns

which are preceded by these particles are considered to be in the genitive case (حَالَةُ الْجَرِّ).

Rule:

1. The noun takes كَسْرَةٌ (ـِ) or تَنْوِيْنُ الْكَسْرِ (ـٍ), when it is preceded by the preposition (حَرْفُ الْجَرِّ).

2. When the noun is preceded by the preposition, it is considered to be in the genitive case.

3. مِنْ, إِلَى, عَنْ, عَلَى, فِيْ, بِ, لِ are some prepositions.

Exercise:

1. Fill in the blanks with suitable nouns given below and put a vowel sign on its last letter.

الْفَصْل - الْجَيْب - الْجُحْر - الْكِتَابَة - الإِبْرِيْق - الطَّاوِلَة
السَّرِيْر - الْحُكُوْمَة - الصَّدْر - الْمُجْرِم - الْقَضِيّة
الرَّصَاص - الطَّرِيْق - الاخْتِتَام - الْغَابَات - الصَّيْد

١ـ أَخْرَجْتُ الشَّايَ مِنَ ـــــ -   ٢ـ التِّلْمِيْذُ فِي ـــــ -

٣ـ وَضَعَ الرِّسَالَةَ عَلَى ـــــ -   ٤ـ قَتَلَ الصَّيَّادُ الشَّاةَ بِـــــ -

٥ـ إِشْتَرَيْتُ الْكُرَّاسَةَ لِـــــ -   ٦ـ ضَلَّ الْغَرِيْبُ عَنِ ـــــ -

٧ـ نَالَ الْمِنْحَةَ مِنَ ـــــ -   ٨ـ الْمَدِيْنَةَ مَحْفُوْفَةٌ بِـــــ -

٩ـ وَضَعْتُ الْفُلُوْسُ فِي ـــــ -   ١٠ـ مَا عَفَا الْقَاضِى عَنِ ـــــ -

١١ـ خَرَجَ الأَمِيْرُ لِـــــ -   ١٢ـ وَصَلَ الْخِطَابُ إِلَى ـــــ -

١٣ـ يَطْرَحُ الرَّجُلُ نَفْسَهُ عَلَى ـــــ -   ١٤ـ بَحَثَتِ الْفَأْرَةُ عَنْ ـــــ -

١٥- فَتَّشَ الْبُولِيسُ عَنِ ـــــ ـ ١٦- ضَمَّتِ الْأُمُّ الطِّفْلَ إِلَى ـــ ـــ -

2. Fill in the blanks with a suitable preposition.

١- اِشْتَرَيْتُ الْخُبْزَ ـــــ الْخَبَّازِ- ٢- وَضَعَ السَّلَّةَ ـــ الْأَرْضِ-

٣- أَجَابَ الشَّابُّ ـــــ عَقْلِهِ- ٤- بَحَثَ ـــــ الْعَمَلِ-

٥- أَقْلَعَتِ الطَّائِرَةُ ـــــ الْمَطَارِ- ٦- لَا تَبْتَعِدُ الْأُمُّ ـــ الصَّبِيِّ-

٧- يَرْجِعُ الْمُسَافِرُ ـــــ الْوَطَنِ- ٨- الْمُغَامَرَةُ ـــ الشُّجَاعِ-

٩- يُوَاصِلُ الطَّالِبُ السَّيْرَ ـــ الْمَدْرَسَةِ-

١٠- يَعْطِفُ الْأَبُ ـــ الْوَلَدِ- ١١-كَسَّرْتُ الْجَوْزَ ـــ الْأَسْنَانِ-

١٢- السَّمَكُ ـــــ النَّهْرِ- ١٣-الْبَضَائِعُ ـــــ التِّرَامِ-

١٤- السَّيْفُ ـــ الْمُحَارِبِ-

3. Use the following words in your own sentences in such a way that they are governed by a preposition.

اللُّغَةُ، الْمَوْضُوعُ، الْكَعْكُ، السِّتَارَةُ، السَّيْفُ
الدَّوَاءُ، الذُّبَابُ، الصُّنْدُوقُ، السِّعْرُ، الْمَعْمَلُ

4. Make two sentences each as directed.

a) with the preposition 'مِنْ'.

b) with the preposition 'إِلَى'.

c) with the preposition 'عَنْ'.

d) with the preposition 'عَلَى'.

e) with the preposition 'فِي'.

f) with the preposition 'بِ'.

g) with the preposition 'لِ'.

5. Translate the following into Arabic.

a) The chairman left for Korea.

b) He went far from his family.

c) On the table are a spoon, a fork and a jug.

d) The traveller visited the places then stayed at a hotel.

e) The bus takes ten minutes from his home to the office.

f) She took the key and put it in her pocket.

g) I saw a drama on the television.

6. Translate the following into English.

١) مَاذَا صَبَبْتَ فِي الْفِنْجَانِ؟

٢) قَدْ دَرَسْنَا الزِّرَاعَةَ مِنْ هٰذَيْنِ الْكِتَابَيْنِ.

٣) اِسْتَقْبَلْتُ الضُّيُوفَ فِي الْمَطَارِ.

٤) هٰذَا الْكِتَابُ لِلْأَطْفَالِ.

٥) كَانَتِ الْقَصِيْدَةُ مُعَلَّقَةً عَلَى جِدَارِ الْكَعْبَةِ.

٦) عَرَفْتُ هَذِهِ الشَّخْصِيَّةَ عَنْ طَرِيْقِ الْإِنْتَرْنَتْ.

٧) لِمَاذَا لَمْ تُتَرْجِمْ هَذِهِ الْفِقْرَةَ مِنَ الْفَرَنْسِيَّةِ إِلَى الْعَرَبِيَّةِ.

GLOSSARY	الْكَلِمَاتُ الْعَسِيْرَةُ
adventure; risk	مُغَامَرَةٌ (مُغَامَرَاتٌ)
tram	تِرَام
surrounded	مَحْفُوْفَةٌ
letter	خِطَابٌ (خِطَابَاتٌ)

embrace	ضَمَّ - يَضُمُّ - ضَمٌّ
cake	كَعْكٌ
factory	مَعْمَلٌ (مَعَامِلُ)
chairman, president	رَئِيْسُ الْجَلْسَةِ
welfare	رَفَاهِيَّةٌ
spoon	مِلْعَقَةٌ (مَلَاعِقُ)
jug	إِبْرِيْقٌ (أَبَارِيْقُ)
by means of, through, by	عَنْ طَرِيْقٍ
internet	إِنْتَرْنَتْ

LESSSON 35

Masculine and Feminine الْمُذَكَّرُ وَالْمُؤَنَّثُ

◄§€►

Feminine With Signs

Examples:

(1)

He is a cultured boy.	هُوَ وَلَدٌ مُؤَدَّبٌ۔
The father is coming.	الْأَبُ قَادِمٌ۔

(2)

The watch is costly.	السَّاعَةُ غَالِيَةٌ۔
The building is old.	الْعِمَارَةُ قَدِيْمَةٌ۔

(3)

The pear is ripe.	الْكُمَّثْرَىٰ نَاضِجَةٌ۔
The sweet is delicious.	الْحَلْوىٰ لَذِيْذَةٌ۔

(4)

The desert is vast.	الصَّحْرَاءُ وَاسِعَةٌ۔
Pride is dispraised.	الْكِبْرِيَاءُ مَذْمُوْمَةٌ۔

Discussion:

Look at the examples above. You will find that the subjects in group (1) i.e. هُوَ and الْأَبُ are masculine nouns while the subjects in the examples of groups (2), (3) and (4) end either with "ة" (اَلتَّاءُ الْمَرْبُوطَةُ) or with "ى" (اَلْأَلِفُ الْمَقْصُوْرَةُ)

or with "اءَ-" (اَلْأَلِفُ الْمَمْدُوْدَةُ). These three signs are called

signs of the feminine gender. Therefore, all these words

which have these signs are considered to be feminine, and

used in making different sentences as feminine e.g. in using

verbs, pronouns and predicates for them and in the construct

phrases to bring attribute for them.

Feminine Without Signs

Examples:

(1)

The mother is busy in the kitchen.	ـاَلْأُمُّ مَشْغُوْلَةٌ فِي الْمَطْبَخِ
The sister is sitting in the room.	ـاَلْأُخْتُ جَالِسَةٌ فِي الْغُرْفَةِ
(2)	
Maryam goes to school.	ـمَرْيَمُ تَذْهَبُ إِلَى الْمَدْرَسَةِ
Suaad studies in the fifth class.	ـسُعَادُ تَدْرُسُ فِي الصَّفِّ الْخَامِسِ
(3)	
Egypt is located in North Africa.	ـمِصْرُ وَاقِعَةٌ فِي شَمَالِ أَفْرِيْقِيَا
Damascus is far from Mumbai.	ـدِمَشْقُ بَعِيْدَةٌ عَنْ مُوْمْبَاى
(4)	
The girl's eyes are blue.	ـعَيْنَا الْبِنْتِ زَرْقَاءُ

The hand is clean.	‫الْيَدُ نَظِيْفَةٌ_‬
(5)	
The sun is rising.	‫الشَّمْسُ طَالِعَةٌ_‬
The earth is round.	‫الْأَرْضُ مُدَوَّرَةٌ_‬

Discussion:

Look at the above examples. You will see that the subject of every sentence is a feminine noun. You will also observe that the subjects of the sentences of group (1) i.e. ‫الْأُمُّ‬ and ‫الْأُخْتُ‬ are feminine by their meanings and the subjects of the sentences of group (2) i.e. ‫مَرْيَم‬ and ‫سُعَادُ‬ are names of females, therefore, they are feminine. But the nouns in group (3), group (4) and group (5) i.e. ‫مِصْرُ‬ and ‫دِمَشْقُ , الْعَيْنُ‬ and ‫الْيَدُ‬ and ‫الشَّمْسُ‬ and ‫الْأَرْضُ‬ - are all feminines and have been used as feminines while they do not have any sign of the feminine gender nor are they feminine by meaning nor are they the names of any female. Then why are they feminine? The answer is that the native speakers use them as feminine without any reason. Therefore, they are called feminine by convention (‫الْمُؤَنَّثُ السَّمَاعِيُّ)‬. In this category you will find the names of countries, cities, parts of the body which exist in pairs and several other words like ‫الشَّمْسُ , الْأَرْضُ‬, etc.

Rule:

1. All nouns and adjectives in Arabic are masculine except those which have signs of the feminine gender.

2. The signs of the feminine are "ة" (اَلتَّاءُ الْمَرْبُوْطَةُ) or "ى" (اَلْأَلِفُ الْمَقْصُوْرَةُ) or "ـاء " (اَلْأَلِفُ الْمَمْدُوْدَةُ) at the end of the word.

3. Feminine words without signs are those that are feminine in meaning or they are the names of females, e.g. أُمٌّ, سُعَادُ ,مَرْيَمُ ,أُخْتٌ, etc.

4. Several words are used by the native speakers as femininefor no reason. They are called "feminine by convention" (اَلْمُؤَنَّثُ السَّمَاعِيُّ). They are:

   i) Names of countries or cities like مِصْرُ ,دِمَشْقُ, etc.

   ii) Parts of body which exist in pairs like الْيَدُ ,الْعَيْنُ, etc.

   iii) There are some other words which are used as feminine by convention like الْأَرْضُ ,الشَّمْسُ, etc.

Note: There are a few words which have "ة" at the end but they are either the names of some persons or are used for males, such as طَرَفَةُ (name of a poet), خَلِيْفَةُ (head of an Islamic state), عَلَّامَةُ (very learned one) etc.

Exercise:

1. Fill in the blanks with suitable feminine nouns and put
   a vowel sign on the last letter.

١ـ هٰذِهِ ــــــ غَالِيَةٌ ـ   ٢ـ ذٰلِكَ ــــــ وَتِلْكَ ــــــ ـ

٣ـ هَلِ الْعَرُوْسُ ــــــ ـ   ٤ـ ــــــ قَاطِعَةٌ ـ

٥ـ الْخَمْرُ ــــــ ـ   ٦ـ ــــــ وَاسِعَةٌ ـ

٧ـ طَبَخَتْ ــــــ الطَّعَامَ ـ   ٨ـ النَّارُ ــــــ ـ

٩ـ ــــــ نَظِيْفَةٌ ـ   ١٠ـ هٰذِهِ الدَّارُ ــــــ ـ

١١ـ دِمَشْقُ ــــــ ـ   ١٢ـ الْعَيْنُ ــــــ ـ

2. Fill in the blanks with suitable nouns given below and put
   a vowel sign on the last letter of each one.

الشَّمْسُ - الْخُطْبَةُ - الْعَجُوْزُ - الْعِمَارَةُ - شَمْسِيَّةٌ

دَبِيْبَةٌ - صَغِيْرَةٌ - الْمَثْيُ - خَفِيْفٌ - السَّمَاءُ

١ـ الْمِحْفَظَةُ ــــــ ـ   ٢ـ هٰذِهِ ــــــ جَمِيْلَةٌ ـ

٣ـ ــــــ ضَعِيْفَةٌ ـ   ٤ـ الْوَرَقُ ــــــ ـ

٥ـ ــــــ طَالِعَةٌ ـ   ٦ـ ــــــ زَرْقَاءُ ـ

٧ـ السُّلَحْفَاة ــــــ ـ   ٨ـ ــــــ طَوِيْلَةٌ جِدًّا ـ

٩ـ ــــــ ضَرُوْرِيٌّ ـ   ١٠ـ ــــــ قَدِيْمَةٌ ـ

3. Write suitable attributes for the following words.

الْجَامِعَةُ - مِصْرُ - الْبَقَرَةُ - النَّفْسُ - سَفِيْنَةٌ

الْمُصِيْبَةُ - سَرِيْعَةٌ - مُجْتَهِدَةٌ - غَالِيَةٌ - الْأَرْمَلَةُ

4. Make two verbal sentences each as follows:

   a) consisting of a doer having 'ة' (تَاءٌ مَرْبُوْطَةٌ) at the end.

   b) consisting of an object having 'ة' (تَاءٌ مَرْبُوْطَةٌ) at the end.

c) consisting of a doer having " ـَـٰ " (أَلِفٌ مَقْصُورَةٌ) at the end.

d) consisting of an object having "ـَاء" (أَلِفٌ مَمْدُودَةٌ) at the end.

e) consisting of a female name.

5. Make two nominal sentences each as follows:

   a) consisting of the names of a city or a country.

   b) consisting of the names of body parts which are found in pairs.

6. Translate the following into Arabic:

   a) The fruit is fresh.

   b) He has large feet.

   c) The mother is baking the bread.

   d) I live in a small village.

   e) The new college is small.

   f) The great scholar is present.

   g) The wretched widow lamented.

7. Translate the following sentences into English.

١) أَصْبَحَتِ الْحَقِيْبَةُ مُبْتَلَّةً۔

٢) مَتَى وَصَلَتِ الطَّالِبَةُ إِلَى الْكُلِّيَّةِ؟

٣) فَقَدَتِ الطَّبِيْبَةُ السَّمَّاعَةَ۔

٤) شَاوَرَتِ الزَّوْجَةُ الزَّوْجَ۔

٥) طَهْرَان تَدْعُو وَزِيْرًا تُرْكِيًّا لِزِيَارَتِهَا۔

٦) تَخْدُمُ الْمُضِيْفَةُ فِي الطَّائِرَةِ۔

٧) الْخَمْرُ فِي الْمَطْعَمِ مَمْنُوْعَةٌ۔

GLOSSARY	الْكَلِمَاتُ الْعَسِيْرَةُ
caliph	خَلِيْفَةٌ (خُلَفَاءُ)
creeping, crawling	دَبِيْبَةٌ
to bake	خَبَزَ - يَخْبِزُ - خَبْزٌ
wretched	بَائِسٌ (بَائِسُوْنَ)
to lament, weep, wail	نَحَبَ - يَنْحَبُ - نَحْبٌ
wet	مُبْتَلَّةٌ
stethoscope	السَّمَّاعَةُ
Tehran (the capital of Iran)	طَهْرَان
air hostess	مُضِيْفَةٌ (مُضِيْفَاتٌ)

LESSON 36

The Quality and the Noun Qualified
النَّعْتُ وَالْمَنْعُوْتُ

Examples:

	(1)
This is a good boy.	هٰذَا وَلَدٌ صَالِحٌ۔
I saw a good boy.	رَأَيْتُ وَلَدًا صَالِحًا۔
I went to a good boy.	ذَهَبْتُ إِلَى وَلَدٍ صَالِحٍ۔
	(2)
This is a beautiful garden.	هٰذِهِ حَدِيْقَةٌ جَمِيْلَةٌ۔
I saw a beautiful garden.	رَأَيْتُ حَدِيْقَةً جَمِيْلَةً۔
I walked in a beautiful garden.	مَشَيْتُ فِي حَدِيْقَةٍ جَمِيْلَةٍ۔
	(3)
The small key was lost.	ضَاعَ الْمِفْتَاحُ الصَّغِيْرُ۔
I held the small key.	أَمْسَكْتُ الْمِفْتَاحَ الصَّغِيْرَ۔
I locked up with the small key.	أَقْفَلْتُ بِالْمِفْتَاحِ الصَّغِيْرِ۔
	(4)
The famous writers came.	جَاءَ الْكُتَّابُ الْمَشَاهِيْرُ۔

| I met the famous writers. | قَابَلْتُ الْكُتَّابَ الْمَشَاهِيرَ۔ |
| I gained from the famous writers. | إِسْتَفَدْتُ مِنَ الْكُتَّابِ الْمَشَاهِيرِ۔ |

Discussion:

Look at the examples above. You will find that the last word in every sentence is an attribute of the noun which precedes it. This word indicates some quality or description or characteristics of the noun, therefore, it is called an attribute 'نَعْتٌ'. The noun which precedes it is called the noun qualified by the adjective 'مَنْعُوتٌ'.

Further observation shows us that all these attributes follow the respective nouns they qualify in all the three cases whether it is the nominative case, accusative case or genitive case.

Hence, the attributes صَالِحٌ in the examples of group (1) follows the substantive in all the three cases. Similarly, the other attributes جَمِيلَةٌ, الصَّغِيْرُ and الْمَشَاهِيرُ follow the respective nouns they qualify.

It should be noted that the attribute follows the noun qualified by it in indefiniteness as in (وَلَدٌ صَالِحٌ) and definiteness as in (الْمِفْتَاحُ الصَّغِيْرُ). It is according to the noun qualified in number also as in (وَلَدٌ صَالِحٌ) where the attribute is singular because the noun qualified is singular and in (الْكُتَّابُ الْمَشَاهِيرُ) where the attribute is in plural form because of the noun it qualifies. The attribute follows the noun qualified in gender also, as in (وَلَدٌ صَالِحٌ) where صَالِحٌ is masculine because وَلَدٌ is a masculine word and in (حَدِيْقَةٌ جَمِيْلَةٌ) where جَمِيْلَةٌ is feminine because the noun qualified is feminine, i.e. حَدِيْقَةٌ.

Rule:

1. The attribute 'نَعْتٌ' is a word that shows the quality or characteristics of someone or something. It is also called صِفَةٌ.

2. The noun qualified 'مَنْعُوْتٌ' is a noun whose quality or characteristics are shown by the attribute 'نَعْتٌ'. It is also called مَوْصُوْفٌ.

3. The attribute always follows the noun it qualifies.

4. The attribute follows the noun qualified in four things:

   i) Case; nominative, accusative and genitive. (See any group).

   ii) Definiteness or Indefiniteness. (See groups 1 and 3).

   iii) Number (See groups 1 and 4).

   iv) Gender (See groups 1 and 2).

Rule:

If the noun qualified is the plural of non-intelligent being (masculine or feminine), its attribute will be feminine singular, e.g. الْبَقَرَاتُ السَّمِيْنَةُ or الْكُتُبُ الْجَدِيْدَةُ.

Exercise:

1. Fill in the blanks with a suitable attribute and put a vowel sign on its last letter.

١ـ فِي الْغَابَةِ أَشْجَارٌ ـــــــ ـ   ٢ـ مَشِيْتُ فِي لَيْلَةٍ ـــــــ

٣ـ لَبِسَ الْوَلَدُ اللِّبَاسَ ـــــــ   ٤ـ يَبْكِي طِفْلٌ ـــــــ

٥ـ ذَهَبْتُ إِلَى رَجُلٍ ـــــــ   ٦ـ الطَّالِبُ ـــــــ مَحْبُوْبٌ

٧ـ يَمْلِكُ التَّاجِرُ قَصْرًا ـــــــ   ٨ـ رَجَعَ مِنْ سَفَرٍ ـــــــ

٩ـ جَلَسَ الضَّيْفُ فِي رَدْهَةٍ ـــــــ   ١٠ـ ذَلِكَ شَخْصٌ ـــــــ

١١ـ صَنَعَ النَّجَّارُ بَابًا ـــــــ   ١٢ـ رَكِبْتُ حِصَانًا ـــــــ

2. Fill in the blanks with a suitable noun given below and put a vowel sign on its last letter.

أُنْشُوْدَة ـ رَجُل ـ حَيَوَان ـ سِكِّيْن ـ غُبَار ـ إِمْرَأَة

عَادَة ـ وَقْت ـ أَسْلِحَة ـ حَشَرَة ـ نَصِيْحَة ـ قَلْعَة

١ـ الدُّبُّ ـــــــ كَبِيْرٌ   ٢ـ النَّامُوْسُ ـــــــ مُوذِيَةٌ

٣ـ زُرْنَا ـــــــ قَدِيْمَةً   ٤ـ قَابَلْتُ ـــــــ شُجَاعًا

٥ـ مَرَّ الْغَنِيُّ بِ ـــــــ فَقِيْرَةٍ   ٦ـ ثَارَ ـــــــ الْكَثِيْفُ

٧ـ الْمُقَامَرَةُ ـــــــ مَكْرُوْهَةٌ   ٨ـ قَطَعْتُ الْحَبْلَ بِ ـــــــ الْحَادِّ

٩ـ جَهَّزَ الْجَيْشُ ـــــــ الْمُمِيْتَةَ   ١٠ـ أَنْشَدَتِ الْبِنْتُ ـــــــ الْجَمِيْلَةَ

١١ـ نَصَحَ الطَّبِيْبُ ـــــــ مُفِيْدَةً   ١٢ـ تَحَادَثْنَا لِ ـــــــ طَوِيْلٍ

3. Write a suitable attribute for each of the following nouns.

مِحْفَظَةٌ ـ نَمْلَةٌ ـ زَوْرَقٌ ـ رَايَةٌ ـ قَارُوْرَةٌ

جَرَسٌ ـ غُصْنٌ ـ نَحْلَةٌ ـ جِسْرٌ ـ دِيْكٌ

4. Write a suitable noun for each of the following attributes.

بَارِعٌ ـ غَاضِبٌ ـ أُوْتُوْمَاتِيكِى ـ مُضِيْئٌ ـ رَخِيْصٌ

صَافِيَةٌ - عَمِيقَةٌ - مَكْسُورَةٌ - وَاضِحَةٌ - كَامِلَةٌ

5. Make three verbal sentences each as directed.

a) with a noun qualified as a doer.

b) with a noun qualified as an object.

6. Make three nominal sentences as directed.

a) with a noun qualified as a subject.

b) with a noun qualified as a predicate.

7. Translate the following sentences into Arabic.

a) He has a beautiful pen.

b) He lost the new bag.

c) The broken watch is on the table.

d) It is a high hill.

e) He drove the sports car to the college.

f) This green grocer sells fresh vegetables.

g) We can find low prices here.

8. Translate the following sentences into English.

١) لَمْ يَقْرَأِ الدَّرْسَ الصَّعْبَ۔

٢) يَرْفَعُ الْعَتَّالُ أَمْتِعَةً ثَقِيلَةً۔

٣) لَبِسَتِ الْعَرُوسُ اللِّبَاسَ الْأَحْمَرَ۔

٤) هَذِه سِلْسِلَةٌ ثَمِينَةٌ۔

٥) كَتَبَ الرِّسَالَةَ بِخَطٍّ حَسَنٍ۔

٦) لَا أُصَاحِبُ الْأَوْلَادَ الْمُهْمَلِينَ۔

٧) مِنْ أَيْنَ اِبْتَعْتَ هَذَا الْمَكْتَبَ الْخَشَبِيَّ۔

GLOSSARY	الْكَلِمَاتُ الْعَسِيْرَةُ
song	أُنْشُوْدَةٌ (أَنَاشِيْدُ)
insect	حَشَرَةٌ (حَشَرَاتٌ)
ant	نَمْلٌ
boat	زَوْرَقٌ (زَوَارِقُ)
flag	رَايَةٌ (رَايَاتٌ)
long-necked bottle	قَارُوْرَةٌ (قَوَارِيْرُ)
automatic	أُوْتُوْمَاتِيكِي

LESSON 37

The Annexation الإِضَافَةُ

+ﻉﺇﻉﺇ+

Examples:

(1)

The student of the school.	طَالِبُ الْمَدْرَسَةِ۔
The pen of the girl	قَلَمُ الْبِنْتِ۔

(2)

The new car of the doctor.	سَيَّارَةُ الطَّبِيْبِ الْجَدِيْدَةُ۔
The big window of the room.	شُبَّاكُ الْحُجْرَةِ الْكَبِيْرُ۔

(3)

These are the two sons of the leader.	هٰذَانِ وَلَدَا الزَّعِيْمِ۔
I saw the two sons of the leader.	رَأَيْتُ وَلَدَيِ الزَّعِيْمِ۔
I went to the two sons of the leader.	ذَهَبْتُ إِلَى وَلَدَيِ الزَّعِيْمِ۔

(4)

These are the teachers of the school.	هٰؤُلَاءِ مُعَلِّمُوْ الْمَدْرَسَةِ۔

I saw the teachers of the school.	‫رَأَيْتُ مُعَلِّمِيْ الْمَدْرَسَةِ.‬
I went to the teachers of the school.	‫ذَهَبْتُ إِلَى مُعَلِّمِيْ الْمَدْرَسَةِ.‬

Discussion:

Look at the above examples. Group (1) has two examples, both of which include two nouns. In the first example, the first noun ‫طَالِبٌ‬ belongs to the second noun ‫الْمَدْرَسَةُ‬. Similarly, in the second example, the first noun ‫قَلَمٌ‬ belongs to the second noun ‫الْبِنْتُ‬. In other words, the first noun is annexed to the other. This kind of relation is called ‫الْإِضَافَةُ‬ (annexation), the first noun is called ‫الْمُضَافُ‬ and the second noun ‫الْمُضَافُ إِلَيْهِ‬ and the construction is known as a construct phrase or genitive phrase.

Group (2) shows two examples: the first one includes two nouns, i.e. ‫'سَيَّارَةٌ‬ and ‫'الطَّبِيْبُ‬ and an adjective ‫الْجَدِيْدَةُ‬ which qualifies the first noun ‫سَيَّارَةٌ‬. This example shows that if there is some quality of ‫الْمُضَافُ‬, it comes after ‫الْمُضَافُ‬ ‫إِلَيْهِ‬. So, this genitive phrase gives the meaning: "The new car of the doctor". The same applies to the second example.

Group (3) shows three examples. In all the three examples a dual noun has been used i.e. ‫الْمُضَافُ‬ in three different cases, the nominative case, the accusative case and the genitive case. What should be noted is that the form of the dual, i.e. 'وَلَدَا' shows that its 'ن' has been dropped because it is الْمُضَاف. In the second and third examples, which show the accusative and genitive cases respectively, the form of the dual is changed into 'وَلَدَيْ' because it is again الْمُضَاف.

Group (4) also has three examples. These three examples show three different cases. Here, الْمُضَاف of the first example shows that 'ن' has been dropped from the noun 'مُعَلِّمُوْنَ' giving the form 'مُعَلِّمُوْ'. In the other two cases, it has changed into 'مُعَلِّمِيْ' because it is again الْمُضَاف.

Rule:

1. The annexation of one noun to another is called 'الْإِضَافَةُ'. In such a construction the first noun is called 'الْمُضَاف' and the second noun is called 'الْمُضَاف إِلَيْهِ'. In English this construct phrase is denoted by the use of "of" or an "apostrophe", e.g. كِتَابُ الْوَلَدِ (The book of the boy or the boy's book).

2. 'الْمُضَاف' neither takes the definite article 'ال' nor does it accept 'تَنْوِيْنٌ'.

3. 'الْمُضَاف إِلَيْهِ' must be in the genitive case (whatever shape would depend on the kind of word).

4. No other word can intercept the construction, therefore, if there is some qualifying adjective (which generally follows the noun) of الْمُضَاف, it must be written after the

construct phrase, e.g.

The new car of the doctor.   سَيَّارَةُ الطَّبِيْبِ الْجَدِيْدَةُ۔

(which was السَّيَّارَةُ الْجَدِيْدَةُ before annexing both words).

5. If there is some adjective qualifying الْمُضَافُ إِلَيْهِ, it will follow the noun as there is no hindrance, e.g.

The book of the hardworking boy.   كِتَابُ الْوَلَدِ الْمُجْتَهِدِ۔

6. If the dual or sound masculine plural (جَمْعُ الْمُذَكَّرِ السَّالِمُ) is 'الْمُضَافُ', its 'ن' is dropped as shown in the examples of groups (3) and (4).

7. The genitive phrase like other phrases comes as a part of the sentence. So, it can be a subject, or a predicate or a doer of a verb etc. The effect of the case is shown only on the first noun which is called الْمُضَافُ while the second noun remains in the genitive case as shown in the following examples.

The student of the school is sitting.	طَالِبُ الْمَدْرَسَةِ جَالِسٌ۔
This is the student of the school.	هٰذَا طَالِبُ الْمَدْرَسَةِ۔
The student of the school came.	جَاءَ طَالِبُ الْمَدْرَسَةِ۔
I saw the student of the school.	رَأَيْتُ طَالِبَ الْمَدْرَسَةِ۔
I went to the student of the school.	ذَهَبْتُ إِلَى طَالِبِ الْمَدْرَسَةِ۔

Exercise:

1. Make a construct phrase by introducing 'اَلْمُضَافُ إِلَيْهِ' for the following 'اَلْمُضَافُ'.

مِفْتَاحٌ - حَاكِمٌ - ثَوْرٌ - حَارِسٌ - فَرِيقٌ - أَرْضٌ

2. Make a construct phrase by introducing 'اَلْمُضَافُ' for the following 'اَلْمُضَافُ إِلَيْهِ'.

بَقَّالٌ - رِوَايَةٌ - وَرْدٌ - كَلِمَةٌ - فَلَّاحٌ - أُخْتٌ - بُرْتُقَالٌ

3. Fill in the blanks with suitable nouns as given below, putting vowel points on the last letter of each and adding the definite article 'ال', if it is needed.

شَجَرَةٌ - وِزَارَةٌ - أَمِيرَةٌ - الْقُرْآنُ - مَاءٌ - الْهِنْد
مُؤْتَمَرٌ - عَمِيدٌ - أَطْفَالٌ - مَدْرَسَةٌ - عُضْوٌ - سِتَارَةٌ

٢- عَاصِمَةُ ـــــ		١- ـــــ الشُّبَّاكِ.	
٤- حُقُوقُ ـــــ		٣- ـــــ الْكُلِّيَّةِ.	
٦- لُغَةُ ـــــ		٥- ـــــ الْمَلِكِ.	
٨- قَاعَةُ ـــــ		٧- ـــــ النَّهْرِ.	
١٠- غُصْنُ ـــــ		٩- ـــــ الْأُسْرَةِ.	
١٢- طَالِبُ ـــــ		١١- ـــــ الصِّحَّةِ.	

4. Rewrite the following sentences and use them in the other two remaining cases. The first two have been done for you.

١- هٰذَا مَسْجِدُ الْمَدِينَةِ.

رَأَيْتُ مَسْجِدَ الْمَدِينَةِ.

صَلَّيْتُ فِي مَسْجِدِ الْمَدِينَةِ.

٢- شَرِبْتُ عَصِيرَ اللَّيْمُوْنِ.

هٰذَا عَصِيرُ اللَّيْمُوْنِ.

نَظَرْتُ إِلَى عصِيرِ اللَّيْمُوْنِ.

٤ ـ إِشْتَرَيْتُ آلَةَ الْكِتَابَةِ.

٣ ـ ذَهَبْتُ إِلَى مُدِيرِ الْمَدْرَسَةِ.

_____

_____

٦ ـ هٰذِهِ الْغُرْفَةُ لِمُوَظَّفِي السِّفَارَةِ.

٥ ـ كَتَبْتُ بِقَلَمِ الْحِبْرِ.

_____

_____

٨ ـ مَدِيْنَةُ الرَّسُوْلِ جَمِيْلَةٌ.

٧ ـ بَكَى طِفْلَا الْجَارِ.

_____

_____

5. Make two sentences using a construct phrase in each as indicated below and translate them into English.

   a) having الْمُضَاف' in the nominative case.

   b) having الْمُضَاف' in the accusative case.

   c) having الْمُضَاف' in the genitive case.

   d) having الْمُضَاف' as a dual.

   e) having الْمُضَاف' as a sound masculine plural.

   f) having الْمُضَاف' with a quality.

6. Translate the following into Arabic.

   a) I forgot your son's name.

   b) Why do not you support his party?

   c) Look! The cover of the copybook is torn.

   d) When is your friend's marriage?

   e) The door of the bus is open.

•

f) Where did you keep the papers of the new car?

g) We are prince's teachers.

7. Translate the following into English.

١) مَشَيْتُ مَعَ صَاحِبِ الشَّرِكَةِ۔

٢) لَا تَضْحَكْ عَلَى فَقْرِ الْفَقِيرِ۔

٣) جَاءَ رَئِيسُ الْجَامِعَةِ إِلَى كُلِّيَّتِنَا۔

٤) أَلْعَبُ كُرَةَ السَّلَّةِ۔

٥) زُرْنَا حَدِيقَةَ الْأَطْفَالِ مَعَ مُعَلِّمِي الْمَدْرَسَةِ۔

٦) تَحَادَثْنَا مَعَ مُهَنْدِسِي الْعِرَاقِ۔

٧) خَافَ الْأَطْفَالُ بِانْفِجَارِ الْقُنْبُلَةِ۔

GLOSSARY	الْكَلِمَاتُ الْعَسِيرَةُ
bull	ثَوْرٌ (ثِيرَانٌ)
juice	عَصِيرٌ
typewriter	آلَةُ الْكِتَابَةِ (آلَاتُ الْكِتَابَةِ)
fountain pen	قَلَمُ الْحِبْرِ
to support	أَيَّدَ - يُؤَيِّدُ - تَأْيِيدٌ
party (political)	حِزْبٌ (أَحْزَابٌ)
cover, wrap, wrapper	غِلَافٌ (غُلُفٌ)
torn	مُمَزَّقٌ
marriage, wedding	زَوَاجٌ

194

Nobel Prize	جَائِزَةُ نُوْبِل
poverty; need	فَقْرٌ
basketball	كُرَةُ السَّلَّةِ
children's garden	حَدِيقَةُ الْأَطْفَالِ
explosion	اِنْفِجَارٌ (اِنْفِجَارَاتٌ)
bomb	قُنْبُلَةٌ (قَنَابِلُ)

Some More Facts about Annexation
مَعْلُوْمَاتٌ أُخْرَى عَنِ الإِضَافَةِ

You have studied الإِضَافَةُ in the previous lesson. But
there are some more rules related to الْمُضَافُ إِلَيْهِ and الْمُضَافُ
which are as follows:

1. When there are more than one 'الْمُضَافُ إِلَيْهِ', only the last
   one may take the definite article 'ال' and others will
   neither take the definite article 'ال' nor will they take
   'تَنْوِيْنٌ' because they are 'الْمُضَافُ' to the following noun,
   e.g.

The door of the house of the
man's sister.   بَابُ بَيْتِ أُخْتِ الرَّجُلِ۔

2. When there are more than one 'الْمُضَافُ', only one
   'الْمُضَافُ' will come before 'الْمُضَافُ إِلَيْهِ' and the other
   'الْمُضَافُ' will follow 'الْمُضَافُ إِلَيْهِ' preceded by a

conjunction ’وَ‘ (وَاوُ الْعَطْفِ) and suffixed by an attached
pronoun (ضَمِيرٌ مُتَّصِلٌ) which agrees with ’الْمُضَافُ إِلَيْهِ‘, e.g.

The book and pen of the boy.   ـ كِتَابُ الْوَلَدِ وَقَلَمُهُ

3. When the construct phrase is preceded by a vocative
   particle and ’الْمُضَافُ‘ becomes the noun in the vocative
   (الْمُنَادَى), it will be in the accusative case, e.g. !يَا تِلْمِيذَ الْكُلِّيَّةِ .

4. When the demonstrative pronoun (اِسْمُ الْإِشَارَةِ) is used for
   ’الْمُضَافُ‘, it comes after ’الْمُضَافُ إِلَيْهِ‘, e.g.

This house of the engineer.   ـ بَيْتُ الْمُهَنْدِسِ هٰذَا

LESSON 38

The Demonstrative Pronouns أَسْمَاءُ الإِشَارَةِ

+§§+

Like any other language, Arabic also has a number of demonstrative pronouns to point to near and distant objects. The table is given below.

(1)

MASCULINE	Singular	الْمُفْرَدُ	this	هٰذَا
	Dual	الْمُثَنَّى	these	هٰذَانِ - هٰذَيْنِ
الْمُذَكَّرُ	Plural	الْجَمْعُ	these	هٰؤُلَاءِ

(2)

FEMININE	Singular	الْمُفْرَدُ	this	هٰذِهِ
	Dual	الْمُثَنَّى	these	هَاتَانِ - هَاتَيْنِ
الْمُؤَنَّثُ	Plural	الْجَمْعُ	these	هٰؤُلَاءِ

(3)

MASCULINE	Singular	الْمُفْرَدُ	that	ذٰلِكَ
	Dual	الْمُثَنَّى	those	ذَانِكَ - ذَيْنِكَ
الْمُذَكَّرُ	Plural	الْجَمْعُ	those	أُوْلَائِكَ

(4)

FEMININE	Singular الْمُفْرَدُ	that	تِلْكَ
	Dual الْمُثَنَّى	those	تَانِكَ - تَيْنِكَ
الْمُؤَنَّثُ	Plural الْجَمْعُ	those	أُوْلَائِكَ

Discussion:

Look at the table above. You will find that group (1) shows the demonstrative pronouns which are meant for pointing to near masculine objects i.e. هٰذَا (Singular), هٰذَانِ or هٰذَيْنِ (Dual) and هٰؤُلَاءِ (Plural) and group (2) shows the demonstrative pronouns which are meant for pointing to near feminine objects i.e. هٰذِهِ (Singular), هَاتَانِ or هَاتَيْنِ (Dual) and هٰؤُلَاءِ (Plural). Similarly, group (3) shows the demonstrative pronouns which are meant to point to distant masculine objects i.e. ذٰلِكَ (Singular), ذَانِكَ or ذَيْنِكَ (Dual) and أُوْلَائِكَ (Plural) while group (4) shows the demonstrative pronouns which are meant to point to distant feminine objects i.e. تِلْكَ (Singular), تَانِكَ or تَيْنِكَ (Dual) and أُوْلَائِكَ (Plural).

Rule:

1. اِسْمُ الْإِشَارَةِ (The Demonstrative Pronoun) is used to point to near or distant objects.

2. The thing to which اِسْمُ الإِشَارَةِ points is called مُشَارٌ إِلَيْهِ.

3. Both اِسْمُ الإِشَارَةِ and مُشَارٌ إِلَيْهِ constitute a part or phrase
(مَفْعُولٌ بِهِ or فَاعِلٌ or مُبْتَدَأٌ) of the sentence, e.g.

هٰذَا الْكِتَابُ جَدِيدٌ.   (مُبْتَدَأٌ)

نَجَحَ ذٰلِكَ الطَّالِبُ.   (فَاعِلٌ)

اِشْتَرَيْتُ تِلْكَ الْمِحْفَظَةَ أَمْسِ.   (مَفْعُولٌ بِهِ)

4. اِسْمُ الإِشَارَةِ, being a definite noun, also functions as the
subject of الْجُمْلَةُ الْاِسْمِيَّةُ.

Exercise:

1. Read and learn all the demonstrative pronouns.

2. Put suitable demonstrative pronouns as the subject of the
following predicates.

٢- _____ وَلَدٌ.   ١- _____ بِنْتٌ.

٤- _____ طُلَّابٌ.   ٣- _____ جِذَاءَانِ.

٦- _____ كَوْكَبَانِ.   ٥- _____ نِسَاءٌ.

٨- _____ كَرَاسِيُّ.   ٧- _____ كِتَابَانِ.

١٠- _____ بِنْتَانِ.   ٩- _____ رِجَالٌ.

١٢- _____ نَجَّارُونَ.   ١١- _____ ثَلَّاجَةٌ.

3. Fill in the blanks with suitable words given below.

هٰذَانِ - أُوْلَائِكَ - تِلْكَ - مُدَرِّسُونَ - هٰذَا - تَانِكَ

قَمَرٌ - هَاتَانِ - ذَانِكَ - هٰذِهِ - هَؤُلَاءِ - خَيَّاطُونَ

٢- ذَلِكَ _____ .   ١- _____ عُصْفُورٌ.

٤- _____ سَائِقُونَ.   ٣- _____ كُرَّاسَتَانِ.

٦- _____ قَلَمَانِ.   ٥- أُوْلَائِكَ _____ .

٧- ـــــ طَيِّبَةٌ.　　٨- ـــــ فَنِّيُّونَ.

٩- هٰؤُلَاءِ ـــــ .　　١٠- ـــــ زُجَاجَتَانِ.

١١- ـــــ قَمِيْصَانِ.　　١٢- ـــــ مَدِيْنَةٌ.

4. Use the following nouns in your own sentences with suitable demonstrative pronouns.

مِذْيَاعٌ - جَرِيْدَةٌ - شَاةٌ - مُهَنْدِسُوْنَ - مِظَلَّتَانِ

بَيْتٌ - مُسْلِمَاتٌ - اِمْرَأَتَانِ - عَالِمٌ - مُتَرْجِمَانِ

5. Make two sentences each as follows.

a) pointing to a near person or thing (masculine).

b) pointing to a near person or thing (feminine).

c) pointing to a distant person or thing (masculine).

d) pointing to a near person or thing (feminine).

6. Translate the following into Arabic.

a) This is a chair.

b) Those are soldiers.

c) This is a girl.

d) That is a garden.

e) These are girl students (dual).

f) These are men.

g) That is a key.

7. Translate the following into English.

١) هَاتَانِ مُعَلِّمَتَانِ.

٢) هٰذَا صَغِيْرٌ وَذٰلِكَ كَبِيْرٌ.

٣) هٰؤُلَاءِ طُلَّابٌ.

٤) هٰذِهِ مِكْنَسَةٌ۔

٥) ذٰلِكَ الرَّجُلُ طَوِيلٌ۔

٦) ذَانِكَ طَالِبَانِ وَتَانِكَ أُمَّانِ۔

٧) أُوْلَائِكَ بَقَّالُوْنَ۔

GLOSSARY	الْكَلِمَاتُ الْعَسِيْرَةُ
shoe	حِذَاءٌ (أَحْذِيَةٌ)
tailor	خَيَّاطٌ (خَيَّاطُوْنَ)
driver	سَائِقٌ (سَائِقُوْنَ)
technician	فَنِّيٌّ (فَنِّيُّوْنَ)
bottle	زُجَاجَةٌ (زُجَاجَاتٌ)
radio	مِذْيَاعٌ (مَذَايِيْعُ)
engineer	مُهَنْدِسٌ (مُهَنْدِسُوْنَ)
umbrella	مِظَلَّةٌ (مِظَلَّاتٌ)
translator	مُتَرْجِمٌ (مُتَرْجِمُوْنَ)

LESSON 39

The Detached Nominative Pronouns
الضَّمَائِرُ الْمَرْفُوْعَةُ الْمُنْفَصِلَةُ

Like any other language, Arabic also has a number of pronouns (he, she, it, I, you, we, they) that serve to replace a noun in the nominative case that has already been mentioned in the sentence or context. The category of pronouns dealt with in this lesson is that of pronouns which are used when detached from any noun, verb or particle. The pronouns which are used when attached will be discussed in the next lesson. The following is the table showing Detached Nominative Pronouns.

(1)

Masculine	Singular	الْمُفْرَدُ	he, it	هُوَ
	Dual	الْمُثَنَّى	they	هُمَا
الْمُذَكَّرُ	Plural	الْجَمْعُ	they	هُمْ
(2)				
Feminine	Singular	الْمُفْرَدُ	she, it	هِيَ
	Dual	الْمُثَنَّى	they	هُمَا
الْمُؤَنَّثُ	Plural	الْجَمْعُ	they	هُنَّ

(3)				
Masculine	Singular	الْمُفْرَدُ	you	أَنْتَ
	Dual	الْمُثَنَّى	you	أَنْتُمَا
الْمُذَكَّرُ	Plural	الْجَمْعُ	you	أَنْتُمْ
(4)				
Feminine	Singular	الْمُفْرَدُ	you	أَنْتِ
	Dual	الْمُثَنَّى	you	أَنْتُمَا
الْمُؤَنَّث	Plural	الْجَمْعُ	you	أَنْتُنَّ
(5)				
Masculine & Feminine الْمُذَكَّرُ وَ الْمُؤَنَّثُ	Singular	الْمُفْرَدُ	I	أَنَا
	Dual	الْمُثَنَّى	we	نَحْنُ
	Plural	الْجَمْعُ	we	نَحْنُ

Discussion:

Look at the table above. You will find that group (1)
shows the detached nominative pronouns which are meant

for the third person masculine i.e. هُوَ, هُمَا and هُم for the singular, dual and plural respectively and group (2) shows the detached nominative pronouns which are meant for the third person feminine i.e. هِيَ, هُمَا and هُنَّ for the singular, dual and plural respectively. Similarly, group (3) shows the detached nominative pronouns which are meant for the second person masculine i.e. أَنْتَ, أَنْتُمَا and أَنْتُمْ for the singular, dual and plural respectively, while group (4) shows the detached nominative pronouns for the second person feminine i.e. أَنْتِ, أَنْتُمَا and أَنْتُنَّ for the singular, dual and plural respectively. Froup (5) shows the detached pronouns for both the first person masculine and feminine, i.e. أَنَا for the singular and نَحْنُ for dual and plural.

Rule:

1. The Detached Nominative Pronouns are used in place of nouns.

2. If the noun is the plural of non-intelligent being (masculine or feminine), the pronoun used for it will be feminine singular, e.g. هِيَ كِلَابٌ (They are dogs).

Exercise:

1. Read and learn all the Detached Nominative Pronouns.

204

2. Fill in the blanks with suitable pronouns.

١- _____ مُؤَلِّفَةٌ۔   ٢- _____ مُدِيْرٌ۔

٣- _____ زُمَلَاءُ۔   ٤- _____ صَرَّافَانِ۔

٥- _____ مُمَثِّلَتَانِ۔   ٦- _____ بَائِعٌ۔

٧- _____ مُصَوِّرُوْنَ۔   ٨- _____ شَاعِرَاتٌ۔

٩- _____ طَيَّارَانِ۔   ١٠- _____ مُغَنِّيَتَانِ۔

١١- _____ عَالِمٌ۔   ١٢- _____ جَارُكَ۔

3. Fill in the blanks with suitable words given below.

هُمَا - هُمْ - أَنْتِ - أَنْتُم - هُوَ - أَنْتُمَا

صُحُفِيٌّ - نَحْنُ - مُفَتِّشُوْنَ - هِيَ - أَنَا - فَلَّاحَاتٌ

١- _____ حَارِسَانِ۔   ٢- أَنْتَ _____ ۔

٣- _____ بَحَّارٌ۔   ٤- _____ مُدَرِّبُوْنَ۔

٥- _____ خَبِيْرَةٌ۔   ٦- هُنَّ _____ ۔

٧- _____ مُجْتَهِدُوْنَ۔   ٨- _____ مُؤَرِّخٌ۔

٩- هُمْ _____ ۔   ١٠- _____ تَاجِرَانِ۔

١١- _____ تَلَامِيْذُ۔   ١٢- _____ خَيَّاطَةٌ۔

4. Use the following nouns in your own sentences with suitable Detached Nominative Pronouns.

نُزُلٌ - عَامِلَانِ - كَاتِبَتَانِ - دُكْتُوْرٌ - خَدَّامَةٌ

مُمَرِّضَاتٌ - مُسْلِمَاتٌ - مُؤَذِّنٌ - مُرَاقِبُوْنَ - سَبَّاكٌ

5. Make two sentences each as follows.

    a) Including a 3rd person singular pronoun.

    b) Including a 3rd person dual pronoun.

c) Including a 3rd person plural.

d) Including a 2nd person singular pronoun.

e) Including a 2nd person plural pronoun.

6. Translate the following into Arabic.

   a) They (masc. dual) are accountants.

   b) She is an assistant.

   c) We are astrologers.

   d) You (fem. plural) are athletes.

   e) He is an ambassador.

   f) I am an agent.

   g) They (fem. plural) are lawyers.

7. Translate the following into English.

١) أَنْتَ مُقَاوِلٌ۔

٢) نَحْنُ مُهَنْدِسُوْنَ۔

٣) هِيَ قَاضِيَةٌ۔

٤) أَنْتُمْ أَصْدِقَاءُ۔

٥) هُمَا سَارِقَانِ۔

٦) هُمْ مُزَارِعُوْنَ۔

٧) أَنَا بَوَّابٌ۔

GLOSSARY	الْكَلِمَاتُ الْعَسِيْرَةُ
author	مُؤَلِّفٌ (مُؤَلِّفُوْنَ)
director	مُدِيْرٌ (مُدَرَاءُ)
cashier	صَرَّافٌ (صَرَّافُوْنَ)
actor	مُمَثِّلٌ (مُمَثِّلُوْنَ)
salesman	بَائِعٌ (بَائِعُوْنَ)
photographer	مُصَوِّرٌ (مُصَوِّرُوْنَ)
pilot	طَيَّارٌ (طَيَّارُوْنَ)
singer	مُغَنٍّ (مُغَنُّوْنَ)
designer	مُصَمِّمٌ (مُصَمِّمُوْنَ)
journalist	صُحُفِيٌّ (صُحُفِيُّوْنَ)
inspector	مُفَتِّشٌ (مُفَتِّشُوْنَ)
sailor	بَحَّارٌ (بَحَّارُوْنَ)
coach, trainer	مُدَرِّبٌ (مُدَرِّبُوْنَ)
historian	مُؤَرِّخٌ (مُؤَرِّخُوْنَ)
waiter	نَادِلٌ (نُدُلٌ)
nurse	مُمَرِّضَةٌ (مُمَرِّضَاتٌ)
supervisor	مُرَاقِبٌ (مُرَاقِبُوْنَ)
plumber	سَبَّاكٌ (سَبَّاكُوْنَ)
assistant	مُسَاعِدٌ (مُسَاعِدُوْنَ)
astrologer	مُنَجِّمٌ (مُنَجِّمُوْنَ)

athlete	رِيَاضِيٌّ (رِيَاضِيُّوْنَ)
ambassador	سَفِيْرٌ (سُفَرَاءُ)
agent	وَكِيْلٌ (وُكَلَاءُ)
lawyer	مُحَامٍ (مُحَامُوْنَ)
contractor	مُقَاوِلٌ (مُقَاوِلُوْنَ)
engineer	مُهَنْدِسٌ (مُهَنْدِسُوْنَ)
judge	قَاضٍ (قُضَاةٌ)
farmer	مُزَارِعٌ (مُزَارِعُوْنَ)
doorman	بَوَّابٌ (بَوَّابُوْنَ)

LESSON 40

The Attached Pronouns
الضَّمَائِرُ الْمُتَّصِلَةُ

+:§:+

Arabic has a number of pronouns which sometimes are attached to nouns to express possession, sometimes to verbs to take the effect of the verb and sometimes to prepositions and particles. See the table below.

(1)

Masculine	Singular	الْمُفْرَدُ	his, him, its, it	هُ
	Dual	الْمُثَنَّى	their, them	هُمَا
الْمُذَكَّرُ	Plural	الْجَمْعُ	their, them	هُمْ

(2)

Feminine	Singular	الْمُفْرَدُ	her, its, it	هَا
	Dual	الْمُثَنَّى	their, them	هُمَا
الْمُؤَنَّثُ	Plural	الْجَمْعُ	their, them	هُنَّ

(3)

Masculine	Singular	الْمُفْرَدُ	your, you	كَ
	Dual	الْمُثَنَّى	your, you	كُمَا
الْمُذَكَّرُ	Plural	الْجَمْعُ	your, you	كُم

(4)			
Feminine	Singular الْمُفْرَدُ	your, you	كِ
	Dual الْمُثَنَّى	your, you	كُمَا
الْمُؤَنَّثُ	Plural الْجَمْعُ	your, you	كُنَّ
(5)			
Masculine and Feminine الْمُذَكَّرُ وَ الْمُؤَنَّثُ	Singular الْمُفْرَدُ	my / me	يْ / نِيْ
	Dual الْمُثَنَّى	our, us	نَا
	Plural الْجَمْعُ	our, us	نَا

Discussion:

Look at the table above. You will find that group (1) shows the attached pronouns which are meant for the third person masculine i.e. هُ, هُمَا and هُم for the singular, dual and plural respectively and group (2) shows the attached pronouns which are meant for the third person feminine i.e. هَا, هُمَا and هُنَّ for the singular, dual and plural respectively. Similarly, the group (3) shows the attached pronouns which are meant for the second person masculine i.e. كَ, كُمَا and كُم for the singular, dual and plural respectively, while group

(4) shows the attached pronouns for the second person feminine i.e. كِ, كُمَا and كُنَّ for the singular, dual and plural respectively. Group (5) shows the attached pronouns both the first person masculine and feminine i.e. يْ (Singular) which is prefixed with nouns or particles (بِيْ or إِلَيْ), نِيْ (Singular) is prefixed with verb or إِنَّ or (عَنِّيْ, مِتِّيْ) and عَنْ مِنْ وَأَخَوَاتُهَا, and pronoun نَا which is used for dual and plural both.

Usage:

1. The attached pronouns are used as direct objects when attached to the verb, e.g. كَسَرَهُ <= كَسَرَ الزُّجَاجَ, etc.

2. The attached pronouns are sometimes attached to particles like إِنَّ وَأَخَوَاتُهَا e.g. إِنَّهُ جَالِسٌ <= إِنَّ الْوَلَدَ جَالِسٌ, etc.

3. The attached pronouns are sometimes attached to nouns to express possession, e.g. بَيْتِيْ, قَلَمُهُ, etc.

4. The attached pronouns are sometimes attached to prepostions, e.g. مِنْهُ <= خَرَجَ مِنَ الْمَسْجِدِ, etc.

5. If the attached pronoun is used for the plural of non-intelligent being (masculine or feminine), it will be used as the feminine singular, e.g.

إِنَّهَا جَدِيدَةٌ <= إِنَّ الْأَقْلَامَ جَدِيدَةٌ

Rule:

1. The pronouns which are suffixed to a verb as objects or a a particle are known as Attached Accusative Pronouns (الضَّمَائِرُ الْمَنْصُوبَةُ الْمُتَّصِلَةُ).

2. The pronouns which are suffixed to a noun or a preposition are known as Attached Genitive Pronouns (الضَّمَائِرُ الْمَجْرُوْرَةُ الْمُتَّصِلَةُ).

3. When هُ or هُمَا or هُمْ or هُنَّ is preceded by a letter which has كَسْرَةٌ (ـِ) under it or is preceded by الْيَاءُ السَّاكِنَةُ (يْ), the ضَمَّةٌ (ـُ) of 'هُ' is replaced with كَسْرَةٌ (ـِ) e.g. فِي بَيْتِهِ, عَلَيْهِنَّ, عَلَيْهِمْ, عَلَيْهِمَا, فِي بَيْتِهِنَّ, عَلَيْهِ, فِي بَيْتِهِمْ, فِي بَيْتِهِمَا.

4. When these pronouns are preceded by a word which has أَلِفٌ مَقْصُوْرَةٌ on its last letter, أَلِفٌ مَقْصُوْرَةٌ is replaced with أَلِفٌ (ا), e.g.

$$ يَرَى + هُ = يَرَاهُ $$

5. When لِ is prefixed to الضَّمَائِرُ الْمُتَّصِلَةُ, its كَسْرَةٌ (ـِ) is replaced with فَتْحَةٌ (ـَ). e.g. لَنَا, لَكُنَّ, لَكَ, لَهَا, لَهُ.

6. When لِ is used with 'يْ', it remains as it is, e.g. لِي.

7. نِيْ is never used with لِ and it is always used with verbs as an object.

8. When هُمْ or كُمْ is joined to the following word, the سُكُوْنٌ (ـْ) of 'مْ' is replaced with ضَمَّةٌ (ـُ), e.g. هُمُ الأَوْلَادُ, وَعَلَيْكُمُ السَّلَامُ.

9. When 'يْ' is joined to the following word, its سُكُوْنٌ (ـْ) is
replaced with فَتْحَةٌ (ـَ) in pronunciation, e.g. رَبِّيَ اللَّهُ.

10. When 'يْ' is preceded by ا or و or ي, its سُكُوْنٌ (ـْ) is
replaced with فَتْحَةٌ (ـَ), e.g. أَبَوَيَّ, فِيَّ, مُعَلِّمُوْيَ, عَصَايَ,
بُنَيَّ, أَبَوَايَ.

11. The extra unpronounced 'ا' which is suffixed to the
masculine plural verb, is dropped when the verb is
followed by الضَّمِيْرُ الْمُتَّصِلُ, e.g. وَجَدُوْنَا, وَجَدُوْكَ, وَجَدُوْهُ.

12. When a verb in the second person masculine plural in
الْمَاضِي is followed by الضَّمِيْرُ الْمُتَّصِلُ, then an extra 'وْ' is
inserted between the two, e.g. وَجَدْتُمْ + هُ = وَجَدْتُمُوْهُ,
وَجَدْتُمُوْنِي, وَجَدْتُمُوْهُنَّ, وَجَدْتُمُوْهَا.

Exercise:

1. Read and learn all the Attached Pronouns.

2. Use all the Attached Accusative Pronouns in your own
sentences.

3. Use all the Attached Genitive Pronouns in your own
sentences.

4. Fill in the blanks with a suitable pronoun given below.

هُ - هُمْ - كَ - كُم - هَا - كُمَا
ى - هُمَا - هُنَّ - لِكِ - نَا - كُنَّ

١- بَيْتٌ + ـ____ = ـ____   ٢- قَامُوْسٌ + ـ____ = ـ____

٣- رِسَالَةٌ + ـ____ = ـ____   ٤- ضَرَبْتُ + ـ____ = ـ____

٥ـ غُرْفَةٌ + ____ = ____ - ٦ـ أُمٌّ + ____ = ____ -

٧ـ يَقْرَأُ + ____ = ____ - ٨ـ هَاتِفٌ + ____ = ____ -

٩ـ شَعْرٌ + ____ = ____ - ١٠ـ أُخْتٌ + ____ = ____ -

١١ـ مَدْرَسَةٌ + ____ = ____ - ١٢ـ شَرِبَتْ + ____ = ____ -

5. Use the following words in your own sentences with suitable Attached Pronouns.

خَادِمٌ - أَقْفَلْتُ - قَمِيصٌ - قَابَلُوا - سَيَّارَةٌ

إِلَى - كُرَّاسَةٌ - لٰكِنَّ - شَرِكَةٌ - تَحْفَظُ

6. Translate the following into Arabic.

a) Their (masc. dual) bus is big.

b) Her dress is red.

c) My teacher is coming.

d) Their (fem. plural) school is far.

e) Hamid is rich, his car is expensive.

f) Our university is big.

g) He did not come today because he is ill.

7. Translate the following into English.

١) بَيْتُكَ وَاسِعٌ۔

٢) قَلَمُهُ جَدِيدٌ۔

٣) اِشْتَرَيْتُ التُّفَّاحَ ثُمَّ نَاوَلْتُهُ۔

٤) هلْ مَطْعَمُهُنَّ جَمِيلٌ۔

٥) جَاءَ إِلَى الْمَدِينَةِ لِيَسْكُنَ فِيهَا۔

٦) حَاسُوبُهُمْ حَدِيثٌ۔

٧) حَقِيبَتُهَا جَمِيلَةٌ۔

GLOSSARY	الْكَلِمَاتُ الْعَسِيرَةُ
telephone	هَاتِفٌ (هَوَاتِفُ)
to lock, shut	أَقْفَلَ - يُقْفِلُ - إِقْفَالٌ
computer	حَاسُوبٌ (حَوَاسِيْبُ)
smile	إبْتِسَامَةٌ

LESSON 41

The Relative Pronouns الْأَسْمَاءُ الْمَوْصُوْلَةُ

٭٭٭

The full paradigm of relative pronouns is as follows:

(1)

Masculine الْمُذَكَّرُ	Singular	who, that, which, whom	الَّذِي
	Dual	who, that, which, whom	اللَّذَانِ اللَّذَيْنِ
	Plural	who, that, which, whom	الَّذِيْنَ

(2)

Feminine الْمُؤَنَّثُ	Singular	who, that, which, whom	الَّتِي
	Dual	who, that, which, whom	اللَّتَانِ اللَّتَيْنِ
	Plural	who, that, which, whom	اللَّاتِي اللَّائِي اللَّوَاتِي

(3)

Masculine & Feminine الْمُذَكَّرُ وَ الْمُؤَنَّثُ	Singular Dual & Plural	who, whom, that, which	مَنْ
	Singular Dual & Plural	what, which, that	مَا

Discussion:

Look at the paradigm above. You will find that group (1) shows the relative pronouns which are meant for masculine i.e. الَّذِي, اللَّذَانِ or اللَّذِينَ and الَّذِينَ for singular, dual and plural respectively. Group (2) shows the relative pronouns which are meant for feminine, i.e. الَّتِي, اللَّتَانِ or اللَّتَيْنِ and اللَّاتِي or اللَّائِي or اللَّوَاتِي for singular, dual and plural respectively. Group (3) also shows the relative pronouns, i.e. مَنْ and مَا, which are meant for both masculine (singular, dual and plural) and feminine (singular, dual and plural).

Rule:

1. The relative pronouns are considered to be definite nouns.

2. The full sense of a relative pronoun is not clear unless it is followed by a sentence (known as a relative sentence or صِلَةٌ), which is a complement to it.

3. The relative sentence (صِلَةٌ) should contain a personal pronoun to refer to it. This pronoun should be according to the relative pronoun with respect to gender and number. This pronoun is called 'عَائِدٌ' returner, e.g.

I read the book which I   قَرَأْتُ الْكِتَابَ الَّذِي اشْتَرَيْتُهُ
purchased yesterday.   بِالْأَمْسِ-

4. This 'عَائِدٌ' is sometimes omitted, particularly when it is the object, e.g.

قَرَأْتُ الْكِتَابَ الَّذِي اشْتَرَيْتُ بِالْأَمْسِ

For

قَرَأْتُ الْكِتَابَ الَّذِي اِشْتَرَيْتُهُ بِالأَمْسِ

5. All the relative pronouns are indeclinable except the duals اللَّذَانِ and اللَّتَانِ which change into اللَّذَيْنِ and اللَّتَيْنِ in the accusative and genitive cases. The following are the details of relative pronouns with examples:

الَّذِي	
جَاءَ الرَّجُلُ الَّذِي دَعَوْتُهُ۔	The man whom I invited came.
اللَّذَانِ	
حَزِنَ الطَّالِبَانِ اللَّذَانِ فَشِلَا فِي الْاِمْتِحَانِ۔	The two students who failed in the examination became sad.
اللَّذَيْنِ	
قَابَلْتُ اللَّاعِبَيْنِ اللَّذَيْنِ سَيَلْعَبَانِ فِي فَرِيْقِنَا۔	I met the two players who are going to play in our team.
الَّذِيْنَ	
أُحِبُّ الرِّجَالَ الَّذِيْنَ يُسَاعِدُوْنَ الْفُقَرَاءَ۔	I like the people who help the poor.
الَّتِي	
الْبِنْتُ الَّتِي تَجْلِسُ فِي الْمَكْتَبَةِ فَازَتْ بِالدَّرَجَةِ الْأُوْلَى ۔	The girl who sits in the library succeeded with a first division.

	اللَّتَانِ
The two lady teachers who teach in the college came out of it.	خَرَجَتْ مِنَ الْكُلِّيَّةِ الْأُسْتَاذَتَانِ اللَّتَانِ تُدَرِّسَانِ فِيهَا۔
	اللَّتَيْنِ
I saw the two women peasants who work in our field.	رَأَيْتُ الْفَلَّاحَتَيْنِ اللَّتَيْنِ تَعْمَلَانِ فِي حَقْلِنَا۔
	اللَّاتِي
The mothers who bring up their children well, render a great service to the nation.	الْأُمَّهَاتُ اللَّاتِي يُرَبِّينَ أَوْلَادَهُنَّ تَرْبِيَةً حَسَنَةً يَخْدُمْنَ الْأُمَّةَ وَالْوَطَنَ خِدْمَةً جَلِيلَةً۔
	مَنْ
I respect the one who respects me.	أَحْتَرِمُ مَنْ يَحْتَرِمُنِي۔
	مَا
Whatsoever you like for yourself, like the same for your brother.	أَحْبِبْ لِأَخِيكَ مَا تُحِبُّ لِنَفْسِكَ۔

----

6. Usually the relative pronoun along with its 'صِلَة' comes as an attribute to a noun contained in the previous sentence. That noun should be definite. If that noun is not definite, there is no need to use a relative pronoun, otherwise the sentence would be wrong, e.g.

I called the man who cooks دَعَوْتُ الرَّجُلَ الَّذِي يَطْبَخُ
food. الطَّعَامَ.

If رَجُلٌ is indefinite, we should say it in this way:

I called the man who cooks دَعَوْتُ رَجُلًا يَطْبَخُ الطَّعَامَ.
food.

We cannot say:

دَعَوْتُ رَجُلًا الَّذِي يَطْبَخُ الطَّعَامَ.

Exercise:

1. Read and learn all the Relative Pronouns.

2. Use all the Relative Pronouns in your own sentences.

3. Fill in the blanks with a suitable relative pronoun.

١ ـ أُحِبُّ _____ يُحِبُّنِي.

٢ ـ صَاحَبْتُ الْمُهَنْدِسِينَ _____ يَعْمَلُونَ فِي شَرِكَتِنَا.

٣ ـ غَسَلَتِ الْأُمُّ السِّتَارَةَ _____ كَانَتْ قَذِرَةً.

٤ ـ أَنْفَقْتُ _____ كَانَ فِي جَيْبِي.

٥ ـ مَا نَجَحَ الطَّالِبَانِ _____ غَابَا عَنِ الدَّرْسِ.

٧ ـ فَرِحَتِ الْأُسْتَاذَةُ مِنَ الْبَنَاتِ _____ أَكْمَلْنَ دُرُوسَهُنَّ.

٨ ـ مَا جَاءَتِ الْخَادِمَتَانِ _____ غَضِبْتُ عَلَيْهِمَا أَمْسِ.

٩ ـ أَ فَهِمْتَ _____ قُلْتُ لَكَ؟

١٠ ـ نَالَ الْجَائِزَةَ _____ اسْتَحَقَّ.

4. Translate the following into Arabic.

a) I did what was easy for me.

220

b) He stole that car which was new.

c) She did not answer the question which was difficult.

d) I will not allow the students to enter the class who behave poorly in the class.

e) I read the novel which won the Nobel prize.

f) The minister gave financial assistance to those widows who could not find a job.

g) The president consoled the families of those who died in the train accident.

5. Translate the following into English.

١) حَزِنَتِ الْبَنَاتُ اللَّاتِي رَسَبْنَ فِي الإِمْتِحَانِ۔

٢) رُدَّ عَلَيَّ الْكِتَابَ الَّذِي أَعْطَيْتُكَ لِلْقِرَاءَةِ۔

٣) لَمْ أَتْرُكِ الرَّجُلَيْنِ اللَّذَيْنِ خَطَفَا حَقِيْبَةَ أُمِّي۔

٤) هٰذِهِ هِيَ الْمَدِيْنَةُ الَّتِي زُرْتُهَا فِي طُفُوْلَتِي۔

٥) مَا جَاءَ إِلَى الْحَفْلَةِ مَنْ كَانَ فِي خَارِجِ الْبِلَادِ۔

٦) إِنْكَسَرَتِ السَّاعَتَانِ اللَّتَانِ وَضَعْتُهُمَا عَلَى الطَّاوِلَةِ۔

٧) هَلْ قَابَلْتَ الأَطْفَالَ الَّذِيْنَ حَفِظُوا الْقُرْآنَ فِي السَّابِعَةِ مِنْ عُمُرِهِمْ۔

GLOSSARY	الْكَلِمَاتُ الْعَسِيرَةُ
to deserve	اِسْتَحَقَّ - يَسْتَحِقُّ - اِسْتِحْقَاقٌ
prize	جَائِزَةٌ (جَوَائِزُ)
to behave poorly	سَلَكَ بِغَيْرِ إِتْقَانٍ
novel	رِوَايَةٌ (رِوَايَاتٌ)
financial assistance	مَعُونَةٌ مَالِيَّةٌ
to console	سَلَّى - يُسَلِّي - تَسْلِيَةٌ
to fail	رَسَبَ - يَرْسُبُ - رُسُوبٌ
to snatch	خَطَفَ - يَخْطِفُ - خَطْفٌ

LESSON 42

Definite and Indefinite الْمَعْرِفَةُ وَالنَّكِرَةُ

←✦→

Examples:

(1)	
Hamid is sleeping.	حَامِدٌ نَائِمٌ۔
Egypt is far away.	مِصْرُ بَعِيْدَةٌ ۔
(2)	
The boy is present.	الْوَلَدُ حَاضِرٌ۔
The girl is standing.	الْبِنْتُ وَاقِفَةٌ۔
(3)	
He is beautiful.	هُوَ جَمِيْلٌ۔
She is coming.	هِيَ قَادِمَةٌ۔
(4)	
This is a bird.	هٰذَا عُصْفُوْرٌ۔
This is a notebook.	هَذِهِ كُرَّاسَةٌ۔
(5)	
The daughter of Hamid is intelligent.	بِنْتُ حَامِدٍ ذَكِيَّةٌ۔
The boy's pen is broken.	قَلَمُ الْوَلَدِ مَكْسُوْرٌ۔
His car is new.	سَيَّارَتُهُ جَدِيْدَةٌ۔

The mosque of this city is big.	مَسْجِدُ هٰذِهِ الْمَدِينَةِ كَبِيرٌ۔

Discussion:

Look at the examples above. You will find that the examples in all the groups are الْجُمْلَةُ الإِسْمِيَّةُ consisting of مُبْتَدَأٌ and خَبَرٌ. on further study, you will find that in the examples of groups (1), (2), (3) and (4) مُبْتَدَأٌ is either a proper noun or a noun prefixed the with the definite article الْ or a pronoun or a demonstrative pronoun. Now because of the fact that مُبْتَدَأٌ needs to be definite, all these are also definite to make a complete sentence.

In group (5), the examples also consist of مُبْتَدَأٌ and خَبَرٌ. Although the first noun is not definite in itself, because it is annexed to a noun which is definite, it will also be considered as definite.

Hence a proper noun, a noun with the definite article, a pronoun, a demonstrative pronoun and an indefinite noun annexed to some definite noun are all considered to be definite.

In addition to it, there are two more things which are also considered to be definite. They are (i) relative pronouns, e.g. الَّذِي, الَّتِي, etc., and (ii) a noun preceded by a حَرْفُ النِّدَاءِ, e.g. يَا رَجُلُ (O man). In this, رَجُلُ is definite because it is the one who is addressed not any other person.

Rule:

1. All nouns in Arabic are indefinite (نَكِرَةٌ) except:

    a) A proper noun (إِسْمُ عَلَمٍ) (a noun with a given name) e.g. حَامِدٌ, مِصْرُ, etc.

    b) A noun prefixed with the definite article 'اَلْ', e.g. الْوَلَدُ, الْبِنْتُ, etc.

    c) A pronoun (إِسْمُ الضَّمِيْرِ), e.g. هُو , هِيَ , هُ , هَا, etc.

    d) A demonstrative pronoun (إِسْمُ إِشَارَةٍ), e.g. هٰذَا, هٰذِهِ etc.

    e) A مُضَافٌ to a definite noun e.g. بِنْتُ حَامِدٍ, قَلَمُ الْوَلَدِ, etc.

    f) A relative pronoun (إِسْمٌ مَوْصُوْلٌ) e.g. الَّتِي, الَّذِي, etc.

    g) A vocative (الْمُنَادَى) e.g. يَا بِنْتُ, يَا تِلْمِيْذُ, etc.

Exercise:

1. Complete the following sentences by putting a suitable subject.

١- _____ جَدِيْدٌ.

٢- _____ رَخِيْصٌ.

٣- _____ غَائِبَةٌ.

٤- _____ بَارِدٌ.

٥- _____ نَفِيْسَةٌ.

٦- _____ ضَيِّقٌ.

٧- _____ قَصِيْرٌ.

٨- _____ مَوْجُوْدَةٌ.

٩- _____ حَسَنٌ.

١٠- _____ بَعِيْدٌ.

١١- _____ عَادِلٌ.

١٢- _____ أَمِيْنَةٌ.

2. State whether the following nouns are definite or indefinite.

١- الْمَكْتَبُ

٢- بِئْرٌ

٤ ـ زَيْنَبُ	٣ ـ مُدَرِّسُوْنَ
٦ ـ بِنْتَانِ	٥ ـ هُمْ
٨ ـ حِذَاءُ عَلِيٍّ	٧ ـ هٰؤُلَاءِ
١٠ ـ عُقَلَاءُ	٩ ـ اللَّتَانِ
١٢ ـ مَكْتَبُكَ	١١ ـ بَيْتٌ

3. Write two proper nouns (أَسْمَاءُ عَلَمٍ).

4. Write two nouns prefixed with the definite article 'الْ'.

5. Make at least 3 sentences containing detached nominative pronouns.

6. Make at least 3 sentences containing demonstrative pronouns.

7. Make at least 3 sentences containing nouns which are مُضَافٌ to a definite noun.

8. Make a list of at least 5 nouns which are indefinite.

9. Translate the following into Arabic.

   a) The room is closed.

   b) Her hand and foot.

   c) Hamid is busy.

   d) This house is big.

   e) O boys! Read.

   f) A ball and a bat.

   g) The buffalo and the cow.

10. Translate the following into English.

١) الدَّرْسُ طَوِيلٌ۔

٢) أُسْتَاذٌ وَتِلْمِيْذٌ۔

٣) عَائِشَةُ ذَكِيَّةٌ۔

٤) لِسَانٌ وَسَيْفٌ۔

٥) الزَّوْجُ والزَّوْجَةُ۔

٦) مَدَائِنُ وَبُلْدَانٌ۔

٧) الشَّمْسُ وَالْقَمَرُ۔

GLOSSARY	الْكَلِمَاتُ الْعَسِيْرَةُ
precious, costly, valuable	نَفِيْسٌ
narrow; tight	ضَيِّقٌ
just	عَادِلٌ
honest	أَمِيْنٌ (أُمَنَاءُ)
well	بِئْرٌ (آبَارٌ)
donkey	حِمَارٌ (حَمِيْرٌ، حُمُرٌ)
lazy, idle, inactive	كَسْلَانٌ (كُسَالَى)
curtain	سِتَارَةٌ (سَتَائِرُ)
globe, ball	كُرَةٌ (كُرَاتٌ)
bat, racket	مِضْرَابٌ
buffalo	جَامُوْسٌ (جَوَامِيْسُ)
cow	بَقَرَةٌ (بَقَرَاتٌ)

LESSON 43

Singular and Dual الْمُفْرَدُ وَالْمُثَنَّى

In order to express number in Arabic, three categories of nouns are used: (i) الْمُفْرَدُ (singular), (ii) الْمُثَنَّى (dual) and (iii) الْجَمْعُ (plural).

الْمُفْرَدُ indicates one thing, الْمُثَنَّى indicates two things and الْجَمْعُ indicates more than two things. In this lesson we will discuss the singular and dual only. As for the plural, it will be discussed in the next lesson.

Examples:

(1)	
A student came.	ـجَاءَ طَالِبٌ.
A student (f.) came.	جَاءَتْ طَالِبَةٌ.
(2)	
Two students came.	جَاءَ طَالِبَانِ.
Two students (f.) came.	جَاءَتْ طَالِبَتَانِ.

Discussion:

Look at the examples above. You will find that by the word 'طَالِبٌ' or 'طَالِبَةٌ' in group (1), we understand only one student. Any word which indicates only one thing is called

مُفْرَدٌ (singular), whether masculine or feminine.

In the examples of group (2), the words 'طَالِبَانِ' or
'طَالِبَتَانِ' means two boy students or two girl students. You
will also observe a slight difference between the examples
of group (1) and group (2). In group (2), the words 'طَالِبٌ'
and 'طَالِبَةٌ' have some extra letters, i.e. 'ان' that have been
suffixed to them. The meaning of "two" comes solely from
this addition. By this addition the word has changed into
مُثَنَّى (dual). Therefore, if we mean two things, we have to
suffix (ان) to the مُفْرَدٌ to convey the meaning of two things.

Rule:

1. Any word that indicates only one thing is called مُفْرَدٌ
   (singular), e.g. طَالِبَةٌ, طَالِبٌ.

2. Any word that indicates two things is called مُثَنَّى (dual),
   e.g. طَالِبَتَانِ, طَالِبَانِ.

3. The dual can be formed by suffixing ان or ين to any
   singular noun, whether masculine or feminine.

4. The أَلِفٌ of the dual is retained in the nominative case. It
   is changed into 'ي' preceded by فَتْحَةٌ in the accusative
   and the genitive cases, e.g.

(Accusative Case)   رَأَيْتُ طَالِبَيْنِ/طَالِبَتَيْنِ۔

(Genitive Case)   ذَهَبْتُ إِلَى طَالِبَيْنِ/طَالِبَتَيْنِ۔

5. If the dual is annexed to another noun, its 'ن' is dropped, e.g.

جَاءَتْ طَالِبَتَا الْمَدْرَسَةِ۔   جَاءَ طَالِبَا الْمَدْرَسَةِ۔

رَأَيْتُ طَالِبَتَيِ الْمَدْرَسَةِ۔   رَأَيْتُ طَالِبَيِ الْمَدْرَسَةِ۔

ذَهَبْتُ إِلَى طَالِبَتَيِ الْمَدْرَسَةِ۔   ذَهَبْتُ إِلَى طَالِبَيِ الْمَدْرَسَةِ۔

Exercise:

1. Fill in the blanks with a suitable singular noun.

٢- _____ كَرِيمٌ۔   ١- _____ بَخِيلٌ۔

٤- _____ هَادِئٌ۔   ٣- _____ ثَمِينَةٌ۔

٦- _____ وَاسِعٌ۔   ٥- _____ زَعْلَانٌ۔

٨- _____ مَشْغُوْلَةٌ۔   ٧- _____ مُهْمِلٌ۔

١٠- _____ سَمِيْنَةٌ۔   ٩- _____ حَزِينٌ۔

١٢- _____ مَتِينَةٌ۔   ١١- _____ بَشِعٌ۔

2. Fill in the blanks with a suitable dual noun.

٢- _____ فَنَّانَانِ۔   ١- _____ سَاذِجَانِ۔

٤- _____ مُقَامِرَانِ۔   ٣- _____ عَلَّامَتَانِ۔

٦- _____ عَمِيْقَانِ۔   ٥- _____ بَائِسَتَانِ۔

٨- _____ ضَجِرَانِ۔   ٧- _____ صَادِقَانِ۔

١٠- _____ هَزِيْلَانِ۔   ٩- _____ جَاهِلَانِ۔

١٢- _____ نَبِيْلَانِ۔   ١١- _____ سَعِيْدَتَانِ۔

3. Make two sentences each as follows.

    a) containing masculine singular nouns in the accusative case.

    b) containing masculine dual nouns in the genitive case.

230

   c) containing feminine singular nouns in the accusative case.

   d) containing feminine dual nouns in the genitive case.

4. Make duals of the nouns given in exercise no. 1.

5. Translate the following into Arabic.

   a) A big army.

   b) Two vast deserts.

   c) A prolific writer.

   d) He sent two letters.

   e) An expert architect.

   f) Two beautiful faces.

   g) A baker and a driver.

6. Translate the following into English.

١) أَدِيبٌ كَبِيرٌ۔

٢) أَكَلَتْ كَعْكَيْنِ لَذِيذَيْنِ۔

٣) سَيَّارَتَانِ سَرِيعَتَانِ۔

٤) دَوَاءٌ مَجَّانِيٌّ۔

٥) الْعَامِلُ تَعْبَانٌ۔

٦) الْجُنْدِيَّانِ شُجَاعَانِ۔

٧) رَجُلٌ مُسِنٌّ۔

GLOSSARY	الْكَلِمَاتُ الْعَسِيرَةُ
miser	بَخِيلٌ (بُخَلَاءُ)
calm, peaceful	هَادِئٌ
annoyed, angry	زَعْلَانٌ
negligent, neglectful; careless	مُهْمِلٌ
ugly	بَشِعٌ
simple; plain	سَاذَجٌ - سَاذِجٌ (سُذَّجٌ)
artist	فَنَّانٌ (فَنَّانُونَ)
gambler	مُقَامِرٌ (مُقَامِرُونَ)
miserable, wretched	بَائِسٌ
deep, profound	عَمِيقٌ
annoyed, irritated	ضَجِرٌ
lean, skinny	هَزِيلٌ (هَزْلَى)
army	جَيْشٌ (جُيُوشٌ)
prolific	مِكْثَارٌ
expert	خَبِيرٌ (خُبَرَاءُ)
cake	كَعْكٌ، كَعْكَةٌ (كَعْكَاتٌ)
free	مَجَّانِيٌّ

LESSON 44

الْجَمْعُ Plural

+3E+

Examples:

Engineers came.	جَاءَ مُهَنْدِسُونَ۔
Engineers (f.) came.	جَاءَتْ مُهَنْدِسَاتٌ۔
The ministers travelled.	سَافَرَ الْوُزَرَاءُ۔
These are mosques.	هٰذِهِ مَسَاجِدُ۔
Those are churches.	تِلْكَ كَنَائِسُ۔

Discussion:

Look at the examples above. You will find that the noun in the first sentence is a plural of مُهَنْدِسٌ (a male engineer). It has been made by adding some letters to its singular form. Those letters are وْنَ. This kind of plural is called sound masculine plural جَمْعُ الْمُذَكَّرِ السَّالِمُ.

The noun in the second sentence مُهَنْدِسَاتٌ (female engineers) is also a plural. It has been made by adding some letters to its singular form مُهَنْدِسَةٌ (female engineer). Those letters are ات (after dropping ة as it is the sign of feminine). This kind of plural is called sound feminine plural جَمْعُ

الْمُؤَنَّثِ السَّالِمُ.

In the other three examples, the nouns مَسَاجِدُ ,وُزَرَاءُ
and كَنَائِسُ are also the plurals of وَزِيرٌ (a minister), مَسْجِدٌ (a
mosque) and كَنِيْسَةٌ (a church) respectively. You will observe
that in all these plurals, the form of the singular word has
changed. This kind of plural, which is made after making
some change in the singular form, is known as broken plural
(جَمْعُ التَّكْسِيْرِ), because the singular form of the word is
broken.

Rule:

1. Any word that indicates more than two persons or things
   is called الْجَمْعُ.

2. Plurals in Arabic are of several kinds

   (i) The sound masculine plural (جَمْعُ الْمُذَكَّرِ السَّالِمُ). This is
       the plural made by suffixing وْنَ to the singular form,
       while the singular form remains intact.

   (ii) The sound feminine plural (جَمْعُ الْمُؤَنَّثِ السَّالِمُ). This is
       the plural made by suffixing ات to the singular form
       while the singular form, remains unchanged (if the
       word is ending with ة, it must be dropped first).

   (iii) Broken Plural (جَمْعُ التَّكْسِيْرِ/ الْجَمْعُ الْمُكَسَّرُ). This is the
        plural that is made by changing the form of the

singular word either by dropping some letters or adding some letters or by making some change in its vowels.

Exercise:

1. Fill in the blanks with suitable plurals and translate them into English.

٢ـ جَلَسَ _____ -	١ـ هٰؤُلَاءِ _____ -
٤ـ فَرَّ _____ -	٣ـ _____ وَاقِفُوْنَ-
٦ـ إِنْكَسَرَتْ _____ -	٥ـ نَامَتْ _____ -
٨ـ هُمْ _____ -	٧ـ هِيَ _____ -
١٠ـ _____ حَارَّةٌ-	٩ـ _____ مَكْسُوْرَةٌ-
١٢ـ هٰذِه _____ -	١١ـ هُنَّ _____ -

2. Separate sound masculine plurals, sound feminine plurals and broken plurals.

٢ـ مُنَجِّمُوْنَ	١ـ أَحْلَامٌ
٤ـ جَامِعَاتٌ	٣ـ صَحَابَةٌ
٦ـ مَرَايَا	٥ـ مُسْلِمُوْنَ
٨ـ كِرَامٌ	٧ـ مُعْجِزَاتٌ
١٠ـ مُضِيْفَاتٌ	٩ـ أَسِنَّةٌ
١٢ـ عُيُوْنٌ	١١ـ سُبُلٌ

3. Make a list of at least 5 words which are sound masculine plurals.

4. Make a list of at least 5 words which are sound feminine

plurals.

5. Make a list of at least 5 words which are broken plurals.

6. Translate the following into Arabic.

  a) The tired workers took a rest.

  b) They are learned people.

  c) The spinsters attended the party.

  d) The authors gathered in a hall.

  e) Teachers and students are present.

  f) These are interesting novels.

  g) Books and magazines.

7. Translate the following into English.

١) الْوَسَائِدُ وَالسَّرَائِرُ۔

٢) جُدُوْدٌ وَجَدَّاتٌ۔

٣) هُمْ حَدَّادُوْنَ۔

٤) الْأَجْنِحَةُ خَفِيْفَةٌ۔

٥) هٰؤُلَاءِ النِّسَاءُ عَفِيْفَاتٌ۔

٦) سَاعَاتٌ مَكْسُوْرَةٌ۔

٧) الرُّفُوْفُ وَالْأَدْرَاجُ۔

GLOSSARY	الْكَلِمَاتُ الْعَسِيرَةُ
dream	حُلْمٌ (أَحْلَامٌ)
astrologer	مُنَجِّمٌ (مُنَجِّمُونَ)
mirror	مِرْآةٌ (مَرَايَا)
miracle (esp. one performed by a prophet)	مُعْجِزَةٌ (مُعْجِزَاتٌ)
spearhead	سِنَانٌ (أَسِنَّةٌ)
way, road, path	سَبِيلٌ (سُبُلٌ)
spinster	عَانِسٌ (عَوَانِسُ)
interesting	مُمْتِعٌ
novel	رِوَايَةٌ (رِوَايَاتٌ)
pillow	وِسَادَةٌ (وَسَائِدُ)
ironsmith, blacksmith	حَدَّادٌ (حَدَّادُونَ)
wing	جَنَاحٌ (أَجْنِحَةٌ)
shelf	رَفٌّ (رُفُوفٌ)
drawer	دُرْجٌ (أَدْرَاجٌ)

LESSON 45

Some More Facts about the Plural
مَعْلُوْمَاتٌ أُخْرَى عَنِ الْجَمْعِ

+‹§§›+

Sound Masculine Plural

1. It was stated in the previous lesson that the sound masculine plural is that which is made by suffixing ون to the singular form, keeping the singular form intact. Here, it is to be noted that ون changes into ـيْنَ when the word is in the accusative or genitive case, e.g.

The engineers came.	جَاءَ الْمُهَنْدِسُوْنَ۔
I saw the engineers	رَأَيْتُ الْمُهَنْدِسِيْنَ۔
I went to the engineers.	ذَهَبْتُ إِلَى الْمُهَنْدِسِيْنَ۔

2. Although this plural is meant solely for rational males, there are some other words whose plurals are formed on this pattern, e.g. عَالَمُوْنَ and أَرْضُوْنَ, سِنُوْنَ are the plurals of سَنَةٌ (year), أَرْضٌ (the earth) and عَالَمٌ (the world) respectively. These words have their other plurals also: سَنَوَاتٌ, أَرَاضِي and عَوَالِمُ.

Sound Feminine Plural

1. The sound feminine plural (with ات at the end) does not accept فَتْحَةٌ. Its nominative case is shown by ضَمَّةٌ and both of its accusative and genitive cases are shown by كَسْرَةٌ, e.g.

The lady teachers came.	جَاءَ ت الْمُعَلِّمَاتُ۔
I saw the lady teachers.	رَأَيْتُ الْمُعَلِّمَاتِ۔
I went to the lady teachers.	ذَهَبْتُ إِلَى الْمُعَلِّمَاتِ۔

2. Although this plural is meant for feminine nouns, some masculine nouns also have this kind of plural, e.g. إِحْسَاسَاتٌ, مَخْزُوْنَاتٌ, جَمَادَاتٌ, مَصْرُوْفَاتٌ, مَوْجُوْدَاتٌ are the plurals of مَوْجُوْدٌ (asset), مَصْرُوْفٌ (expenditure), جَمَادٌ (inanimate body), مَخْزُوْنٌ (stock) and إِحْسَاسٌ (feeling) respectively.

3. Likewise some feminine nouns with ة at the end are not made sound feminine plurals, e.g. قَوَاعِدُ, فَوَاكِهُ, حَوَادِثُ, كَوَارِثُ, قَبَائِلُ, رَسَائِلُ, جَوَائِزُ, حَادِثَةٌ are the plurals of (incident), فَاكِهَةٌ (fruit), قَاعِدَةٌ (rule), جَائِزَةٌ (prize), قَبِيْلَةٌ (tribe), رِسَالَةٌ (letter) and كَارِثَةٌ (calamity) respectively.

The Broken Plural

1. This is the plural which is made by breaking the singular form of the word.

2. As there is no rule for making this plural, one should
   know the plural of every word one comes across. There
   are, however some common patterns which the plurals of
   particular nouns follow. The following is the list of nouns
   and their plural patterns.

Most Commonly Used Patterns of the Broken Plural

فُعُلٌ	كُتُبٌ (كِتَابٌ)	سُفُنٌ (سَفِينَةٌ)	رُسُلٌ (رَسُولٌ)
فُعَلٌ	أُسَرٌ (أُسْرَةٌ)	غُرَفٌ (غُرْفَةٌ)	جُمَلٌ (جُمْلَةٌ)
فِعَلٌ	قِطَعٌ (قِطْعَةٌ)	إِبَرٌ (إِبْرَةٌ)	مِهَنٌ (مِهْنَةٌ)
فُعُولٌ	دُرُوسٌ (دَرْسٌ)	فُصُولٌ (فَصْلٌ)	بُيُوتٌ (بَيْتٌ)
فُعُولَاتٌ	(فُتُوحَاتٌ) (فَتْحٌ)	شُبُوكَاتٌ (شُبَّاكٌ)	سُحُوبَاتٌ (سَحْبٌ)
فِعَالٌ	بِلَادٌ (بَلَدٌ)	جِمَالٌ (جَمَلٌ)	بِحَارٌ (بَحْرٌ)
فِيعَالٌ	حِيطَانٌ (حَائِطٌ)	ثِيرَانٌ (ثَوْرٌ)	جِيرَانٌ (جَارٌ)
فُعَّلٌ	جُهَّلٌ (جَاهِلٌ)	مُلَّكٌ (مَالِكٌ)	كُهَّلٌ (كَامِلٌ)
فُعَّالٌ	عُمَّالٌ (عَامِلٌ)	كُتَّابٌ (كَاتِبٌ)	قُرَّاءٌ (قَارِئٌ)
فَعَّالَةٌ	جَزَّارَةٌ (جَزَّارٌ)	عَلَّافَةٌ (عَلَّافٌ)	بَقَّالَةٌ (بَقَّالٌ)
أَفْعُلٌ	أَلْسُنٌ (لِسَانٌ)	أَشْهُرٌ (شَهْرٌ)	أَزْهُرٌ (زَهْرٌ)
أَفْعَالٌ	أَثْقَالٌ (ثِقْلٌ)	أَعْمَالٌ (عَمَلٌ)	أَشْجَارٌ (شَجَرٌ)
أَفَاعِلَةٌ	أَسَاتِذَةٌ (أُسْتَاذٌ)	أَسَاكِفَةٌ (إِسْكَافٌ)	أَسَاوِرَةٌ (سِوَارٌ)
فَعَلَةٌ	طَلَبَةٌ (طَالِبٌ)	حَمَلَةٌ (حَامِلٌ)	قَتَلَةٌ (قَاتِلٌ)
أَفْعِلَةٌ	أَلْسِنَةٌ (لِسَانٌ)	أَسْئِلَةٌ (سُؤَالٌ)	أَلْبِسَةٌ (لِبَاسٌ)
فُعْلَانٌ	بُلْدَانٌ (بَلَدٌ)	فُرْسَانٌ (فَارِسٌ)	رُهْبَانٌ (رَاهِبٌ)

فِعْلَانٌ	جِرْذَانٌ (جُرَذٌ)	تِرْبَانٌ (تُرَابٌ)	جِحْشَانٌ (جَحْشٌ)
فَعَاعِلَةٌ	زَبَابِنَةٌ (زِبَّانٌ)	جَبَابِرَةٌ (جَبَّارٌ)	دَجَاجِلَةٌ (دَجَّالٌ)
فَعَالِلَةٌ	أَسَاقِفَةٌ (أُسْقُفٌ)	فَلَاسِفَةٌ (فَيْلَسُوفٌ)	أَرَاخِنَةٌ (أُرْخَنٌ)

3. There are some patterns of broken plurals which are
diptote. Here is the list of diptote plurals.

The Broken Plural (Diptote)

فَعَائِلُ	عَرَائِسُ (عَرُوسٌ)	قَبَائِلُ (قَبِيلَةٌ)	رَسَائِلُ (رِسَالَةٌ)
أَفَاعِلُ	أَرَامِلُ (أَرْمَلَةٌ)	أَمَاكِنُ (مَكَانٌ)	أَقَارِبُ (قَرِيبٌ)
فُعَلَاءُ	نُشَطَاءُ (نَاشِطٌ)	كُرَمَاءُ (كَرِيمٌ)	حُكَمَاءُ (حَاكِمٌ)
أَفْعِلَاءُ	أَقْوِيَاءُ (قَوِيٌّ)	أَقْرِبَاءُ (قَرِيبٌ)	أَغْنِيَاءُ (غَنِيٌّ)
فَوَاعِلُ	عَوَامِلُ (عَامِلٌ)	شَوَارِعُ (شَارِعٌ)	فَوَاكِهُ (فَاكِهَةٌ)
فَيَاعِلُ	عَيَالِمُ (عَيْلَمٌ)	دَيَانِمُ (دَيْنَمٌ)	بَيَارِقُ (بَيْرَقٌ)
فَعَاعِيلُ	كَتَاتِيبُ (كُتَّابٌ)	كَدَادِيسُ (كُدَّاسٌ)	بَلَالِيصُ (بَلَّاصٌ)
فَوَاعِيلُ	قَوَامِيسُ (قَامُوسٌ)	جَوَامِيسُ (جَامُوسٌ)	كَوَابِيسُ (كَابُوسٌ)
مَفَاعِلُ	مَدَارِسُ (مَدْرَسَةٌ)	مَكَاتِبُ (مَكْتَبٌ)	مَكَانِسُ (مِكْنَسَةٌ)
مَفَاعِيلُ	مَفَاتِيحُ (مِفْتَاحٌ)	مَصَابِيحُ (مِصْبَاحٌ)	مَنَاشِيرُ (مِنْشَارٌ)
أَفَاعِيلُ	أَنَاشِيدُ (نَشِيدٌ)	أَكَاذِيبُ (أُكْذُوبَةٌ)	أَبَاهِيمُ (إِبْهَامٌ)
تَفَاعِيلُ	تَمَاثِيلُ (تَمْثِيلٌ)	تَلَاحِينُ (تَلْحِينٌ)	تَلَابِيبُ (تَلْبِيبٌ)
فَعَالِلُ	بَرَاقِعُ (بُرْقُعٌ)	عَنَاصِرُ (عُنْصُرٌ)	بَرَاعِمُ (بُرْعُمٌ)
فَعَاعِيلُ	دَبَابِيسُ (دَبُوسٌ)	بَلَالِيغُ (بَلَّاغَةٌ)	سَكَاكِينُ (سِكِّينٌ)
فَعَالِيلُ	زَغَالِيلُ (زُغْلُولٌ)	رَعَادِيدُ (رِعْدِيدٌ)	زَعَارِيرُ (زُعْرُورٌ)

فَعَائِلُ	سَلَالِمُ (سُلَّمٌ)	جَبَابِرُ (جَبَّارٌ)	سَمَامِنُ (سُمُنٌ)

4. Sometimes there is ة (which is called تَاءُ الْجَمْعِ) at the end of a plural word but the word remains masculine, e.g. فَلَاسِفَةٌ, عَمَالِقَةٌ, أَسَاقِفَةٌ, جَزَّارَةٌ, بَحَّارَةٌ, بَقَّالَةٌ, أَسَاتِذَةٌ are the plurals of أُسْتَاذ (teacher), بَقَّالٌ (grocer), بَحَّارٌ (seaman), جَزَّارٌ (butcher), أُسْقُفٌ (bishop), عِمْلَاقٌ (huge) and فَيْلَسُوف (philosopher) respectively.

5. For the broken plural we can use the feminine verb also, although the word is masculine, e.g.

سَافَرَ الْوُزَرَاءُ   جَلَسَ الرِّجَالُ

سَافَرَتِ الْوُزَرَاءُ   جَلَسَتِ الرِّجَالُ

General Rules

1. Many words have more than one plural which give the same meaning, but there are some other words which have different patterns of plurals to give different meanings, e.g.

  a) The word بَحْرٌ has two plurals of different patterns, one is أَبْحَارٌ which means oceans and the other is بُحُورٌ which means metres of poetry.

  b) The word بَيْتٌ also has two plurals of different patterns, one is بُيُوتٌ which means houses and the other is أَبْيَاتٌ which means verses.

2. Some words though singular, give the meaning of the plural and are used as plural, e.g. قَوْمٌ (people).

هٰؤُلَاءِ الْقَوْمُ جَاءُوْا مِنَ الْخَارِجِ

(These people have come from abroad)

3. Some words have their plural form on their singular pattern, e.g. فُلْكٌ (ship) and فُلْكٌ (ships).

4. Sometimes the plural of a word is not from the radicals of the singular word but from other new words, e.g. نِسَاءٌ and نِسْوَةٌ are the plurals of اِمْرَأَةٌ.

5. The following plurals must be noted and remembered:

(Broken Plural) أَبْنَاءٌ	<=	اِبْنٌ
(Sound Plural) بَنُوْنَ		
بَنَاتٌ	<=	اِبْنَةٌ
إِخْوَةٌ، إِخْوَانٌ	<=	أَخٌ
أَخَوَاتٌ	<=	أُخْتٌ
أُمَّهَاتٌ	<=	أُمٌّ

6. Collective nouns (أَسْمَاءُ الْجَمْعِ) like بَيْضٌ, شَجَرٌ, زَهْرٌ, تَمْرٌ, سَمَكٌ, لُؤْلُؤٌ, تُفَّاحٌ etc. need not be put in their plural forms. They serve, as they are, as plurals also. See the examples below.

The dates are cheap in this country.	التَّمْرُ رَخِيْصٌ فِي هٰذَا الْبَلَدِ.

There are many apples on the tree.	عَلَى الشَّجَرِ تُفَّاحٌ كَثِيْرٌ۔
The basket is full of flowers.	السَّلَّةُ مَمْلُوْءَةٌ بِالزَّهْرِ۔
I want a tray of eggs.	أَطْلُبُ طَبَقًا مِنَ الْبَيْضِ۔
There are precious pearls in the box.	فِي الصُّنْدُوْقِ لُؤْلُؤٌ ثَمِيْنٌ۔
I saw many fish in the pool.	رَأَيْتُ فِي الْحَوْضِ سَمَكًا كَثِيْرًا۔

However, in case the number is to be mentioned specifically, ة (which is called تَاءُ الْوَحْدَةِ) should be added to the nouns for the singular, ان with ة for the dual and the plural form is used for more than two. See the examples below.

My friend plucked a flower and I plucked two flowers, so we have three flowers.	قَطَفَ صَدِيْقِى زَهْرَةً وَقَطَفْتُ زَهْرَتَيْنِ فَعِنْدَنَا ثَلَاثَةُ زُهُوْرٍ۔
Her teeth appeared as if they were shining pearls.	بَرَزَتْ سِنَاهَا كَأَنَّهُمَا لُؤْلُؤَتَانِ لَامِعَتَانِ۔
There was an apple in the refrigerator and I put in two apples, now there are three apples in it.	كَانَتْ فِي الثَّلَاجَةِ تُفَّاحَةٌ وَوَضَعْتُ تُفَّاحَتَيْنِ فَالْآنَ فِيْهَا ثَلَاثُ تُفَّاحَاتٍ۔
We caught three fish.	صِدْنَا ثَلَاثَ سَمَكَاتٍ۔
We broke the fast together, my sister ate a date, my brother ate two and I ate many dates.	أَفْطَرْنَا مَعًا، أَكَلَتْ أُخْتِي تَمْرَةً وَأَخِي أَكَلَ تَمْرَتَيْنِ وَأَنَا أَكَلْتُ تُمُوْرًا كَثِيْرَةً۔

Every morning my breakfast is two eggs, two sandwiches and a glass of milk.	فَطُوْرِي كُلَّ صَبَاحٍ بَيْضَتَانِ وَشَطِيْرَتَانِ وَكُوْبُ لَبَنٍ۔

Exercise:

1. Fill in the blanks with suitable plurals and translate them into English.

٢ ـ هٰؤُلَاءِ _____ - ١ ـ أُوْلَائِكَ _____ -

٤ ـ غَضِبَ _____ - ٣ ـ _____ حَاضِرُوْنَ۔

٦ ـ اِسْتَيْقَظَ _____ - ٥ ـ هُمْ _____ -

٨ ـ _____ دَارِسَاتٌ۔ ٧ ـ هُمْ _____ -

١٠ ـ _____ بَطِيْئَةٌ۔ ٩ ـ _____ فَرِحُوْنَ۔

١٢ ـ نَحْنُ _____ - ١١ ـ أَنْتُم _____ -

2. Write plurals of the following words.

٢ ـ جَالِسَةٌ ١ ـ مَدْهُوْشٌ

٤ ـ بَائِعٌ ٣ ـ وَكِيْلٌ

٦ ـ صَدِيْقٌ ٥ ـ خَادِمَةٌ

٨ ـ حَافِظَةٌ ٧ ـ نَجَّارٌ

١٠ ـ مُخْتَرَعٌ ٩ ـ مِقْدَارٌ

١٢ ـ مُعْجَمٌ ١١ ـ نَجِيْبَةٌ

3. Make three sentences each to show all the three cases of the following nouns.

مُوَظَّفُوْنَ - أَصْحَابٌ - فَلَّاحَاتٌ - خَادِمَتَانِ

4. Translate the following into Arabic.

a) The accountants are busy.

b) Her sons are clever and smart.

c) He always asks his teachers for advice.

d) Did you bring the certificates?

e) The painters and plumbers arrived an hour ago.

f) The air hostesses did not get their salaries.

g) Our workers are honest and trustworthy.

h) They met the doctors.

i) These rosaries belong to me.

j) These students (f.) are successful.

5. Translate the following into English.

١) وَصَلَ الصُّحُفِيُّونَ إِلَى مَوْقِعِ الْحَادِثِ۔

٢) أَيْنَ الْكُرَّاسَاتُ الْجَدِيْدَةُ؟

٣) مَتَى أَنْشَأَتِ الْحُكُومَةُ هٰذِهِ الْجُسُوْرَ؟

٤) الْخَادِمُوْنَ مُطِيْعُوْنَ۔

٥) تُعْقَدُ الْمَعَارِضُ فِي ثَلَاثِ مُدُنٍ فِى هَذَا الشَّهْرِ۔

٦) أَرْسَلَتِ الْأُمَّهَاتُ أَطْفَالَهُنَّ إِلَى الْحَضَانَاتِ۔

٧) قَدْ حَفِظْتُ قَوَاعِدَ النَّحْوِ۔

٨) أَقْلَعَ الْبَحَّارُوْنَ فِي الْمُحِيْطِ الْأَطْلَسِي۔

٩) هٰذِهِ الْعِمَارَاتُ لِلشَّرِكَاتِ الْأَجْنَبِيَّةِ۔

١٠) جَمِيْعُ الْمَطَاعِمِ مُغْلَقَةٌ الْيَوْمَ۔

١١) اِلْتَقَطَ الْمُصَوِّرُوْنَ صُوَرًا جَمِيْلَةً۔

١٢) هَلِ الطَّبَّاخَاتُ حَاضِرَاتٌ؟

GLOSSARY	الْكَلِمَاتُ الْعَسِيرَةُ
slow	بَطِيْئٌ (بِطَاءٌ، بَطِيْؤُوْنَ)
astonished, surprised	مَدْهُوْشٌ (مَدْهُوْشُوْنَ)
noble	نَجِيْبَةٌ (نَجِيْبَاتٌ)
accountant	مُحَاسِبٌ (مُحَاسِبُوْنَ)
clever	شَاطِرٌ (شَاطِرُوْنَ)
smart	نَبِيْهٌ (نُبَهَاءُ) or ذَكِيٌّ (أَذْكِيَاءُ)
to ask s.o. for advice, be advised, consult (s.o.)	اِسْتَنْصَحَ - يَسْتَنْصِحُ - اِسْتِنْصَاحٌ
certificate, testimonial	شَهَادَة (شَهَادَاتٌ)
painter	دَهَّانٌ (دَهَّانُوْنَ)
plumber	سَبَّاكٌ (سَبَّاكُوْنَ)
air hostess	مُضِيْفَةٌ (مُضِيْفَاتٌ)
salary, pay	رَاتِبٌ (رَوَاتِبُ)
honest	أَمِيْنٌ (أُمَنَاءُ)
dancer	رَقَّاصٌ (رَقَّاصُوْنَ)
rosary	سُبْحَةٌ (سُبْحَاتٌ)
journalist	صُحُفِيٌّ (صُحُفِيُّوْنَ)
bridge	جِسْرٌ (جُسُوْرٌ)
obedient	مُطِيْعٌ (مُطِيْعُوْنَ)
exhibition; fair	مَعْرِضٌ (مَعَارِضُ)
nursery school	حَضَانَةٌ (حَضَانَاتٌ)

to sail (set sail)	أَقْلَعَ - يُقْلِعُ - إِقْلَاعٌ
Atlantic Ocean	الْمُحِيْطُ الْأَطْلَسِي
to take a picture	اِلْتَقَطَ - يَلْتَقِطُ - اِلْتِقَاطٌ (صُوْرَةً)

LESSON 46

The Case الْحَالَةُ الْإِعْرَابِيَّةُ

Case is the function of a noun in the sentence. There are three cases in Arabic, namely Nominative Case (حَالَةُ الرَّفْعِ), Accusative Case (حَالَةُ النَّصْبِ) and Genitive Case (حَالَةُ الْجَرِّ) to which a noun can belong. The case of the noun can be represented by a vowel sign on or below the last letter, which is known as declension by vowel (إِعْرَابٌ بِالْحَرَكَةِ) or it could be represented by some letters which is known as declension by letters (إِعْرَابٌ بِالْحُرُوْفِ).

Examples:

(1)

The teacher came.	جَاءَ الْمُدَرِّسُ-
I saw the teacher.	رَأَيْتُ الْمُدَرِّسَ-
I went to the teacher.	ذَهَبْتُ إِلَى الْمُدَرِّسِ-

(2)

The teacher is standing.	الْمُدَرِّسُ وَاقِفٌ-
This is a teacher.	هٰذَا مُدَرِّسٌ-
The teacher stood	وَقَفَ الْمُدَرِّسُ-

The teacher was standing.	ـكَانَ الْمُدَرِّسُ وَاقِفًا
Indeed, he is a teacher.	إِنَّهُ مُدَرِّسٌ۔
(3)	
I saw the teacher.	ـرَأَيْتُ الْمُدَرِّسَ
His brother was a teacher.	ـكَانَ أَخُوهُ مُدَرِّسًا
Indeed, the teacher is available.	ـإِنَّ الْمُدَرِّسَ مَوْجُودٌ
(4)	
I went to the teacher.	ـذَهَبْتُ إِلَى الْمُدَرِّسِ
The car of the teacher is new.	ـسَيَّارَةُ الْمُدَرِّسِ جَدِيدَةٌ

Discussion:

Look at the examples above. You will find that the group (1) has three examples. Each example contains the word الْمُدَرِّس'. In the first example the word 'الْمُدَرِّسُ' has ضَمَّةٌ (—ُ) on the last letter, and is considered to be in the Nominative case because this case is generally shown by simply putting ضَمَّةٌ on the last letter of the word. In the second example it appeared with فَتْحَةٌ (—َ), and is considered to be in the Accusative case, as it is shown by putting فَتْحَةٌ on the last letter of the word. In the third example, it appeared with كَسْرَةٌ (—ِ), and is considered to be in the Genitive case because this case is generally shown by كَسْرَةٌ

under the last letter. It may be noted that the last vowel sign of the word 'الْمُدَرِّس' is changed due to its function (case) in the sentence.

One should note the things which are said to be in the Nominative case or in Accusative case or in Genitive case.

If a noun happens to be the subject (of a nominal sentence), or a predicate, or a subject (doer) of a verb or a noun of كَانَ وَأَخَوَاتُهَا or a predicate of إِنَّ وَأَخَوَاتُهَا, etc. it is considered to be in the Nominative case as shown in the examples of group (2).

If a noun is the object or predicate of كَانَ وَأَخَوَاتُهَا or a noun of إِنَّ وَأَخَوَاتُهَا it is considered to be in the Accusative case as shown in the examples of group (3).

If a noun is الْمُضَافُ إِلَيْهِ or is governed by a preposition, it is considered to be in the Genitive case as shown in the examples of group (4).

Rule:

1. Case is the function of a noun as used in the sentence.

2. There are three cases in Arabic

   (i)   Nominative Case (حَالَةُ الرَّفْعِ)

   (ii) Accusative Case (حَالَةُ النَّصْبِ)

(iii) Genitive Case (حَالَةُ الْجَرِّ)

3. The case is sometimes, represented by a vowel sign. This
is called declension by vowel (إِعْرَابٌ بِالْحَرَكَةِ) and
sometimes it is represented by letters. This is called
declension by letter (إِعْرَابٌ بِالْحُرُوفِ).

Declension of Different Categories of Words

Normal Noun

If the noun is a singular or a declinable broken plural,
its nominative case is shown by ضَمَّةٌ, the accusative case by
فَتْحَةٌ and the genitive case by كَسْرَةٌ, e.g.

(Nominative Case)	جَاءَ الرِّجَالُ۔	جَاءَ الرَّجُلُ۔
(Accusative Case)	رَأَيْتُ الرِّجَالَ۔	رَأَيْتُ الرَّجُلَ۔
(Genitive Case)	ذَهَبْتُ إِلَى الرِّجَالِ۔	ذَهَبْتُ إِلَى الرَّجُلِ۔

Dual

If the noun is a dual, its nominative case is shown by
(الْأَلِفُ وَالنُّونُ) انِ and its accusative as well as genitive cases
are shown by ـَيْنَ (الْيَاءُ وَالنُّونُ) preceded by فَتْحَةٌ), e.g.

(Nominative Case)	جَاءَ الْمُدَرِّسَانِ۔
(Accusative Case)	رَأَيْتُ الْمُدَرِّسَيْنِ۔
(Genitive Case)	ذَهَبْتُ إِلَى الْمُدَرِّسَيْنِ۔

As you have learned earlier, the 'ن' of the dual is

dropped, if it is annexed to another noun, e.g.

(Nominative Case)   جَاءَ مُدَرِّسَا الْمَدْرَسَةِ۔

(Accusative Case)   رَأَيْتُ مُدَرِّسَيْ الْمَدْرَسَةِ۔

(Genitive Case)   ذَهَبْتُ إِلَى مُدَرِّسَيْ الْمَدْرَسَةِ۔

Sound Masculine Plural

If the word is جَمْعُ الْمُذَكَّرِ السَّالِمُ, its nominative case
is shown by ـُـ وْنَ while its accusative case as well as its
genitive case are shown by ـِـ يْنَ, e.g.

(Nominative Case)   جَاءَ الْمُدَرِّسُوْنَ۔

(Accusative Case)   رَأَيْتُ الْمُدَرِّسِيْنَ۔

(Genitive Case)   ذَهَبْتُ إِلَى الْمُدَرِّسِيْنَ۔

As you have learned earlier that 'ن' of the sound
masculine plural is dropped, if it is annexed to another noun,
e.g.

(Nominative Case)   جَاءَ مُدَرِّسُوْ الْمَدْرَسَةِ۔

(Accusative Case)   رَأَيْتُ مُدَرِّسِي الْمَدْرَسَةِ۔

(Genitive Case)   ذَهَبْتُ إِلَى مُدَرِّسِي الْمَدْرَسَةِ۔

Sound Feminine Plural

If the word is جَمْعُ الْمُؤَنَّثِ السَّالِمُ, its nominative case
is shown by ضَمَّةٌ while its accusative as well as genitive
cases are shown by كَسْرَةٌ, e.g.

(Nominative Case)   جَاءَتِ الْمُعَلِّمَاتُ

(Accusative Case) رَأَيْتُ الْمُعَلِّمَاتِ

(Genitive Case) ذَهَبْتُ إِلَى الْمُعَلِّمَاتِ

Diptote

If the noun is a diptote (غَيْرُ مُنْصَرِفٍ) its nominative case is shown by a single ضَمَّةٌ and both its accusative and genitive cases are shown by a single فَتْحَةٌ, e.g.

(Nominative Case) هٰذِهِ مَكَّةُ۔

(Accusative Case) زُرْتُ مَكَّةَ۔

(Genitive Case) ذَهَبْتُ إِلَى مَكَّةَ۔

The Noun Ending in Alif (ا) and the Noun Annexed to First Person Pronoun 'ي'

If the noun is الْاِسْمُ الْمَقْصُورُ (which ends with أَلِفٌ) or a noun annexed to a pronoun of first person 'ي', no sign will be used to show the case. These nouns are assumed to be in some particular case without any sign, e.g.

جَاءَ مُوسَى، رَأَيْتُ مُوسَى، ذَهَبْتُ إِلَى مُوسَى

هٰذَا كِتَابِي، قَرَأْتُ كِتَابِي، قَرَأْتُ سَطْرًا مِنْ كِتَابِي

The Noun Ending in 'ي' preceded by (ـِ) كَسْرَةٌ

If the noun is الْاِسْمُ الْمَنْقُوصُ (like الْقَاضِي), there is nothing to express this in the nominative and genitive cases, however, to show its accusative case, فَتْحَةٌ is placed over its last letter, e.g.

جَاءَ الْقَاضِي، رَأَيْتُ الْقَاضِيَ، ذَهَبْتُ إِلَى الْقَاضِي

Exercise:

1. Fill in the blanks with a suitable noun with a vowel sign
   on its last letter.

١ـ الْكُلِّيَّةُ ـــــــ ـ   ٢ـ السُّكَّرُ فِي ـــــــ ـ

٣ـ كَتَبَ الطَّالِبُ ـــــــ ـ   ٤ـ جَاءَ ـــــــ ـ

٥ـ نَالَتْ ـــــــ مِنْحَةً ـ   ٦ـ فَرِحَ ـــــــ ـ

٧ـ نَامَ الْكَلْبُ خَلْفَ ـــــــ ـ   ٨ـ رَأَيْتُ الْفَلَّاحَاتِ ـــــــ ـ

٩ـ لَوْنُ التُّفَّاحِ ـــــــ ـ   ١٠ـ جَلَسَ ـــــــ الْكِرَامُ ـ

١١ـ قَطَعَ الْحَبْلَ بِالـ ـــــــ ـ   ١٢ـ لِلْبَيْتِ ـــــــ كَبِيرَانِ ـ

2. State whether the underlined nouns are in the nominative
   case or the accusative case or the genitive case and
   translate them into English.

١ـ أَطْلَقَ الْبُولِيصُ النَّارَ ـ   ٢ـ اِصْطَدَمَتِ السَّيَّارَةُ بِالشَّاحِنَةِ ـ

٣ـ يَعْدُو الْحِصَانُ ـ   ٤ـ خَرَجَ مِنْ غُرْفَتِهِ ـ

٥ـ زُرْتُ الْجَامِعَاتِ الْقَدِيمَةَ ـ   ٦ـ وَلَدَا هٰذَا الرَّجُلِ ذَكِيَّانِ ـ

٧ـ حَسِبَ أَحْمَدُ عُثْمَانَ رَجُلاً ثَرِيًّا ـ   ٨ـ اللُّغَةُ الْعَرَبِيَّةُ صَعْبَةٌ ـ

٩ـ سَبَحْتُ فِي نَهْرٍ جَارٍ ـ   ١٠ـ هَلْ أَخْبَرَ عِيسَى مُوسَى ـ

١١ـ أَنْتَظِرُ لِلصُّحُفِيَّيْنَ ـ   ١٢ـ اِشْتَرَيْتُهُ فِي الشَّهْرِ الْمَاضِي ـ

3. Make 3 sentences which show the nominative case.

4. Make 3 sentences which show the accusative case.

5. Make 3 sentences which show the genitive case.

6. Translate the following into Arabic.

   a) The weather is warm.

b) The lion killed the goat.

c) I come by bus.

d) Who invented radio?

e) The biggest girl is present.

f) I lost my card.

g) Two employees were absent.

7. Translate the following into English.

١) أَبْدَأُ السَّفَرَ فِي الصَّبَاحِ۔

٢) مَا جَاءَ طَرْدَانِ مِنْ الْعِرَاقِ۔

٣) تَرَكْتُ مِصْرَ وَقَدِمْتُ مَكَّةَ۔

٤) سَقَطَ مِنَ الْمَبْنَى الْعَالِي۔

٥) أَنْتَمِي إِلَى الطَّبَقَةِ الْوُسْطَىٰ۔

٦) الْمُعَالِجُونَ مُغْضَبُونَ مِنَّا۔

٧) سَكَتَتِ الشَّرِيفَاتُ الْعَفِيفَاتُ۔

GLOSSARY	الْكَلِمَاتُ الْعَسِيرَةُ
sugar	سُكَّرٌ
scholarship	مِنْحَةٌ دِرَاسِيَّةٌ
to fire, to shoot at	أَطْلَقَ - يُطْلِقُ - إِطْلَاقٌ
to collide, clash, hit	اِصْطَلَدَمَ - يَصْطَلِدِمُ - اِصْطِلَدَامٌ
truck, lorry	شَاحِنَةٌ (شَاحِنَاتٌ)
to run, race	عَدَا - يَعْدُو - عَدْوٌ

journalist	صُحُفِيٌّ (صُحُفِيُّوْنَ)
weather	جَوٌّ (أَجْوَاءٌ)
card	بِطَاقَةٌ (بِطَاقَاتٌ)
parcel	طَرْدٌ (طُرُوْدٌ)
the middle class	الطَّبَقَةُ الْوُسْطَى
noble	شَرِيْفٌ (شُرَفَاءُ، أَشْرَافٌ)
chaste, modest	عَفِيْفٌ (أَعِفَّاءُ، أَعِفَّةٌ)

Some More Grammatical Rules
to Remember

قَوَاعِدُ نَحْوِيَّةٌ أُخْرَى لِلْحِفْظِ

1. The 'Hamza' of Joining and the 'Hamza' of Separation

2. The Detached Accusative Pronoun

3. The Verbal Noun

4. The Adverb of Time and Place

(1)

The 'Hamza' of Joining and the 'Hamza' of Separation

هَمْزَةُ الْوَصْلِ وَهَمْزَةُ الْقَطْعِ

هَمْزَةُ الْوَصْلِ is a هَمْزَةٌ which is used at the beginning of the word whose first letter is vowelless (سَاكِنٌ) for pronouncing it. If there is another word before such a word, this هَمْزَةٌ is not pronounced and nothing is written on it. Instead, the last letter of the preceding word is joined to the following word in pronounciation, e.g.

مِنَ الْبَيْتِ (الْبَيْتُ) - يَا وَلَدُ اكْتُبْ (أُكْتُبْ) - هُوَ ابْنهُ (اِبْنُهُ)

The هَمْزَةٌ of the following is هَمْزَةُ الْوَصْلِ:

1) The هَمْزَةٌ of the definite article is الْ.

2) The هَمْزَةٌ present in the imperatives made from the simple triliteral verbs.

3) The هَمْزَةٌ of the imperatives, the perfect verbs, and the verbal nouns of the following extended triliteral verbs.

    a) اِنْفَعَلَ   b) اِفْتَعَلَ   c) اِسْتَفْعَلَ   d) اِفْعَلَّ

    e) اِفْعَالَّ   f) اِفْعَوْعَلَ   g) اِفْعَلَلَ   h) اِفْعَلَّ

4) The هَمْزَةٌ of the following words:

اِسْمٌ - اِمْرُؤٌ - اِبْنٌ - اِبْنَةٌ - اِثْنَانِ - اِثْنَتَانِ

هَمْزَةُ الْقَطْعِ is a هَمْزَةٌ which is always pronounced whether there is any other word before it or not, e.g.

أَحْمَرُ - أَحْمَدُ - أَشْجَارٌ - أَخْرَجَ - أَخْرِجْ - إِخْرَاجٌ

----

(2)

Detached Accusative Pronouns
الضَّمَائِرُ الْمُنْفَصِلَةُ الْمَنْصُوبَةُ

The table of the Detached Accusative Pronouns is given below.

Masculine	Singular المُفْرَدُ	him, it	إِيَّاهُ
	Dual الْمُثَنَّى	them	إِيَّاهُمَا
المُذَكَّرُ	Plural الْجَمْعُ	them	إِيَّاهُمْ

Feminine	Singular المُفْرَدُ	her, it	إِيَّاهَا
	Dual الْمُثَنَّى	them	إِيَّاهُمَا
المُؤَنَّثُ	Plural الْجَمْعُ	them	إِيَّاهُنَّ

Masculine	Singular المُفْرَدُ	you	إِيَّاكَ
	Dual الْمُثَنَّى	you	إِيَّاكُمَا
المُذَكَّرُ	Plural الْجَمْعُ	you	إِيَّاكُمْ

Feminine	Singular المُفْرَدُ	you	إِيَّاكِ
	Dual الْمُثَنَّى	you	إِيَّاكُمَا
المُؤَنَّثُ	Plural الْجَمْعُ	you	إِيَّاكُنَّ

Masculine and Feminine المُذَكَّرُ وَ المُؤَنَّثُ	Singular المُفْرَدُ	me	إِيَّايَ
	Dual المُثَنَّى	us	إِيَّانَا
	Plural الجَمْعُ	us	إِيَّانَا

Rule:

The Detached Accusative Pronouns are used on such occasions where it is difficult or not proper to use attached pronouns, e.g.

آلَمَنِي ضَرْبُ الأُسْتَاذِ إِيَّاهُ

(It pained me that the teacher beat him)

----

(3)

The Verbal Noun الْمَصْدَرُ

For every verb that we use in our speech or writing there is a noun form which is called a verbal noun (مَصْدَرٌ). It gives the meaning of actions as a verb does but it is not a verb because it does not show the tense (or time of action).

The verbal nouns are like other nouns and are used just as other nouns are used with or without definite article and are declined in all the three cases, e.g.

Reading is useful.	الْقِرَاءَةُ مُفِيْدَةٌ.
I like reading.	أُحِبُّ الْقِرَاءَةَ۔
I benefitted from reading.	أَنَا اِسْتَفَدْتُ بِالْقِرَاءَةِ۔

In the above examples the word الْقِرَاءَة is the verbal noun of the verb قَرَأَ - يَقْرَأُ.

There is no particular pattern of a verbal noun for a particular verb, which means there can be two different patterns of verbal nouns of the same form of the verb, for example, the verbal nouns of ذَهَبَ, قَرَأَ and جَمَعَ are ذَهَابٌ, قِرَاءَةٌ and جَمْعٌ respectively and the verbal nouns of فَرِحَ, لَبِسَ and عَلِمَ are فَرَحٌ, عِلْمٌ and فَهْمٌ respectively. Similarly, the verbal nouns of كِتَابَةٌ, أَكَلَ and دَخَلَ are أَكْلٌ, دُخُوْلٌ and كَتَبَ respectively, and so on.

A verb may have a verbal noun on any pattern of the verbal nouns and it may also have more than one verbal nouns. Some of the patterns of verbal nouns of triliteral verbs are given below.

a) فَعْلٌ : نَصْرٌ

b) فُعُولٌ : جُلُوسٌ

c) فِعَالٌ : صِيَامٌ

d) فَعَلٌ : عَمَلٌ

e) فَعَالٌ : سَمَاعٌ

f) فُعْلٌ : شُرْبٌ

g) فِعْلٌ : كِذْبٌ

i) فِعَالَةٌ : كِتَابَةٌ

j) فَعَالِيَةٌ : كَرَاهِيَةٌ

As far as the extended triliteral verbs are concerned, their verbal noun are derived on set patterns as follows.

Form	Verb	Verbal Noun	Example
II	فَعَّلَ - يُفَعِّلُ	تَفْعِيْلٌ	تَقْدِيْمٌ
III	فَاعَلَ - يُفَاعِلُ	مُفَاعَلَةٌ ، فِعَالٌ	مُقَابَلَةٌ ، قِتَالٌ
IV	أَفْعَلَ - يُفْعِلُ	إِفْعَالٌ	إِكْرَامٌ
V	تَفَعَّلَ - يَتَفَعَّلُ	تَفَعُّلٌ	تَجَهُّزٌ
VI	تَفَاعَلَ - يَتَفَاعَلُ	تَفَاعُلٌ	تَجَاهُلٌ
VII	اِنْفَعَلَ - يَنْفَعِلُ	اِنْفِعَالٌ	اِنْعِقَادٌ
VIII	اِفْتَعَلَ - يَفْتَعِلُ	اِفْتِعَالٌ	اِفْتِتَاحٌ
IX	اِفْعَلَّ - يَفْعَلُّ	اِفْعِلَالٌ	اِحْمِرَارٌ
X	اِسْتَفْعَلَ - يَسْتَفْعِلُ	اِسْتِفْعَالٌ	اِسْتِقْبَالٌ

----

(4)

The Adverb of Time and Place ظَرْفُ الزَّمَانِ وَالْمَكَانِ

1) The Adverb of Time (ظَرْفُ الزَّمَانِ)

2) The Adverb of Place (ظَرْفُ الْمَكَانِ)

ظَرْفُ الزَّمَانِ is a noun in the accusative case which tells the time when the action takes place, e.g.

The stars appear at night. تَظْهَرُ النُّجُوْمُ لَيْلًا۔

I went to school in the morning. ذَهَبْتُ إِلَى الْمَدْرَسَةِ صَبَاحًا۔

The heat is severe in summer. تَشْتَدُّ الْحَرَارَةُ صَيْفًا۔

ظَرْفُ الْمَكَانِ is a noun in accusative case which tells the place where the action takes place, e.g.

يَقَعُ الْبَيْتُ أَمَامَ الْمَسْجِدِ۔

The house is situated in front of the mosque.

وَضَعَ الطَّالِبُ الْكُرَّاسَةَ فَوْقَ الطَّاوِلَةِ۔

The student kept the copy book on the table.

اِسْتَرَاحَ الْمُسَافِرُ تَحْتَ الشَّجَرَةِ۔

The traveller took rest under the tree.

GLOSSARY
ENGLISH-ARABIC

A

accountant	مُحَاسِبٌ (مُحَاسِبُوْنَ)
acid	حَامِضٌ
acquainted with	مُطَّلِعٌ (عَلَى)
active	نَشِيْطٌ (نِشَاطٌ)
actor	مُمَثِّلٌ (مُمَثِّلُوْنَ)
adventure	مُغَامَرَةٌ (مُغَامَرَاتٌ)
aeroplane	طَائِرَةٌ (طَائِرَاتٌ)
affair	قَضِيَّةٌ (قَضَايَا)، أَمْرٌ (أُمُوْرٌ)
agent	وَكِيْلٌ (وُكَلَاءُ)
air	جَوٌّ (أَجْوَاءٌ)
air-hostess	مُضِيْفَةٌ (مُضِيْفَاتٌ)
allow	سَمَحَ - يَسْمَحُ - سَمَاحٌ (بِ، لِ)
ambassador	سَفِيْرٌ (سُفَرَاءُ)
angry	زَعْلَانٌ، غَاضِبٌ
annoyed	زَعْلَانٌ، ضَجِرٌ
anonymous	مَجْهُوْلٌ
ant	نَمْلٌ، نَمْلَةٌ
approach (time)	حَانَ - يَحِيْنُ - حَيْنٌ

apricot	مِشْمِش
armlet	سِوَارٌ (أَسْوِرَةٌ)
army	جَيْشٌ (جُيُوْشٌ)
arrange	رَتَّبَ - يُرَتِّبُ - تَرْتِيْبٌ
arrest	قَبَضَ - يَقْبِضُ - قَبْضٌ (عَلَى)
artist	رَسَّامٌ (رَسَّامُوْنَ) فَنَّانٌ (فَنَّانُوْنَ)
(be) ashamed	خَجِلَ - يَخْجَلُ - خَجَلٌ
ask	سَأَلَ - يَسْأَلُ - سُؤَالٌ
assistant	مُسَاعِدٌ (مُسَاعِدُوْنَ)
astonished	مَدْهُوْشٌ (مَدْهُوْشُوْنَ)
astrologer	مُنَجِّمٌ (مُنَجِّمُوْنَ)
athlete	رِيَاضِيٌّ (رِيَاضِيُّوْنَ)
Atlantic Ocean	الْمُحِيْطُ الأَطْلَسِي
atmosphere	جَوٌّ (أَجْوَاءٌ)
attack	هَجَمَ - يَهْجُمُ - هُجُوْمٌ
author	مُؤَلِّفٌ (مُؤَلِّفُوْنَ)
automatic	أُوْتُوْمَاتِيْكِي

B

bag	حَقِيْبَةٌ (حَقَائِبُ)

English	Arabic
bake	خَبَزَ - يَخْبِزُ - خَبْزٌ
(be) bald	صَلِعَ - يَصْلَعُ - صَلَعٌ
ball	كُرَةٌ (كُرَاتٌ)
bangle	سِوَارٌ (أَسْوِرَةٌ)
barber	حَلَّاقٌ (حَلَّاقُوْنَ)
basketball	كُرَةُ السَّلَّةِ
bat	مِضْرَابٌ
bear	قَاسَى - يُقَاسِي - مُقَاسَاةٌ
beat	ضَرَبَ - يَضْرِبُ - ضَرْبٌ
behave poorly	سَلَكَ بِغَيْرِ إِتْقَانٍ
bell	جَرَسٌ (أَجْرَاسٌ)
benefit	رَبِحَ - يَرْبَحُ - رِبْحٌ
betray	خَانَ - يَخُوْنُ - خِيَانَةٌ
bill	فَاتُوْرَةٌ (فَاتُوْرَاتٌ)
bird (young)	فَرْخٌ (أَفْرَاخٌ)
(become) black	إِسْوَدَّ - يَسْوَدُّ - اِسْوِدَادٌ
(be) beneficial	نَفَعَ - يَنْفَعُ - نَفْعٌ
blacksmith	حَدَّادٌ (حَدَّادُوْنَ)
blood	دَمٌ (دِمَاءٌ)

blooming	مُزْهِرٌ
boat	زَوْرَقٌ (زَوَارِقُ)
boil	غَلَى - يَغْلِي - غَلْيٌ
bomb	قُنْبُلَةٌ (قَنَابِلُ)
boss	مُدِيْرٌ (مُدَرَاءُ)
bottle (long necked)	قَارُوْرَةٌ (قَوَارِيْرُ)
bottle (glass bottle)	زُجَاجَةٌ (زُجَاجَاتٌ)
box	صُنْدُوْقٌ (صَنَادِيْقُ)
boy	غُلَامٌ (غِلْمَانٌ)
bracelet	سِوَارٌ (أَسْوِرَةٌ)
bread	خُبْزٌ (أَخْبَازٌ)
bread (flat loaf of bread)	رَغِيْفٌ (أَرْغِفَةٌ)
break	كَسَرَ - يَكْسِرُ - كَسْرٌ
break	اِنْكَسَرَ - يَنْكَسِرُ - اِنْكِسَارٌ
breakfast	فَطُوْرٌ
(be out of) breath	لَهَثَ - يَلْهَثُ - لَهْثٌ
bribe	رِشْوَةٌ
bride	عَرُوْسٌ (عَرَائِسُ)
bridge	جِسْرٌ (جُسُوْرٌ)

bucket	سَطْلٌ (سُطُوْلٌ)
buffalo	جَامُوْسٌ (جَوَامِيْسُ)
buffalo (she)	جَامُوْسَةٌ
building	بِنَاءٌ (أَبْنِيَةٌ)
bull	ثَوْرٌ (ثِيْرَانٌ)
bun	رَغِيْفٌ (أَرْغِفَةٌ)
bundle	حُزْمَةٌ (حُزَمٌ)
(do) business	اِتَّجَرَ - يَتَّجِرُ - اِتِّجَارٌ
butcher	جَزَّارٌ (جَزَّارُوْنَ) قَصَّابٌ (قَصَّابُوْنَ)
butterfly	فَرَاشَةٌ (فَرَاشَاتٌ)
buy	اِبْتَاعَ - يَبْتَاعُ - اِبْتِيَاعٌ

C

cake	كَعْكٌ، كَعْكَةٌ (كَعْكَاتٌ)
caliph	خَلِيْفَةٌ (خُلَفَاءُ)
(telephonic) call	مُكَالَمَةٌ (مُكَالَمَاتٌ)
calm	هَادِئٌ
card	بِطَاقَةٌ (بِطَاقَاتٌ)
careless	مُهْمِلٌ
carelessness	إِهْمَالٌ

carpenter	نَجَّارٌ (نَجَّارُونَ)
carpet	سَجَّادَةٌ (سَجَّادَاتٌ)
carry out	قَامَ - يَقُومُ - قِيَامٌ (بِ)
case	قَضِيَّةٌ (قَضَايَا)
cashier	صَرَّافٌ (صَرَّافُونَ)
castle	قَصْرٌ (قُصُورٌ)
cat	قِطَّةٌ (قِطَطٌ)
catch	اِصْطَادَ - يَصْطَادُ - اِصْطِيَادٌ
(cause to) cease	أَزَالَ - يُزِيلُ - إِزَالَةٌ
cereals	حَبٌّ (حُبُوبٌ)
certain	مُوقِنٌ (مُوقِنُونَ)
certificate	شَهَادَةٌ (شَهَادَاتٌ)
chairman	رَئِيسُ الْجَلْسَةِ
change	بَدَّلَ - يُبَدِّلُ - تَبْدِيلٌ
charity	صَدَقَةٌ (صَدَقَاتٌ)
chase	طَارَدَ - يُطَارِدُ - مُطَارَدَةٌ
chaste	عَفِيفٌ (أَعِفَّاءُ، أَعِفَّةٌ)
child	طِفْلٌ (أَطْفَالٌ)
children's garden	حَدِيقَةُ الْأَطْفَالِ

chirp	تَغَنَّى - يَتَغَنَّى - تَغَنٍّ
cigarette	سِيجَارَةٌ (سَجَائِرُ)
circular	مُسْتَدِيرَةٌ
citizen	مُوَاطِنٌ (مُوَاطِنُونَ)
clash	اِصْطَدَمَ - يَصْطَدِمُ - اِصْطِدَامٌ
class	حَلَقَةٌ دِرَاسِيَّةٌ
clean	نَظَّفَ - يُنَظِّفُ - تَنْظِيفٌ
(be) clean	طَهُرَ - يَطْهُرُ - طُهْرٌ، طَهَارَةٌ
clean	نَظِيفٌ
clever	شَاطِرٌ (شَاطِرُونَ)
climb	صَعِدَ - يَصْعَدُ - صُعُودٌ
cloak	رِدَاءٌ (أَرْدِيَةٌ)
cloth	قُمَاشٌ (أَقْمِشَةٌ)
clothe	كَسَا - يَكْسُو - كَسْوٌ
clown	مُهَرِّجٌ
coach	مُدَرِّبٌ (مُدَرِّبُونَ)
cobbler	إِسْكَافٌ، إِسْكَافِيٌّ (أَسَاكِفَةٌ)
coffee	قَهْوَةٌ
collect	جَمَعَ - يَجْمَعُ - جَمْعٌ

collide	اِصْطَدَمَ - يَصْطَدِمُ - اِصْطِدَامٌ
come	جَاءَ - يَجِيءُ - مَجِيْءٌ
	أَتَى - يَأْتِي - إِتْيَانٌ
come (here)!	تَعَالَ
command	أَمَرَ - يَأْمُرُ - أَمْرٌ
commander	قَائِدٌ (قُوَّادٌ)
commence	بَدَأَ - يَبْدَأُ - بَدْءٌ
compose poetry	قَرَضَ - يَقْرِضُ - قَرْضٌ
computer	حَاسُوْبٌ (حَوَاسِيْبُ)
conquer	فَتَحَ - يَفْتَحُ - فَتْحٌ
consider	حَسِبَ - يَحْسِبُ - حِسْبَانٌ
console	سَلَّى - يُسَلِّي - تَسْلِيَةٌ
consult (s.o.), (seek advice)	اِسْتَنْصَحَ - يَسْتَنْصِحُ - اِسْتِنْصَاحٌ
contractor	مُقَاوِلٌ (مُقَاوِلُوْنَ)
convinced	مُوْقِنٌ (مُوْقِنُوْنَ)
cook	طَبَخَ - يَطْبَخُ - طَبْخٌ
cooperation	تَعَاوُنٌ
cost	أُجْرَةٌ، ثَمَنٌ (أَثْمَانٌ)
costly	نَفِيْسٌ، ثَمِيْنٌ

cotton	قُطْنٌ
cover	غِطَاءٌ (أَغْطِيَةٌ) غِلَافٌ (غُلُفٌ)
cow	بَقَرَةٌ (بَقَرَاتٌ)
coward	جَبَانٌ (جُبَنَاءُ)
crawl	زَحَفَ - يَزْحَفُ - زَحْفٌ
crawling	دَبِيبَةٌ
create	خَلَقَ - يَخْلُقُ - خَلْقٌ
creep	زَحَفَ - يَزْحَفُ - زَحْفٌ
creeping	دَبِيبَةٌ
crocodile	تِمْسَاحٌ (تَمَاسِيْحُ)
cross	عَبَرَ - يَعْبُرُ - عُبُوْرٌ
crow	غُرَابٌ (غِرْبَانٌ)
cry	بَكَى - يَبْكِي - بُكَاءٌ
cultivate	زَرَعَ - يَزْرَعُ - زَرْعٌ
cure	شَفَى - يَشْفِي - شِفَاءٌ
curtain	سِتَارَةٌ (سَتَائِرُ)
cutting (sharp)	قَاطِعٌ

D

dais	مِنَصَّةٌ

dancer	رَقَّاصٌ (رَقَّاصُوْنَ)
date palm	نَخْلٌ، نَخِيْلٌ
deep	عَمِيْقٌ
delegation	وَفْدٌ (وُفُوْدٌ)
delicate	رَقِيْقٌ (رِقَاقٌ)
deliver a speech	أَدْلَى بِخِطَابٍ
deserve	اِسْتَحَقَّ - يَسْتَحِقُّ - اِسْتِحْقَاقٌ
design	صَمَّمَ - يُصَمِّمُ - تَصْمِيْمٌ
designer	مُصَمِّمٌ (مُصَمِّمُوْنَ)
destined	مَحْتُوْمٌ
diagnose a disease	شَخَّصَ - يُشَخِّصُ - تَشْخِيْصٌ
dictionary	قَامُوْسٌ (قَوَامِيْسُ)، مُعْجَمٌ (مَعَاجِمُ)
difficulty	ضِيْقٌ، صُعُوْبَةٌ
dig	حَفَرَ - يَحْفِرُ - حَفْرٌ
dinner	عَشَاءٌ
diplomat	دِبْلُوْمَاسِي
director	مُدِيْرٌ (مُدَرَاءُ)
disapprove	أَنْكَرَ - يُنْكِرُ - إِنْكَارٌ
dispatched	مُرْسَلٌ

distinction	اِمْتِيَازٌ
dive (into)	غَاصَ - يَغُوصُ - غَوْصٌ
doctor	طَبِيبٌ (أَطِبَّاءُ)
donkey	حِمَارٌ (حَمِيرٌ، حُمُرٌ)
doorman	بَوَّابٌ (بَوَّابُونَ)
dove	يَمَامَةٌ
drawer	دُرْجٌ (أَدْرَاجٌ)
drawing room	غُرْفَةُ الْاِسْتِقْبَالِ
dream	حُلْمٌ (أَحْلَامٌ)
drink	شَرِبَ - يَشْرَبُ - شُرْبٌ
drive (an automobile)	سَاقَ - يَسُوقُ - سِيَاقَةٌ
driver	سَائِقٌ (سَائِقُونَ)
drought	قَحْطٌ
during	خِلَالَ، أَثْنَاءَ
duty	وَاجِبٌ (وَاجِبَاتٌ)
dweller	سَاكِنٌ (سَاكِنُونَ)

E

eagle	عُقَابٌ (عِقْبَانٌ)
earth	أَرْضٌ (أَرَاضٍ)

eat	أَكَلَ - يَأْكُلُ - أَكْلٌ
e-mail	الْبَرِيدُ الإِلَكْتِرَوْنِي
embrace	ضَمَّ - يَضُمُّ - ضَمٌّ
encompass	أَحَاطَ - يُحِيطُ - إِحَاطَةٌ (بِ)
enemy	عَدُوٌّ (أَعْدَاءٌ)
engineer	مُهَنْدِسٌ (مُهَنْدِسُوْنَ)
England	انْجِلْتِرَا
enjoy	تَمَتَّعَ - يَتَمَتَّعُ - تَمَتُّعٌ (بِ)
escape	إِفْلَاتٌ
event	حَفْلَةٌ (حَفْلَاتٌ)
execute	قَامَ - يَقُوْمُ - قِيَامٌ (بِ)
execute (s.o.)	أَعْدَمَ - يُعْدِمُ - إِعْدَامٌ
exhibition	مَعْرِضٌ (مَعَارِضُ)
expert	خَبِيْرٌ (خُبَرَاءُ)
explain	أَوْضَحَ - يُوْضِحُ - إِيْضَاحٌ
explosion	انْفِجَارٌ (انْفِجَارَاتٌ)

F

fabric	قُمَاشٌ (أَقْمِشَةٌ)
face	وَاجَهَ - يُوَاجِهُ - مُوَاجَهَةٌ

factory	مَصْنَعٌ (مَصَانِعُ) مَعْمَلٌ (مَعَامِلُ)
fail	رَسَبَ - يَرْسُبُ - رُسُوبٌ
fair	مَعْرِضٌ (مَعَارِضُ)، عَادِلٌ (عَادِلُوْنَ)
falcon	صَقْرٌ (صُقُوْرٌ)
fall	هَوَى - يَهْوِي - هُوِيٌّ
family	عَائِلَةٌ (عَائِلَاتٌ)
farmer	مُزَارِعٌ (مُزَارِعُوْنَ)
(one who) fasts	صَائِمٌ (صَائِمُوْنَ)
fence	سُوْرٌ (أَسْوَارٌ)
fight	قَاتَلَ - يُقَاتِلُ - مُقَاتَلَةٌ
fighter	مُجَاهِدٌ (مُجَاهِدُوْنَ)
fill	مَلَا - يَمْلَأُ - مَلْءٌ
financial assistance	مَعُوْنَةٌ مَالِيَّةٌ
find	وَجَدَ - يَجِدُ - وِجْدَانٌ
fine	رَقِيْقٌ (رِقَاقٌ)
fire	أَطْلَقَ - يُطْلِقُ - إِطْلَاقٌ (النَّارَ)
fisherman	صَيَّادُ السَّمَكِ
flag	رَايَةٌ (رَايَاتٌ)
flash of lightning	بَرْقٌ (بُرُوْقٌ)

flee	فَرَّ - يَفِرُّ - فِرَارٌ
flour	دَقِيْقٌ
flow	جَرَى - يَجْرِي - جَرْيٌ
flower	زَهْرٌ (زُهُوْرٌ)
fog	ضَبَابٌ
food	طَعَامٌ (أَطْعِمَةٌ)
footpath	مَمَرُّ الْمُشَاةِ
forest	غَابَةٌ (غَابَاتٌ)
forget	نَسِيَ - يَنْسَى - نِسْيَانٌ
fork	شَوْكَةٌ (أَشْوَاكٌ)
(bring) forth	نَتَجَ - يَنْتِجُ - نِتَاجٌ
fountain pen	قَلَمُ الْحِبْرِ
fox	ثَعْلَبٌ (ثَعَالِبٌ)
free	مَجَّانِيٌّ
fruit	ثَمَرٌ (ثِمَارٌ)
fruit seller	فَاكِهَانِيٌّ
fry	قَلَى - يَقْلِيْ - قَلْيٌ

G

gain	رَبِحَ - يَرْبَحُ - رِبْحٌ

gambler	مُقَامِرٌ (مُقَامِرُوْنَ)
gardener	بُسْتَانِيٌّ
gather	جَمَعَ - يَجْمَعُ - جَمْعٌ
gazelle	غَزَالٌ (غِزْلَانٌ)
generation	جِيْلٌ (أَجْيَالٌ)
(be) generous	كَرُمَ - يَكْرُمُ - كَرَمٌ
Germany	أَلْمَانِيَا
get broken	اِنْكَسَرَ - يَنْكَسِرُ - اِنْكِسَارٌ
ghat (place for bathing and washing clothes in India)	الْغَاطُ
girth	حَزَمَ - يَحْزِمُ - حَزْمٌ
give	أَعْطَى - يُعْطِي - إِعْطَاءٌ
glass bottle	زُجَاجَةٌ (زُجَاجَاتٌ)
globe	كُرَةٌ (كُرَاتٌ)
go	ذَهَبَ - يَذْهَبُ - ذَهَابٌ
good	جَيِّدٌ
goose	إِوَزٌّ
governor	مُحَافِظٌ (مُحَافِظُوْنَ)
grab	أَخَذَ - يَأْخُذُ - أَخْذٌ

grains	حَبٌّ (حُبُوبٌ)
grand father	جَدٌّ (أَجْدَادٌ)
grant	مَنَحَ - يَمْنَحُ - مَنْحٌ
grapes	عِنَبٌ (أَعْنَابٌ)
grass	عُشْبٌ (أَعْشَابٌ)
grow	نَمَا - يَنْمُو - نُمُوٌّ
guard	خَفِيرٌ (خُفَرَاءُ)

H

hall		قَاعَةٌ (قَاعَاتٌ)
hand	fem.	يَدٌ (أَيْدٍ، أَيَادٍ)
happen		حَدَثَ - يَحْدُثُ - حُدُوثٌ
hawk		صَقْرٌ (صُقُورٌ)
hear		سَمِعَ - يَسْمَعُ - سَمْعٌ
heat		حَرٌّ
(be) heavy		ثَقُلَ - يَثْقُلُ - ثِقَلٌ
help		نَصَرَ - يَنْصُرُ - نَصْرٌ
historian		مُؤَرِّخٌ (مُؤَرِّخُونَ)
hit		ضَرَبَ - يَضْرِبُ - ضَرْبٌ
honest		أَمِينٌ (أُمَنَاءُ)، نَزِيهٌ (نُزَهَاءُ)

honouring	كَرَّمَ - يُكَرِّمُ - تَكْرِيمٌ
horse	حِصَانٌ (حُصُنٌ)
horse shoe	نَعْلٌ (نِعَالٌ)
hospital	مُسْتَشْفَى (مُسْتَشْفَيَاتٌ)
host	مُسْتَضِيفٌ (مُسْتَضِيفُونَ)
household things	الأَدَوَاتُ الْمَنْزِلِيَّةُ
hover	حَلَّقَ - يُحَلِّقُ - تَحْلِيقٌ
hungry	جَائِعٌ (جَائِعُونَ)
hunt	اِصْطَادَ - يَصْطَادُ - اِصْطِيَادٌ
hurry	هَرَعَ - يَهْرَعُ - هَرَعٌ
hut	كُوخٌ (أَكْوَاخٌ)
hyena	fem. ضَبُعٌ (ضِبَاعٌ)

I

ice	ثَلْجٌ (ثُلُوجٌ)
ice-cream	ايْسْكِرِيمُ
idle	كَسْلَانٌ (كُسَالَى)
inactive	كَسْلَانٌ (كُسَالَى)
incline	مَالَ - يَمِيْلُ - مَيْلٌ
inclining	مَائِلٌ (مَائِلُونَ)

inevitable	مَحْتُوْمٌ
inhabitant	سَاكِنٌ (سَاكِنُوْنَ)
injured	مُصَابٌ (مُصَابُوْنَ)
innocent	بَرِيْءٌ (أَبْرِيَاءُ)
insect	حَشَرَةٌ (حَشَرَاتٌ)
inspector	مُفَتِّشٌ (مُفَتِّشُوْنَ)
instruct	لَقَّنَ - يُلَقِّنُ - تَلْقِيْنٌ
interesting	مُمْتِعٌ
internet	إِنْتَرْنَت
ironsmith	حَدَّادٌ (حَدَّادُوْنَ)
irrigate	سَقَى - يَسْقِي - سَقْيٌ
irritated	ضَجِرٌ

J

jackal	ذِئْبٌ (ذِئَابٌ)
journalist	صُحُفِيٌّ (صُحُفِيُّوْنَ)
judge	قَاضٍ (قُضَاةٌ)
jug	إِبْرِيْقٌ (أَبَارِيْقُ)
juice	عَصِيْرٌ
just	عَادِلٌ

K

keep	ذَخَرَ - يَذْخَرُ - ذَخْرٌ
key	مِفْتَاحٌ (مَفَاتِيحُ)
kick	ضَرَبَ بِالْقَدَمِ
kill	قَتَلَ - يَقْتُلُ - قَتْلٌ
king	مَلِكٌ (مُلُوكٌ)
kiss	لَثَمَ - يَلْثِمُ - لَثْمٌ
kitchen	مَطْبَخٌ (مَطَابِخُ)
knead (flour)	عَجَنَ - يَعْجِنُ - عَجْنٌ
knock	طَرَقَ - يَطْرُقُ - طَرْقٌ

L

lamb	حَمَلٌ (حُمْلَانٌ)
lament	نَحَبَ - يَنْحَبُ - نَحْبٌ
large rat	جُرَذٌ (جِرْذَانٌ)
late	مُتَأَخِّرٌ (مُتَأَخِّرُونَ)
lawyer	مُحَامٍ (مُحَامُونَ)
lay	وَضَعَ - يَضَعُ - وَضْعٌ
lazy	كَسْلَانٌ (كُسَالَى)
(be) leafy	أَوْرَقَ - يُورِقُ - إِيْرَاقٌ

lean	مَالَ - يَمِيلُ - مَيْلٌ
lean	هَزِيلٌ (هَزْلَى)
learn by heart	حَفِظَ - يَحْفَظُ - حِفْظٌ
leave	غَادَرَ - يُغَادِرُ - مُغَادَرَةٌ
Lebanese	لُبْنَانِيٌّ
letter	خِطَابٌ (خِطَابَاتٌ)
(give) light (shine)	زَهَرَ - يَزْهَرُ - زُهُورٌ
light	خَفِيفٌ (خِفَافٌ)
lightning	بَرْقٌ (بُرُوقٌ)
lioness	لَبُؤَةٌ (لَبُؤَاتٌ)
listen	سَمِعَ - يَسْمَعُ - سَمْعٌ
lock	أَقْفَلَ - يُقْفِلُ - إِقْفَالٌ
(become) long	طَالَ - يَطُولُ - طُولٌ
long	طَوِيلٌ (طِوَالٌ)
lorry	شَاحِنَةٌ (شَاحِنَاتٌ)
lose	فَقَدَ - يَفْقِدُ - فُقْدَانٌ
love	أَحَبَّ يُحِبُّ إحْبَاباً

M

magazine	مَجَلَّةٌ (مَجَلَّاتٌ)

make	جَعَلَ - يَجْعَلُ - جَعْلٌ
	صَنَعَ - يَصْنَعُ - صَنْعٌ
male sheep	كَبْشٌ
man	رَجُلٌ (رِجَالٌ)
mark	عَلَامَةٌ (عَلَامَاتٌ)
marriage	زَوَاجٌ
matter	قَضِيَّةٌ (قَضَايَا)
(by) means of	عَنْ طَرِيق
medicine	دَوَاءٌ (أَدْوِيَةٌ)
meet	قَابَلَ - يُقَابِلُ - مُقَابَلَةٌ
melt	ذَابَ - يَذُوبُ - ذَوْبٌ، ذَوَبَانٌ
members of the family	أَعْضَاءُ الأُسْرَةِ
memorize	حَفِظَ - يَحْفَظُ - حِفْظٌ
merit	فَضِيلَةٌ (فَضَائِلُ)
middle class	الطَّبَقَةُ الْوُسْطَى
milk an animal	حَلَبَ - يَحْلِبُ - حَلْبٌ
miracle (esp. one performed by a prophet)	مُعْجِزَةٌ (مُعْجِزَاتٌ)
mirage	سَرَابٌ

mirror	مِرآةٌ (مَرَايَا)
miser	بَخِيلٌ (بُخَلاَءُ)
miserable	بَائِسٌ (بَائِسُونَ)
misguided	غَاوٍ (غَاوُونَ)
modest	عَفِيفٌ (أَعِفَّاءُ، أَعِفَّةٌ)، مُتَوَاضِعٌ
monument	عِمَارَةٌ (عِمَارَاتٌ)
mother	أُمٌّ (أَمَهَاتٌ)
mouse	فَأْرٌ (فِيْرَانٌ)
museum	مَتْحَفٌ (مَتَاحِفٌ)
music	مُوسِيقَى

N

narrow	ضَيِّقٌ
necklace	قِلاَدَةٌ (قَلاَئِدُ)
need	فَقْرٌ، عَوَزٌ
negligent	مُهْمِلٌ
neglectful	مُهْمِلٌ
nest	عُشٌّ (أَعْشَاشٌ)
net	شَبَكَةٌ (شَبَكَاتٌ)
new	جَدِيدٌ (جُدَدٌ)

nightingale	هَزَارٌ (هَزَارَاتٌ) عَنْدَلِيْبُ (عَنَادِلُ)
Nobel Prize	جَائِزَةُ نُوْبِل
(be) noble	كَرُمَ - يَكْرُمُ - كَرَمٌ، كَرَامَةٌ
noble	شَرِيْفٌ (شُرَفَاءُ، أَشْرَافٌ)
novel	رِوَايَةٌ (رِوَايَاتٌ)
nurse (male)	مُمَرِّضٌ (مُمَرِّضُوْنَ)
nurse (female)	مُمَرِّضَةٌ (مُمَرِّضَاتٌ)
nursery school	حَضَانَةٌ (حَضَانَاتٌ)

O

obedient	مُطِيْعٌ (مُطِيْعُوْنَ)
obligation	وَاجِبٌ (وَاجِبَاتٌ)
occur	حَدَثَ - يَحْدُثُ - حُدُوْثٌ
offer	قَدَّمَ - يُقَدِّمُ - تَقْدِيْمٌ
official	رَسْمِيٌّ
official authorized by the Qadi to perform civil marriages	الْمَأْذُوْنُ الشَّرْعِيُّ
old	قَدِيْمٌ (قُدَمَاءُ)
old monuments	الْآثَارُ الْقَدِيْمَةُ

open	فَتَحَ - يَفْتَحُ - فَتْحٌ
opera	أُوبِيرَا
oppress	ظَلَمَ - يَظْلِمُ - ظُلْمٌ
orange	بُرْتُقَالٌ
order	أَمَرَ - يَأْمُرُ - أَمْرٌ
order	أَمْرٌ (أَوَامِرُ)
ornament	حِلْيَةٌ (حِلًى)
other	آخَرُ (آخَرُوْنَ)

P

(house) painter	دَهَّانٌ (دَهَّانُوْنَ)
painting	رَسْمٌ (رُسُوْمٌ، رُسُوْمَاتٌ)
Palestine	فِلَسْطِيْنُ
pant	لَهَثَ - يَلْهَثُ - لَهْثٌ
paragraph	فِقْرَةٌ (فِقْرَاتٌ)
parcel	طَرْدٌ (طُرُوْدٌ)
particular	خَاصٌّ
party	حِزْبٌ (أَحْزَابٌ)
pass	مَضَى - يَمْضِي - مُضِيٌّ
passage	فِقْرَةٌ (فِقْرَاتٌ)

passenger	مُسَافِرٌ (مُسَافِرُونَ)
passport	جَوَازٌ (جَوَازَاتٌ)
pastry	فَطِيرٌ
paternal uncle	عَمٌّ (أَعْمَامٌ)
path	سَبِيلٌ (سُبُلٌ)
pay	دَفَعَ - يَدْفَعُ - دَفْعٌ
pay	رَاتِبٌ (رَوَاتِبُ)
pay in cash	نَقَدَ - يَنْقُدُ - نَقْدٌ
peaceful	هَادِئٌ
photographer	مُصَوِّرٌ (مُصَوِّرُونَ)
(take) a picture	اِلْتَقَطَ - يَلْتَقِطُ - اِلْتِقَاطٌ (صُوْرَةً)
pillow	وِسَادَةٌ (وِسَادَاتٌ)
pilot	طَيَّارٌ (طَيَّارُونَ)
place	يَضَعُ - وَضْعٌ
plain	سَاذِجٌ (سُذَّجٌ)
plant	زَرَعَ - يَزْرَعُ - زَرْعٌ
play (absent mindedly)	عَبِثَ - يَعْبَثُ - عَبَثٌ
pleasant	هَنِيئٌ
pleasing	مُرْضٍ

plumber	سَبَّاكٌ (سَبَّاكُونَ)
potato	بَطَاطِسُ
poverty	ضِيْقٌ
poverty	فَقْرٌ
precious	نَفِيْسٌ، ثَمِيْنٌ
(be) prepared	تَجَهَّزَ - يَتَجَهَّزُ - تَجَهُّزٌ
preserve	ذَخَرَ - يَذْخَرُ - ذَخْرٌ
president	رَئِيْسُ الْجَلْسَةِ
price	أُجْرَةٌ، ثَمَنٌ
priest	كَاهِنٌ (كُهَّانٌ)
prince	أَمِيْرٌ (أُمَرَاءُ)
princess	أَمِيْرَةٌ (أَمِيْرَاتٌ)
principle	مَبْدَأٌ (مَبَادِئُ)
principal of the school	نَاظِرُ الْمَدْرَسَةِ
prize	جَائِزَةٌ (جَوَائِزُ)
profit	رَبِحَ - يَرْبَحُ - رِبْحٌ
profound	عَمِيْقٌ
project	مَشْرُوْعٌ (مَشَارِيْعُ)
prolific	مِكْثَارٌ

protect	حَفِظَ - يَحْفَظُ - حِفْظٌ
pull	جَرَّ - يَجُرُّ - جَرٌّ
purchase	اِبْتَاعَ - يَبْتَاعُ - اِبْتِيَاعٌ
(be) pure	طَهُرَ - يَطْهُرُ - طُهْرٌ
	رَاقَ - يَرُوقُ - رَوْقٌ
push	دَفَعَ - يَدْفَعُ - دَفْعٌ
put	وَضَعَ - يَضَعُ - وَضْعٌ

<h1 style="text-align:center">R</h1>

rabbit	fem.	أَرْنَبٌ (أَرَانِبُ)
race		عدَا - يَعْدُو - عَدْوٌ
racket		مِضْرَابٌ
radio set		مِذْيَاعٌ (مَذَايِيْعُ)
rain		مَطَرٌ (أَمْطَارٌ)
reach		وَصَلَ - يَصِلُ - وُصُوْلٌ
(get) ready		تَجَهَّزَ - يَتَجَهَّزُ - تَجَهُّزٌ
receive		اِسْتَلَمَ - يَسْتَلِمُ - اِسْتِلَامٌ
receptionist (lady)		مُوَظَّفَةُ الاِسْتِقْبَالِ
reception room		غُرْفَةُ الاِسْتِقْبَال
(turn) red		اِحْمَرَّ - يَحْمَرُّ - اِحْمِرَارٌ

red	أَحْمَرُ (حُمْرٌ)
refrigerator	ثَلَّاجَةٌ (ثَلَّاجَاتٌ)
refuse	أَنْكَرَ - يُنْكِرُ - إِنْكَارٌ
regard	حَسِبَ - يَحْسِبُ - حِسْبَانٌ
reliable	أَمِيْنٌ (أُمَنَاءُ)
relief	فَرَجٌ
remain	بَقِيَ - يَبْقَى - بَقَاءٌ
remove	أَزَالَ - يُزِيْلُ - إِزَالَةٌ
renewed	مُجَدَّدٌ
renounce pleasure	زَهَدَ - يَزْهَدُ - زُهْدٌ
rent	أُجْرَةٌ
replace	بَدَّلَ - يُبَدِّلُ - تَبْدِيْلٌ
repute	صِيْتٌ
(take) rest	اِسْتَرَاحَ - يَسْتَرِيْحُ - اِسْتِرَاحَةٌ
result	نَتَجَ - يَنْتِجُ - نِتَاجٌ
rickshaw puller	سَائِقُ الْعَرَبَةِ الْهَوَائِيَّةِ
rise	نَهَضَ - يَنْهَضُ - نُهُوْضٌ
	أَشْرَقَ - يُشْرِقُ - إِشْرَاقٌ
risk	مُغَامَرَةٌ (مُغَامَرَاتٌ)

river	نَهْرٌ (أَنْهَارٌ)
road	سَبِيلٌ (سُبُلٌ)، طَرِيقٌ (طُرُقٌ)
roam	جَالَ - يَجُولُ - جَوْلٌ
robber	لِصٌّ (لُصُوصٌ)
room	حُجْرَةٌ (حُجُرَاتٌ)
rosary	سُبْحَةٌ (سُبُحَاتٌ)
round	مُسْتَدِيرَةٌ
routine work	الْعَمَلُ الرَّتِيبُ
rude	فَظٌّ (أَفْظَاظٌ)
ruler	حَاكِمٌ (حُكَّامٌ، حَاكِمُوْنَ)
run	عَدَا - يَعْدُو - عَدْوٌ
rusty	صَدِئٌ

S

sack	جِرَابٌ (أَجْرِبَةٌ، جُرُبٌ)
safe	خِزَانَةٌ (خَزَائِنُ)
sail (set sail)	أَقْلَعَ - يُقْلِعُ - إِقْلَاعٌ
sailor	مَلَّاحٌ، بَحَّارٌ (بَحَّارُوْنَ)
salary	رَاتِبٌ (رَوَاتِبُ)
salesman	بَائِعٌ (بَائِعُوْنَ)

satisfactory	مُرْضٍ
save	ذَخَرَ - يَذْخَرُ - ذَخْرٌ
say	قَالَ - يَقُوْلُ - قَوْلٌ
scholarship	مِنْحَةٌ دِرَاسِيَّةٌ
search	بَحَثَ - يَبْحَثُ - بَحْثٌ (عن)
sea-shore	سَاحِلُ الْبَحْرِ
see	رَأَى - يَرَى - رُؤْيَةٌ
seize	قَبَضَ - يَقْبِضُ - قَبْضٌ (عَلَى)
sell	بَاعَ - يَبِيْعُ - بَيْعٌ
serve	قَدَّمَ - يُقَدِّمُ - تَقْدِيْمٌ
severe	شَدِيْدٌ
shed (tears)	ذَرَفَ - يَذْرِفُ - ذَرْفٌ
sheep (male)	كَبْشٌ
sheep	غَنَمٌ (أَغْنَامٌ)
shelf	رَفٌّ (رُفُوْفٌ)
shepherd	رَاعٍ (رُعَاةٌ)
shine	زَهَرَ - يَزْهَرُ - زُهُوْرٌ
ship	سَفِيْنَةٌ (سُفُنٌ)
shoe	حِذَاءٌ (أَحْذِيَةٌ)، نَعْلٌ (نِعَالٌ)

shoot	فَرْخٌ (أَفْرَاخٌ)
shoot at	أَطْلَقَ - يُطْلِقُ - إِطْلَاقٌ
short	قَصِيرٌ (قِصَارٌ)
show mercy	رَأَفَ - يَرْأَفُ - رَأْفَةٌ (بِ)
sick	مَرِيْضٌ (مَرْضَى)
silken	حَرِيْرِيٌّ
simple	سَاذَجٌ - سَاذِجٌ (سُذَّجٌ)
sincerity	صِدْقٌ، خُلُوْصٌ
singer	مُغَنٍّ (مُغَنُّوْنَ)
sinner	مُذْنِبٌ (مُذْنِبُوْنَ)
sketch	رَسْمٌ (رُسُوْمٌ، رُسُوْمَاتٌ)
skinny	هَزِيْلٌ (هَزْلَى)
sky	سَمَاءٌ
slow	بَطِيْئٌ (بِطَاءٌ، بَطِيْئُوْنَ)
slowly	بِبُطْءٍ
smart	نَبِيْهٌ (نُبَهَاءُ)، ذَكِيٌّ (أَذْكِيَاءُ)
smile	اِبْتِسَامَةٌ
snake	أَفْعَى (أَفَاعٍ)
snatch	خَطَفَ - يَخْطِفُ - خَطْفٌ

sneeze	عَطَسَ - يَعْطِسُ - عَطْسٌ
snow	ثَلْجٌ (ثُلُوجٌ)
soap	صَابُونٌ (صَابُونَاتٌ)
society	مُجْتَمَعٌ (مُجْتَمَعَاتٌ)
sock	جَوْرَبٌ (جَوَارِبُ)
sofa	أَرِيكَةٌ (أَرَائِكُ)
soft	نَاعِمٌ
soldier	جُنْدِيٌّ (جُنُودٌ)
song	أُنْشُودَةٌ (أَنَاشِيدُ)
sour	حَامِضٌ
sow	زَرَعَ - يَزْرَعُ - زَرْعٌ
sparrow	عُصْفُورٌ (عَصَافِيرُ)
speak	تَكَلَّمَ - يَتَكَلَّمُ - تَكَلُّمٌ
spearhead	سِنَانٌ (أَسِنَّةٌ)
special	خَاصٌّ
(deliver) speech	أَدْلَى بِخِطَابٍ
spinster	عَانِسٌ (عَوَانِسُ)
sponsor	كَفَلَ - يَكْفُلُ - كَفَالَةٌ
spoon	مِلْعَقَةٌ (مَلَاعِقُ)

spy	جَاسُوسٌ (جَوَاسِيسُ)
squeeze	عَصَرَ - يَعْصِرُ - عَصْرٌ
stand	وَقَفَ - يَقِفُ - وُقُوفٌ
star	نَجْمٌ (نُجُومٌ)، كَوْكَبٌ (كَوَاكِبُ)
station	مَحَطَّةٌ (مَحَطَّاتٌ)
stay	بَقِيَ - يَبْقَى - بَقَاءٌ مَكَثَ - يَمْكُثُ - مُكُوثٌ
stethoscope	سَمَّاعَةٌ
stick	عَصًا (عِصِيٌّ)
stocking	جَوْرَبٌ (جَوَارِبُ)
stop	أَوْقَفَ - يُوقِفُ - إِيْقَافٌ
strike	ضَرَبَ - يَضْرِبُ - ضَرْبٌ
string	سِلْكٌ (أَسْلَاكٌ)
suffer	قَاسَى - يُقَاسِي - مُقَاسَاةٌ
sugar	سُكَّرٌ
supervisor	مُرَاقِبٌ (مُرَاقِبُونَ)
support	أَيَّدَ - يُؤَيِّدُ - تَأْيِيدٌ
sure	مُوقِنٌ (مُوقِنُونَ)
surprised	مَدْهُوشٌ (مَدْهُوشُونَ)

surround	أَحَاطَ - يَحِيْطُ - إِحَاطَةٌ (بِ)
surrounded	مَحْفُوْفَةٌ
swell	وَرِمَ - يَرِمُ - وَرَمٌ
switch on	شَغَّلَ - يُشَغِّلُ - تَشْغِيْلٌ
sword	سَيْفٌ (سُيُوْفٌ)

T

tailor	خَيَّاطٌ (خَيَّاطُوْنَ)
take	أَخَذَ - يَأْخُذُ - أَخْذٌ
take (a picture)	اِلْتَقَطَ - يَلْتَقِطُ - اِلْتِقَاطٌ (صُوْرَةً)
take place	حَدَثَ - يَحْدُثُ - حُدُوْثٌ
take rest	اِسْتِرَاحَ - يَسْتَرِيْحُ - اِسْتِرَاحَةٌ
teach	عَلَّمَ - يُعَلِّمُ - تَعْلِيْمٌ
tear	مَزَّقَ - يُمَزِّقُ - تَمْزِيْقٌ
technician	فَنِّيٌّ (فَنِّيُوْنَ)
Tehran (the capital of Iran)	طَهْرَانُ
telephone	هَاتِفٌ (هَوَاتِفُ)
tell	حَكَى - يَحْكِي - حِكَايَةٌ
testimonial	شَهَادَةٌ (شَهَادَاتٌ)
(become) thick	غَلُظَ - يَغْلُظُ - غِلَظٌ

thief	سَارِقٌ (سَرَقَةٌ، سَارِقُوْنَ)
thin	خَفِيْفٌ (خِفَافٌ)
think	حَسِبَ - يَحْسِبُ - حِسْبَانٌ
through	عَنْ طَرِيْقٍ
throughout	طِوَالَ، طِيْلَةَ
throw	رَمَى - يَرْمِي - رَمْيٌ
ticket	تَذْكِرَةٌ (تَذَاكِرُ)
tiger	نَمِرٌ (نُمُرٌ)
tight	ضَيِّقٌ
time	وَقْتٌ (أَوْقَاتٌ)
(become) tired	تَعِبَ - يَتْعَبُ - تَعَبٌ
tired	تَعْبَانٌ (تَعْبَانُوْنَ)
torn	مُمَزَّقٌ
tower	بُرْجٌ (بُرُوْجٌ، أَبْرَاجٌ)
trade	اِتَّجَرَ - يَتَّجِرُ - اِتِّجَارٌ
tradition	تَقْلِيْدٌ (تَقَالِيْدُ)
train	قِطَارٌ (قُطُرٌ)
(be) trained	تَدَرَّبَ - يَتَدَرَّبُ - تَدَرُّبٌ
trainer	مُدَرِّبٌ (مُدَرِّبُوْنَ)

tram	تِرَام
translate	تَرْجَمَ - يُتَرْجِمُ - تَرْجَمَةً
translator	مُتَرْجِمٌ (مُتَرْجِمُونَ)
travel	سَافَرَ - يُسَافِرُ - مُسَافَرَةٌ
traveller	مُسَافِرٌ (مُسَافِرُونَ)
travelling bag	جِرَابٌ (أَجْرِبَةٌ، جُرُبٌ)
tribute	كَرَّمَ - يُكَرِّمُ - تَكْرِيمٌ
troops	جَيْشٌ (جُيُوشٌ)
truck	شَاحِنَةٌ (شَاحِنَاتٌ)
trustworthy	أَمِينٌ (أُمَنَاءُ)
truth	صِدْقٌ
turn red	اِحْمَرَّ - يَحْمَرُّ - اِحْمِرَارٌ
typewriter	آلَةُ الْكِتَابَةِ (آلَاتُ الْكِتَابَةِ)

U

ugly	بَشِعٌ
umbrella	مِظَلَّةٌ (مِظَلَّاتٌ)
uniform	زِيٌّ (أَزْيَاءُ)
unknown	مَجْهُولٌ
useless	عَدِيمُ الْفَائِدَةِ

useless talk	الْكَلَامُ الْفَارِغُ
(be) upset	قَلِقَ - يَقْلَقُ - قَلَقٌ
(be of) use	نَفَعَ - يَنْفَعُ - نَفْعٌ

V

valuable	نَفِيسٌ
value	ثَمَنٌ (أَثْمَانٌ)
village	قَرْيَةٌ (قُرَى)
viper	أَفْعَى (أَفَاعٍ)
virtue	فَضِيلَةٌ (فَضَائِلُ)
volcano	بُرْكَانٌ (بَرَاكِينُ)
vowelize	ضَبَطَ - يَضْبِطُ - ضَبْطٌ (الْكَلِمَةَ)

W

wage	أَجْرٌ (أُجُورٌ)
wail	نَحَبَ - يَنْحَبُ - نَحْبٌ
waiter	نَادِلٌ (نُدُلٌ)
walk	مَشَى - يَمْشِي - مَشْيٌ
wall	سُورٌ (أَسْوَارٌ)، حَائِطٌ (حِيطَانٌ)
wander about	جَالَ - يَجُولُ - جَوْلٌ
wash	غَسَلَ - يَغْسِلُ - غَسْلٌ

washerman	غَسَّالٌ (غَسَّالُونَ)
washing machine	غَسَّالَةٌ (غَسَّالاَتٌ)
washing soda	صُوْدَا الْغَسِيْلِ
watchman	خَفِيْرٌ (خُفَرَاءُ)
way	سَبِيْلٌ (سُبُلٌ)
wear	لَبِسَ - يَلْبَسُ - لُبْسٌ
weather	جَوٌّ (أَجْوَاءٌ)
wedding	زَوَاجٌ
weep	نَحَبَ - يَنْحَبُ - نَحْبٌ
welfare	رَفَاهِيَّةٌ
well	بِئْرٌ (آبَارٌ)
(become) wet	اِبْتَلَّ - يَبْتَلُّ - اِبْتِلاَلٌ
wet	مُبَلَّلٌ، مُبْتَلَّةٌ
whistle	صَفَّارَةٌ (صَفَّارَاتٌ)
whistle	صَفَرَ - يَصْفِرُ - صَفِيْرٌ
wing	جَنَاحٌ (أَجْنِحَةٌ)
winter	شِتَاءٌ
wipe off	مَحَا - يَمْحُو - مَحْوٌ
wire	سِلْكٌ (أَسْلاَكٌ)

wolf	ذِئْبٌ (ذِئَابٌ)
woollen	صُوفِيٌّ
work	عَمِلَ - يَعْمَلُ - عَمَلٌ
worker	عَامِلٌ (عُمَّالٌ)
worship	عَبَدَ - يَعْبُدُ - عِبَادَةٌ
wound (v)	جَرَحَ - يَجْرَحُ - جَرْحٌ
wound (n)	جُرْحٌ (جِرَاحٌ، جُرُوحٌ)
wrap	غِلَافٌ (غُلُفٌ)
wrapper	غِلَافٌ (غُلُفٌ)
wrestler	مُصَارِعٌ (مُصَارِعُوْنَ)
wretched	بَائِسٌ (بَائِسُوْنَ)
write	كَتَبَ - يَكْتُبُ - كِتَابَةٌ

X

x-ray	أَشِعَّةٌ سِيْنِيَّةٌ

Y

year	سَنَةٌ (سَنَوَاتٌ)

Z

zoological garden	حَدِيْقَةُ الْحَيَوَانَاتِ

GLOSSARY
ARABIC-ENGLISH

buy, purchase		اِبْتَاعَ - يَبْتَاعُ - اِبْتِيَاعٌ
smile		اِبْتِسَامٌ
become wet		اِبْتَلَّ - يَبْتَلُّ - اِبْتِلَالٌ
jug		إِبْرِيقٌ (أَبَارِيقُ)
trade, do business		اِتَّجَرَ - يَتَّجِرُ - اِتِّجَارٌ
come		أَتَى - يَأْتِي - اِتْيَانٌ
the old monuments		الْآثَارُ الْقَدِيمَةُ
wage		أَجْرٌ (أُجُورٌ)
rent; price		أُجْرَةٌ
surround, encompass		أَحَاطَ - يُحِيطُ - إِحَاطَةٌ (بِ)
red		أَحْمَرُ (حُمْرٌ)
red	fem.	حَمْرَاءُ (حُمْرٌ)
turn red		اِحْمَرَّ - يَحْمَرُّ - اِحْمِرَارٌ
take		أَخَذَ - يَأْخُذُ - أَخْذٌ
other		آخَرُ (آخَرُونَ)
deliver a speech		أَدْلَى بِخِطَابٍ
household things		الْأَدَوَاتُ الْمَنْزِلِيَّةُ
earth	fem.	أَرْضٌ (أَرَاضٍ)
rabbit	fem.	أَرْنَبٌ (أَرَانِبُ)

sofa	أَرِيكَةٌ (أَرَائِكُ)
cause to cease, stop, remove	أَزَالَ - يُزِيلُ - إِزَالَةٌ
deserve	اِسْتَحَقَّ - يَسْتَحِقُّ - اِسْتِحْقَاقٌ
take rest	اِسْتَرَاحَ - يَسْتَرِيحُ - اِسْتِرَاحَةٌ
receive	اِسْتَلَمَ - يَسْتَلِمُ - اِسْتِلَامٌ
consult (s.o.), seek advice	اِسْتَنْصَحَ - يَسْتَنْصِحُ - اِسْتِنْصَاحٌ
cobbler	إِسْكَافٌ، إِسْكَافِيٌّ (أَسَاكِفَةٌ)
become black	اِسْوَدَّ - يَسْوَدُّ - اِسْوِدَادٌ
saw	أَشَرَ - يَأْشُرُ - أَشْرٌ
rise	أَشْرَقَ - يُشْرِقُ - إِشْرَاقٌ
x-ray	أَشِعَّةٌ سِينِيَّةٌ
catch, hunt	اِصْطَادَ - يَصْطَادُ - اِصْطِيَادٌ
collide, clash, hit	اِصْطَدَمَ - يَصْطَدِمُ - اِصْطِدَامٌ
fire, to shoot at	أَطْلَقَ - يُطْلِقُ - إِطْلَاقٌ (النَّارَ)
execute (s.o)	أَعْدَمَ - يُعْدِمُ - إِعْدَامٌ
members of the family	أَعْضَاءُ الْأُسْرَةِ
viper, snake	أَفْعَى (أَفَاعٍ)
escape	إِفْلَاتٌ
lock, shut	أَقْفَلَ - يُقْفِلُ - إِقْفَالٌ
sail (set sail)	أَقْلَعَ - يُقْلِعُ - إِقْلَاعٌ

eat	أَكَلَ - يَأْكُلُ - أَكْلٌ
typewriter	آلَةُ الْكِتَابَةِ (آلَاتُ الْكِتَابَةِ)
take a picture	اِلْتَقَطَ - يَلْتَقِطُ - اِلْتِقَاطٌ (صُوْرَةً)
put, throw	أَلْقَى - يُلْقِي - إِلْقَاءٌ
Germany	أَلْمَانِيَا
mother	أُمٌّ (أُمَّهَاتٌ)
order, command	أَمَرَ - يَأْمُرُ - أَمْرٌ
matter	أَمْرٌ (أُمُوْرٌ)
order	أَمْرٌ (أَوَامِرُ)
prince	أَمِيْرٌ (أُمَرَاءُ)
princess	أَمِيْرَةٌ (أَمِيْرَاتٌ)
honest, reliable, trustworthy	أَمِيْنٌ (أُمَنَاءُ)
internet	إِنْتَرْنَتْ
England	إِنْجِلْتَرَا
song	أُنْشُوْدَةٌ (أَنَاشِيْدُ)
explosion	اِنْفِجَارٌ (اِنْفِجَارَاتٌ)
refuse, disapprove	أَنْكَرَ - يُنْكِرُ - إِنْكَارٌ
break, get broken	اِنْكَسَرَ - يَنْكَسِرُ - اِنْكِسَارٌ
carelessness	إِهْمَالٌ
opera	أُوْبِيْرَا

automatic	أُوتُومَاتِيكِي
be leafy (tree)	أَوْرَقَ - يُورِقُ - إِيرَاقٌ
goose	إِوَزٌّ
explain	أَوْضَحَ - يُوضِحُ - إِيضَاحٌ
support	أَيَّدَ - يُؤَيِّدُ - تَأْيِيدٌ
ice-cream	ايْسْكِرِيم

ب

well	بِئْرٌ (آبَارٌ)
with distinction	بِالِامْتِيَازِ
wretched, miserable	بَائِسٌ (بَائِسُونَ)
salesman	بَائِعٌ (بَائِعُونَ)
sell	بَاعَ - يَبِيعُ - بَيْعٌ
slowly	بِبُطْءٍ
sailor	بَحَّارٌ (بَحَّارُونَ)
search	بَحَثَ - يَبْحَثُ - بَحْثٌ (عَنْ)
miser	بَخِيلٌ (بُخَلَاءُ)
commence	بَدَأَ - يَبْدَأُ - بَدْءٌ
change, replace	بَدَّلَ - يُبَدِّلُ - تَبْدِيلٌ
orange	بُرْتُقَالٌ
tower; castle	بُرْجٌ (بُرُوجٌ، أَبْرَاجٌ)

lightning, flash of lightning	بَرْقٌ (بُرُوْقٌ)
volcano	بُرْكَانٌ (بَرَاكِيْنُ)
innocent	بَرِيْءٌ (أَبْرِيَاءُ)
e-mail	الْبَرِيدُ الْإِلَكْتِرُوْنِي
gardener	بُسْتَانِيٌّ
ugly	بَشِعٌ
potato	بَطَاطِسُ
card	بِطَاقَةٌ (بِطَاقَاتٌ)
slow	بَطِيْءٌ (بِطَاءٌ، بَطِيْئُوْنَ)
cow	بَقَرَةٌ (بَقَرَاتٌ)
remain, stay	بَقِيَ - يَبْقَى - بَقَاءٌ
cry	بَكَى - يَبْكِي - بُكَاءٌ
building	بِنَاءٌ (أَبْنِيَةٌ)
doorman	بَوَّابٌ (بَوَّابُوْنَ)

ت

be ready, be prepared	تَجَهَّزَ - يَتَجَهَّزُ - تَجَهُّزٌ
be trained	تَدَرَّبَ - يَتَدَرَّبُ - تَدَرُّبٌ
ticket	تَذْكِرَةٌ (تَذَاكِرُ)
tram	تِرَام
translate	تَرْجَمَ - يُتَرْجِمُ - تَرْجَمَةٌ

come (here)!	تَعَالَ
cooperation	تَعَاوُنٌ
be or become tired	تَعِبَ - يَتْعَبُ - تَعَبٌ
tired	تَعْبَانٌ (تَعْبَانُونَ)
chirp, sing	تَغَنَّى - يَتَغَنَّى - تَغَنٍّ
custom, tradition	تَقْلِيْدٌ (تَقَالِيْدُ)
enjoy	تَمَتَّعَ - يَتَمَتَّعُ - تَمَتُّعٌ (بِ)
crocodile	تِمْسَاحٌ (تَمَاسِيْحُ)

ث

fox	ثَعْلَبٌ (ثَعَالِبُ)
be heavy	ثَقُلَ - يَثْقُلُ - ثِقَلٌ
refrigerator	ثَلَّاجَةٌ (ثَلَّاجَاتٌ)
snow, ice	ثَلْجٌ (ثُلُوجٌ)
fruit	ثَمَرٌ (ثِمَارٌ)
price, cost; value	ثَمَنٌ (أَثْمَانٌ)
bull	ثَوْرٌ (ثِيْرَانٌ)

ج

come	جَاءَ - يَجِيْءُ - مَجِيْئٌ
spy	جَاسُوْسٌ (جَوَاسِيْسُ)
roam, wander about	جَالَ - يَجُوْلُ - جَوْلٌ

buffalo	جَامُوسٌ (جَوَامِيْسُ)
she buffalo	جَامُوسَةٌ
prize	جَائِزَةٌ (جَوَائِزُ)
Nobel Prize	جَائِزَةُ نُوْبِل
hungry	جَائِعٌ (جَائِعُوْنَ)
coward	جَبَانٌ (جَبَانُوْنَ)
grandfather	جَدٌّ (أَجْدَادٌ)
new	جَدِيْدٌ (جُدُدٌ)
sack, bag, travelling bag	جِرَابٌ (أَجْرِبَةٌ، جُرُبٌ)
pull	جَرَّ - يَجُرُّ - جَرٌّ
wound	جَرَحَ - يَجْرَحُ - جَرْحٌ
wound	جُرْحٌ (جِرَاحٌ، جُرُوْحٌ)
large rat	جُرَذٌ (جِرْذَانٌ)
bell	جَرَسٌ (أَجْرَاسٌ)
flow, run	جَرَى - يَجْرِي - جَرْيٌ
butcher	جَزَّارٌ (جَزَّارُوْنَ)
bridge	جِسْرٌ (جُسُوْرٌ)
gather, collect	جَمَعَ - يَجْمَعُ - جَمْعٌ
wing	جَنَاحٌ (أَجْنِحَةٌ)
soldier	جُنْدِيٌّ (جُنُوْدٌ)

weather, air, atmosphere	جَوٌّ (أَجْوَاءٌ)
passport	جَوَازٌ (جَوَازَاتٌ)
stocking; sock	جَوْرَبٌ (جَوَارِبُ)
army, troops	جَيْشٌ (جُيُوشٌ)
generation	جِيلٌ (أَجْيَالٌ)

ح

computer	حَاسُوبٌ (حَوَاسِيْبُ)
ruler	حَاكِمٌ (حُكَّامٌ، حَاكِمُوْنَ)
sour	حَامِضٌ
approach (time)	حَانَ - يَحِيْنُ - حَيْنٌ
grains, cereals	حَبٌّ (حُبُوْبٌ)
room	حُجْرَةٌ (حُجُرَاتٌ)
ironsmith, blacksmith	حَدَّادٌ (حَدَّادُوْنَ)
happen, occur, take place	حَدَثَ - يَحْدُثُ - حُدُوْثٌ
children's garden	حَدِيْقَةُ الْأَطْفَالِ
zoological garden	حَدِيْقَةُ الْحَيَوَانَاتِ
shoe	حِذَاءٌ (أَحْذِيَةٌ)
heat	حَرٌّ
silken	حَرِيْرِيٌّ
party (political)	حِزْبٌ (أَحْزَابٌ)

girth	حَزَمَ - يَحْزِمُ - حَزْمٌ
bundle	حُزْمَةٌ (حُزَمٌ)
think, consider	حَسِبَ - يَحْسِبُ - حِسْبَانٌ
insect	حَشَرَةٌ (حَشَرَاتٌ)
horse	حِصَانٌ (حُصُنٌ)
nursery school	حَضَانَةٌ (حَضَانَاتٌ)
to dig	حَفَرَ - يَحْفِرُ - حَفْرٌ
protect; learn by heart	حَفِظَ - يَحْفَظُ - حِفْظٌ
event	حَفْلَةٌ (حَفَلَاتٌ)
tell	حَكَى - يَحْكِي - حِكَايَةٌ
barber	حَلَّاقٌ (حَلَّاقُونَ)
milk an animal	حَلَبَ - يَحْلِبُ - حَلْبٌ
hover	حَلَّقَ - يُحَلِّقُ - تَحْلِيقٌ
class	حَلَقَةٌ دِرَاسِيَّةٌ
dream	حُلْمٌ (أَحْلَامٌ)
ornament	حِلْيَةٌ (حِلًى)
donkey	حِمَارٌ (حَمِيرٌ، حُمُرٌ)
lamb	حَمَلٌ (حُمْلَانٌ)

خ

| particular, special | خَاصٌّ |

betray	خَانَ - يَخُونُ - خِيَانَةٌ
bake	خَبَزَ - يَخْبِزُ - خَبْزٌ
bread	خُبْزٌ (أَخْبَازٌ)
expert	خَبِيرٌ (خُبَرَاءُ)
be ashamed	خَجِلَ - يَخْجَلُ - خَجَلٌ
safe	خِزَانَةٌ (خَزَائِنُ)
letter	خِطَابٌ (خِطَابَاتٌ)
snatch	خَطَفَ - يَخْطِفُ - خَطْفٌ
watchman, guard	خَفِيرٌ (خُفَرَاءُ)
light, thin	خَفِيفٌ (خِفَافٌ)
during	خِلَالَ
create, make	خَلَقَ - يَخْلُقُ - خَلْقٌ
caliph	خَلِيفَةٌ (خُلَفَاءُ)
tailor	خَيَّاطٌ (خَيَّاطُونَ)

د

diplomat	دِبْلُومَاسِي
creeping, crawling	دَبِيبٌ
drawer	دُرْجٌ (أَدْرَاجٌ)
pay, push	دَفَعَ - يَدْفَعُ - دَفْعٌ
the clock struck four	دَقَّتِ السَّاعَةُ الرَّابِعَةَ

flour	دَقِيْقٌ
blood	دَمٌ (دِمَاءٌ)
painter	دَهَّانٌ (دَهَّانُوْنَ)
medicine	دَوَاءٌ (أَدْوِيَةٌ)
cupboard	دُوْلَابٌ (دَوَالِيْبُ)

ذ

melt	ذَابَ - يَذُوْبُ - ذَوْبٌ، ذَوَبَانٌ
keep, preserve, save	ذَخَرَ - يَذْخَرُ - ذَخْرٌ
shed (tears)	ذَرَفَ - يَذْرِفُ - ذَرْفٌ
smart, intelligent	ذَكِيٌّ (أَذْكِيَاءُ)
go	ذَهَبَ - يَذْهَبُ - ذَهَابٌ
jackal, wolf	ذِئْبٌ (ذِئَابٌ)

ر

salary, pay	رَاتِبٌ (رَوَاتِبُ)
shepherd	رَاعٍ (رُعَاةٌ)
show mercy	رَأَفَ - يَرْأَفُ - رَأْفَةٌ
be clear, be pure	رَاقَ - يَرُوْقُ - رَوْقٌ
see	رَأَى - يَرَى - رُؤْيَةٌ
flag	رَايَةٌ (رَايَاتٌ)
benefit, gain, profit	رَبِحَ - يَرْبَحُ - رِبْحٌ

arrange	رَتَّبَ - يُرَتِّبُ - تَرْتِيْبٌ
man	رَجُلٌ (رِجَالٌ)
cloak	رِدَاءٌ
artist	رَسَّامٌ (رَسَّامُوْنَ)
fail	رَسَبَ - يَرْسُبُ - رُسُوْبٌ
painting, sketch	رَسْمٌ (رُسُوْمٌ، رُسُوْمَاتٌ)
official	رَسْمِيٌّ
bribe	رِشْوَةٌ
flat loaf of bread; bun	رَغِيْفٌ (أَرْغِفَةٌ)
shelf	رَفٌّ (رُفُوْفٌ)
welfare	رَفَاهِيَّةٌ
dancer	رَقَّاصٌ (رَقَّاصُوْنَ)
fine, delicate	رَقِيْقٌ (رِقَاقٌ)
throw	رَمَى - يَرْمِي - رَمْيٌ
novel	رِوَايَةٌ (رِوَايَاتٌ)
athlete	رِيَاضِيٌّ (رِيَاضِيُّوْنَ)
chairman, president	رَئِيْسُ الْجَلْسَةِ

ز

uniform	زِيٌّ (أَزْيَاءٌ)
glass bottle	زُجَاجَةٌ (زُجَاجَاتٌ)

creep, crawl	زَحَفَ - يَزْحَفُ - زَحْفٌ
sow, plant, cultivate	زَرَعَ - يَزْرَعُ - زَرْعٌ
annoyed, angry	زَعْلَانٌ
renounce pleasure	زَهَدَ - يَزْهَدُ - زُهْدٌ
shine, give light	زَهَرَ - يَزْهَرُ - زُهُورٌ
flower	زَهْرَةٌ (زُهُورٌ)
marriage, wedding	زَوَاجٌ
boat	زَوْرَقٌ (زَوَارِقُ)

س

sea-shore	سَاحِلُ الْبَحْرِ
simple; plain	سَاذَجٌ - سَاذِجٌ (سُذَّجٌ)
thief	سَارِقٌ (سَارِقُوْنَ، سَرَقَةٌ)
travel	سَافَرَ - يُسَافِرُ - مُسَافَرَةٌ
dweller, inhabitant	سَاكِنٌ (سَاكِنُوْنَ)
drive (an automobile)	سَاقَ - يَسُوْقُ - سِيَاقَةٌ
ask	سَأَلَ - يَسْأَلُ - سُؤَالٌ
driver	سَائِقٌ (سَائِقُوْنَ)
rickshaw puller	سَائِقُ الْعَرَبَةِ الْهَوَائِيَّةِ
plumber	سَبَّاكٌ (سَبَّاكُوْنَ)
rosary	سُبْحَةٌ (سُبْحَاتٌ)

way, road, path; assess	سَبِيلٌ (سُبُلٌ)
curtain	سِتَارَةٌ (سَتَائِرُ)
carpet	سَجَّادٌ (سَجَّادَاتٌ)
mirage	سَرَابٌ
bucket	سَطْلٌ (سُطُولٌ)
ambassador	سَفِيرٌ (سُفَرَاءُ)
ship	سَفِينَةٌ (سُفُنٌ)
irrigate	سَقَى - يَسْقِي - سَقْيٌ
sugar	سُكَّرٌ
string, wire	سِلْكٌ (أَسْلَاكٌ)
behave poorly	سَلَكَ بِغَيْرِ إِتْقَانٍ
console	سَلَّى - يُسَلِّي - تَسْلِيَةٌ
hear, listen	سَمِعَ - يَسْمَعُ - سَمْعٌ
stethoscope	السَّمَّاعَةُ
sky	سَمَاءٌ
allow	سَمَحَ - يَسْمَحُ - سَمَاحٌ (بِ، لِ)
hear, listen	سَمِعَ - يَسْمَعُ - سَمْعٌ
spearhead	سِنَانٌ (أَسِنَّةٌ)
year	سَنَةٌ (سَنَوَاتٌ)
bracelet, armlet, bangle; cuff	سِوَارٌ (أَسْوِرَةٌ)

wall; enclosure	سُوْرٌ (أَسْوَارٌ)
cigarette	سِيْجَارَةٌ (سَجَائِرُ)
sword	سَيْفٌ (سُيُوْفٌ)

ش

truck, lorry	شَاحِنَةٌ (شَاحِنَاتٌ)
clever	شَاطِرٌ (شَاطِرُوْنَ)
net	شَبَكَةٌ (شَبَكَاتٌ)
winter	شِتَاءٌ
diagnose a disease	شَخَّصَ - يُشَخِّصُ - تَشْخِيْصٌ
severe	شَدِيْدٌ
noble	شَرِيْفٌ (شُرَفَاءُ، أَشْرَافٌ)
switch on	شَغَّلَ - يُشَغِّلُ - تَشْغِيْلٌ
cure	شَفَى - يَشْفِي - شِفَاءٌ
certificate, testimonial	شَهَادَةٌ (شَهَادَاتٌ)
fork	شَوْكَةٌ (أَشْوَاكٌ)

ص

soap	صَابُوْنٌ (صَابُوْنَاتٌ)
one who fasts	صَائِمٌ (صَائِمُوْنَ)
journalist	صُحُفِي (صُحُفِيُّوْنَ)
truth; sincerity	صِدْقٌ

charity	صَدَقَةٌ (صَدَقَاتٌ)
rusty	صَدِئٌ
cashier	صَرَّافٌ (صَرَّافُونَ)
rise, climb	صَعِدَ - يَصْعَدُ - صُعُودٌ
whistle	صَفَّارَةٌ (صَفَّارَاتٌ)
whistle	صَفَرَ - يَصْفِرُ - صَفِيرٌ
falcon, hawk	صَقْرٌ (صُقُورٌ)
be bald	صَلِعَ - يَصْلَعُ - صَلْعٌ
design	صَمَّمَ - يُصَمِّمُ - تَصْمِيمٌ
box	صُنْدُوقٌ (صَنَادِيقُ)
washing soda	صُودَا الْغَسِيلِ
woollen	صُوفِيٌّ
fisherman	صَيَّادُ السَّمَكِ
repute	صِيْتٌ

ض

fog	ضَبَابٌ
vowelize	ضَبَطَ - يَضْبِطُ - ضَبْطٌ (الْكَلِمَةَ)
hyena	ضَبُعٌ (ضِبَاعٌ) fem.
annoyed, irritated	ضَجِرٌ
beat, strike, hit	ضَرَبَ - يَضْرِبُ - ضَرْبٌ

kick	ضَرَبَ بِالْقَدَمِ
he kicked the football	ضَرَبَ كُرَةَ الْقَدَمِ بِرِجْلِهِ
embrace	ضَمَّ - يَضُمُّ - ضَمٌّ
poverty, difficulty	ضِيقٌ
narrow; tight	ضَيِّقٌ

ط

chase	طَارَدَ - يُطَارِدُ - مُطَارَدَةٌ
aeroplane	طَائِرَةٌ (طَائِرَاتٌ)
be or become long	طَالَ - يَطُولُ - طُوْلٌ
cook	طَبَخَ - يَطْبَخُ - طَبْخٌ
the middle class	الطَّبَقَةُ الْوُسْطَى
doctor	طَبِيبٌ (أَطِبَّاءُ)
parcel	طَرْدٌ (طُرُودٌ)
knock	طَرَقَ - يَطْرُقُ - طَرْقٌ
food	طَعَامٌ (أَطْعِمَةٌ)
child	طِفْلٌ (أَطْفَالٌ)
be clear, pure	طَهَرَ - يَطْهُرُ - طُهْرٌ
Tehran (the capital of Iran)	طَهْرَانُ
throughout	طِوَالَ
long	طَوِيلٌ (طِوَالٌ)

pilot	طَيَّارٌ (طَيَّارُونَ)
throughout	طِيْلَةَ

ظ

oppress	ظَلَمَ - يَظْلِمُ - ظُلْمٌ

ع

family	عَائِلَةٌ (عَائِلَاتٌ)
just, fair, honest	عَادِلٌ
worker	عَامِلٌ (عُمَّالٌ)
spinster	عَانِسٌ (عَوَانِسُ)
play (absent mindedly)	عَبِثَ - يَعْبَثُ - عَبَثٌ
worship	عَبَدَ - يَعْبُدُ - عِبَادَةٌ
cross	عَبَرَ - يَعْبُرُ - عُبُورٌ
knead (flour)	عَجَنَ - يَعْجِنُ - عَجْنٌ
run, race	عَدَا - يَعْدُو - عَدْوٌ
enemy	عَدُوٌّ (أَعْدَاءٌ)
useless	عَدِيْمُ الْفَائِدَةِ
bride	عَرُوْسٌ (عَرَائِسُ)
nest	عُشٌّ (أَعْشَاشٌ)
dinner	عَشَاءٌ
grass	عُشْبٌ (أَعْشَابٌ)

stick	fem.	عَصًا (عِصِيٌّ)
squeeze		عَصَرَ - يَعْصِرُ - عَصْرٌ
sparrow		عُصْفُورٌ (عَصَافِيْرُ)
juice		عَصِيْرٌ
sneeze		عَطَسَ - يَعْطِسُ - عَطْسٌ
chaste, modest		عَفِيْفٌ (أَعِفَّاءُ، أَعِفَّةٌ)
eagle		عُقَابٌ (عِقْبَانٌ)
mark		عَلَامَةٌ (عَلَامَاتٌ)
teach		عَلَّمَ - يُعَلِّمُ - تَعْلِيْمٌ
paternal uncle		عَمٌّ (أَعْمَامٌ)
monument		عِمَارَةٌ (عِمَارَاتٌ)
work		عَمِلَ - يَعْمَلُ - عَمَلٌ
routine work		الْعَمَلُ الرَّتِيْبُ
deep, profound		عَمِيْقٌ
by means of, through, by		عَنْ طَرِيْقٍ
grapes		عِنَبٌ (أَعْنَابٌ)
nightingale		عَنْدَلِيْبٌ (عَنَادِلُ)

غ

| forest | | غَابَةٌ (غَابَاتٌ) |
| leave | | غَادَرَ - يُغَادِرُ - مُغَادَرَةٌ |

dive (into)	غَاصَ - يَغُوْصُ - غَوْصٌ
ghat (place for bathing and washing clothes in India)	الْغَاطُ
misguided	غَاوٍ (غَاوُوْنَ)
crow	غُرَابٌ (غِرْبَانٌ)
reception room, drawing room	غُرْفَةُ الْإِسْتِقْبَالِ
gazelle	غَزَالٌ (غِزْلَانٌ)
washerman	غَسَّالٌ (غَسَّالُوْنَ)
washing machine	غَسَّالَةٌ (غَسَّالَاتٌ)
wash	غَسَلَ - يَغْسِلُ - غَسْلٌ
oppress	غَشَمَ - يَغْشِمُ - غَشْمٌ
cover	غِطَاءٌ (أَغْطِيَةٌ)
cover, wrap, wrapper, box	غِلَافٌ (غُلُفٌ)
boy	غُلَامٌ (غِلْمَانٌ)
be or become thick	غَلُظَ - يَغْلُظُ - غِلَظٌ
boil	غَلَى - يَغْلِي - غَلْيٌ
sheep	غَنَمٌ (أَغْنَامٌ)

ف

bill	فَاتُوْرَةٌ (فَاتُوْرَاتٌ)
mouse	فَأْرٌ (فِيْرَانٌ)

Fruit seller	فَاكِهَاني
open; conquer	فَتَحَ - يَفْتَحُ - فَتْحٌ
flee	فَرَّ - يَفِرُّ - فِرَارٌ
butterfly	فَرَاشَةٌ (فَرَاشَاتٌ)
relief	فَرَجٌ
young bird, shoot	فَرْخٌ (أَفْرَاخٌ)
virtue; merit	فَضِيلَةٌ (فَضَائِلُ)
breakfast	فَطُورٌ
pastry	فَطِيرٌ
rude	فَظٌّ (أَفْظَاظٌ)
lose	فَقَدَ - يَفْقِدُ - فُقْدَانٌ
poverty; need	فَقْرٌ
section, paragraph, passage	فِقْرَةٌ (فِقْرَاتٌ)
Palestine	فِلَسْطِينُ
technician	فَنِّي (فَنِّيُّونَ)
artist	فَنَّانٌ (فَنَّانُونَ)
hotel	فُنْدُقٌ (فَنَادِقُ)

ق

commander	قَائِدٌ (قُوَّادٌ)
meet	قَابَلَ - يُقَابِلُ - مُقَابَلَةٌ

fight	قَاتَلَ - يُقَاتِلُ - مُقَاتَلَةٌ
long necked bottle	قَارُورَةٌ (قَوَارِيْرُ)
suffer, bear	قَاسَى - يُقَاسِي - مُقَاسَاةٌ
judge	قَاضٍ (قُضَاةٌ)
cutting (sharp)	قَاطِعٌ
hall	قَاعَةٌ (قَاعَاتٌ)
carry out, execute	قَامَ - يَقُوْمُ - قِيَامٌ (بِ)
dictionary	قَامُوْسٌ (قَوَامِيْسُ)
arrest, sieze	قَبَضَ - يَقْبِضُ - قَبْضٌ (عَلَى)
kill	قَتَلَ - يَقْتُلُ - قَتْلٌ
drought	قَحْطٌ
offer, serve	قَدَّمَ - يُقَدِّمُ - تَقْدِيْمٌ
old	قَدِيْمٌ (قُدَمَاءُ)
compose poetry	قَرَضَ - يَقْرِضُ - قَرْضٌ
village	قَرْيَةٌ (قُرًى)
butcher	قَصَّابٌ (قَصَّابُوْنَ)
short	قَصِيْرٌ (قِصَارٌ)
case, matter, affair	قَضِيَّةٌ (قَضَايَا)
train	قِطَارٌ (قُطُرٌ)
cat	قِطَّةٌ (قِطَطٌ)

cotton	قُطْنِيٌّ
necklace	قِلَادَةٌ (قَلَائِدُ)
be upset	قَلِقَ - يَقْلَقُ - قَلَقٌ
fountain pen	قَلَمُ الْحِبْرِ
to fry	قَلَى - يَقْلِي - قَلْيٌ
fabric, cloth	قُمَاشٌ (أَقْمِشَةٌ)
bomb	قُنْبَلَةٌ (قَنَابِلُ)
coffee	قَهْوَةٌ

ك

priest	كَاهِنٌ (كُهَّانٌ)
male sheep	كَبْشٌ
to write	كَتَبَ - يَكْتُبُ - كِتَابَةٌ
globe, ball	كُرَةٌ (كُرَاتٌ)
basketball	كُرَةُ السَّلَّةِ
honour, tribute	كَرَّمَ - يُكَرِّمُ - تَكْرِيمٌ
be noble; be generous	كَرُمَ - يَكْرُمُ - كَرَامَةٌ، كَرَمٌ
clothe	كَسَا - يَكْسُو - كَسْوٌ
break	كَسَرَ - يَكْسِرُ - كَسْرٌ
lazy, idle, inactive	كَسْلَانٌ (كُسَالَى)
cake	كَعْكٌ، كَعْكَةٌ (كَعْكَاتٌ)

sponsor, support	كَفَلَ - يَكْفُلُ - كَفَالَةٌ
useless talk	الْكَلَامُ الْفَارِغُ
hut	كُوْخٌ (أَكْوَاخٌ)
star	كَوْكَبٌ (كَوَاكِبُ)

ل

wear	لَبِسَ - يَلْبَسُ - لُبْسٌ
Lebanese	لُبْنَانِيٌّ
lioness	لَبُؤَةٌ (لَبَآتٌ)
kiss	لَثَمَ - يَلْثِمُ - لَثْمٌ
thief, robber	لِصٌّ (لُصُوْصٌ)
teach, instruct	لَقَّنَ - يُلَقِّنُ - تَلْقِيْنٌ
be out of breath, pant	لَهَثَ - يَلْهَثُ - لَهْثٌ

م

official authorized by the Qadi to perform civil marriages	الْمَأْذُوْنُ الشَّرْعِيُّ
inclining	مَائِلٌ (مَائِلُوْنَ)
incline	مَالَ - يَمِيْلُ - مَيْلٌ
wet	مُبْتَلَّةٌ
principle	مَبْدَأٌ (مَبَادِئُ)

wet	مُبَلَّلٌ
late	مُتَأَخِّرٌ (مُتَأَخِّرُونَ)
museum	مَتْحَفٌ (مَتَاحِفُ)
translator	مُتَرْجِمٌ (مُتَرْجِمُونَ)
free	مَجَّانِيٌّ
fighter	مُجَاهِدٌ (مُجَاهِدُونَ)
society	مُجْتَمَعٌ (مُجْتَمَعَاتٌ)
renewed	مُجَدَّدٌ
magazine	مَجَلَّةٌ (مَجَلَّاتٌ)
unknown; anonymous	مَجْهُولٌ
wipe off	مَحَا - يَمْحُو - مَحْوٌ
accountant	مُحَاسِبٌ (مُحَاسِبُونَ)
governor	مُحَافِظٌ (مُحَافِظُونَ)
lawyer	مُحَامٍ (مُحَامُونَ)
inevitable, destined	مَحْتُومٌ
station	مَحَطَّةٌ (مَحَطَّاتٌ)
surrounded	مَحْفُوفٌ
Atlantic Ocean	الْمُحِيطُ الأَطْلَسِي
coach, trainer	مُدَرِّبٌ (مُدَرِّبُونَ)
astonished, surprised	مَدْهُوشٌ (مَدْهُوشُونَ)

director, boss	مُدِيْرٌ (مُدَرَاءُ)
sinner	مُذْنِبٌ (مُذْنِبُوْنَ)
radio	مِذْيَاعٌ (مَذَايِيْعُ)
mirror	مِرْآةٌ (مَرَايَا)
supervisor	مُرَاقِبٌ (مُرَاقِبُوْنَ)
dispatched	مُرْسَلٌ
satisfactory, pleasing	مُرْضٍ
farmer	مُزَارِعٌ (مُزَارِعُوْنَ)
tear	مَزَّقَ - يُمَزِّقُ - تَمْزِيْقٌ
blooming	مُزْهِرٌ
assistant	مُسَاعِدٌ (مُسَاعِدُوْنَ)
round; circular	مُسْتَدِيْرٌ
hospital	مُسْتَشْفَى (مُسْتَشْفَيَاتٌ)
host	مُسْتَضِيْفٌ
project	مَشْرُوْعٌ (مَشَارِيْعُ)
apricot	مِشْمِشٌ
walk	مَشَى - يَمْشِي - مَشْيٌ
injured, sick	مُصَابٌ (مُصَابُوْنَ)
wrestler	مُصَارِعٌ (مُصَارِعُوْنَ)
designer	مُصَمِّمٌ (مُصَمِّمُوْنَ)

factory	مَصْنَعٌ (مَصَانِعُ)
photographer	مُصَوِّرٌ (مُصَوِّرُونَ)
bat, racket	مِضْرَابٌ
pass	مَضَى - يَمْضِي - مُضِيٌّ
air hostess	مُضِيْفَةٌ (مُضِيْفَاتٌ)
kitchen	مَطْبَخٌ (مَطَابِخُ)
rain	مَطَرٌ (أَمْطَارٌ)
acquainted with	مُطَّلِعٌ (عَلَى)
obedient	مُطِيعٌ (مُطِيْعُوْنَ)
umbrella	مِظَلَّةٌ (مِظَلَّاتٌ)
miracle (esp. one performed by a prophet)	مُعْجِزَةٌ (مُعْجِزَاتٌ)
exhibition; fair	مَعْرِضٌ (مَعَارِضُ)
factory	مَعْمَلٌ (مَعَامِلُ)
financial assistance	مَعُوْنَةٌ مَالِيَةٌ
adventure; risk	مُغَامَرَةٌ (مُغَامَرَاتٌ)
singer	مُغَنٍّ (مُغَنُّوْنَ)
key	مِفْتَاحٌ (مَفَاتِيْحُ)
inspector	مُفَتِّشٌ (مُفَتِّشُوْنَ)
gambler	مُقَامِرٌ (مُقَامِرُوْنَ)

contractor	مُقَاوِلٌ (مُقَاوِلُوْنَ)
telephonic call	مُكَالَمَةٌ (مُكَالَمَاتٌ)
stay	مَكَثَ - يَمْكُثُ - مُكُوْثٌ
prolific	مِكْثَارٌ
fill	مَلَأَ - يَمْلَأُ - مَلْأٌ
spoon	مِلْعَقَةٌ (مَلَاعِقُ)
king	مَلِكٌ (مُلُوْكٌ)
interesting	مُمْتِعٌ
actor	مُمَثِّلٌ (مُمَثِّلُوْنَ)
footpath	مَمَرُّ الْمُشَاةِ
nurse (male)	مُمَرِّضٌ (مُمَرِّضُوْنَ)
nurse (female)	مُمَرِّضَةٌ (مُمَرِّضَاتٌ)
torn	مُمَزَّقٌ
astrologer	مُنَجِّمٌ (مُنَجِّمُوْنَ)
grant, give	مَنَحَ - يَمْنَحُ - مَنْحٌ
scholarship	مِنْحَةٌ دِرَاسِيَّةٌ
dais	مِنَصَّةٌ
clown	مُهَرِّجٌ
negligent, neglectful; careless	مُهْمِلٌ
engineer	مُهَنْدِسٌ (مُهَنْدِسُوْنَ)

citizen	مُوَاطِنٌ (مُوَاطِنُوْنَ)
historian	مُؤَرِّخٌ (مُؤَرِّخُوْنَ)
music	مُوْسِيْقَى
receptionist (lady)	مُوَظَّفَةُ الْإِسْتِقْبَالِ
convinced, certain, sure	مُوْقِنٌ (مُوْقِنُوْنَ)
author	مُؤَلِّفٌ (مُؤَلِّفُوْنَ)

ن

waiter	نَادِلٌ (نُدُلٌ)
the principal of the school	نَاظِرُ الْمَدْرَسَةِ
soft	نَاعِمٌ
smart, clever	نَبِيْهٌ (نُبَهَاءُ)
result, bring forth	نَتَجَ - يَنْتِجُ - نِتَاجٌ
carpenter	نَجَّارٌ (نَجَّارُوْنَ)
star	نَجْمٌ (نُجُوْمٌ)
noble, distinguished	نَجِيْبَةٌ (نَجِيْبَاتٌ)
lament, weep, wail	نَحَبَ - يَنْحَبُ - نَحْبٌ
date palm	نَخْلٌ، نَخِيْلٌ
honest	نَزِهٌ (نُزَهَاءُ)
forget	نَسِيَ - يَنْسَى - نِسْيَانٌ
active	نَشِيْطٌ (نِشَاطٌ)

help	نَصَرَ - يَنْصُرُ - نَصْرٌ
clean	نَظَّفَ - يُنَظِّفُ - تَنْظِيْفٌ
clean	نَظِيْفٌ
shoe; horseshoe	نَعْلٌ (نِعَالٌ)
be of use, be beneficial	نَفَعَ - يَنْفَعُ - نَفْعٌ
precious, costly, valuable	نَفِيْسٌ
pay in cash	نَقَدَ - يَنْقُدُ - نَقْدٌ
grow	نَمَا - يَنْمُوْ - نُمُوٌّ
tiger	نَمِرٌ (نُمُرٌ)
river	نَهْرٌ (أَنْهَارٌ)
rise	نَهَضَ - يَنْهَضُ - نُهُوْضٌ

ه

telephone	هَاتِفٌ (هَوَاتِفُ)
calm, peaceful	هَادِئٌ
attack	هَجَمَ - يَهْجُمُ - هُجُوْمٌ
hurry	هَرَعَ - يَهْرَعُ - هَرَعٌ
nightingale	هَزَارٌ (هَزَارَاتٌ)
lean, skinny	هَزِيْلٌ (هَزْلَى)
pleasant, good	هَنِيْئٌ
fall	هَوَى - يَهْوِي - هُوِيٌّ

love	هَوِيَ - يَهْوَى - هَوًى

و

duty, obligation	وَاجِبٌ (وَاجِبَاتٌ)
face (problem)	وَاجَهَ - يُوَاجِهُ - مُوَاجَهَةٌ
find	وَجَدَ - يَجِدُ - وِجْدَانٌ
be swollen, swell	وَرِمَ - يَرِمُ - وَرَمٌ
pillow	وِسَادَةٌ (وَسَائِدُ)
reach	وَصَلَ - يَصِلُ - وُصُوْلٌ
put	وَضَعَ - يَضَعُ - وَضْعٌ
delegation	وَفْدٌ (وُفُوْدٌ)
time	وَقْتٌ (أَوْقَاتٌ)
stand	وَقَفَ - يَقِفُ - وُقُوْفٌ
agent	وَكِيْلٌ (وُكَلَاءُ)

ي

hand	fem.	يَدٌ (أَيْدٍ، أَيَادٍ)
dove		يَمَامَةٌ

Notes

....
....
....
....
....
....
....
....
....
....
....
....
....
....
....
....
....
....
....
....
....
....
....
....
....
....